# *Eugene Morel*

*Pioneer of Public Libraries in France*

# *Eugene Morel*

## *Pioneer of Public Libraries in France*

### By Gaetan Benoit

Litwin Books, LLC
Duluth, Minnesota

Copyright Gaetan Benoit, 1976

Published in 2008

Litwin Books, LLC
P.O. Box 3320
Duluth, MN 55803
http://litwinbooks.com/

This book is printed on acid-free paper that meets all present ANSI standards for archival preservation.

Cover design by Topher McCulloch

Cover portrait of Eugène Morel by Felix Valloton (1865-1925)

Library of Congress Cataloging-in-Publication Data

Benoit, Gaetan M.
  Eugene Morel : pioneer of public libraries in France / by Gaetan Benoit.
    p. cm.
  Includes bibliographical references and index.
  ISBN 978-0-9778617-8-1 (alk. paper)
  1. Morel, Eugène, 1869-1934. 2. Librarians--France--Biography. 3. Public libraries--France--History--19th century. 4. Public libraries--France--History--20th century. I. Title.
  Z720.M6835B46 2008
  020.92--dc22
  [B]
                                                              2007047228

# Contents

| | |
|---|---|
| Contents | v. |
| Acknowledgments | vii. |
| Author's Abstract | ix. |
| | |
| The Early Years | 1. |
| The Making of a Librarian: 1892-1900 | 11. |
| Moving Spirits in the French Library Movement | 43. |
| Morel and Library Education | 63. |
| Morel and Children's Libraries | 85. |
| Advocacy of Public Libraries | 101. |
| Morel and Legal Deposit in France | 147. |
| | |
| Notes | 195. |
| Bibliography | 223. |
| Index | 241. |

# Acknowledgments

I would like to express my gratitude to Mr. N.A. Webber, Senior Lecturer in Library History at the School of Librarianship, Polytechnic of North London, for his initial help and encouragement in the selection of this topic, and also to my supervisor, Dr. W.A. Nunford, N.B.E. Ph.D., F.L.A., B.So., for his infinite patience and his most valuable suggestions.

It is also my pleasure and duty to record and acknowledge the special help received from the following:

Miss Marguerite Gruny, Ex-Children's Librarian of *L'Heure Joyeuse*, Paris, and niece of Eugene Morel.

The British Council in Mauritius.

The French Embassy in Mauritius.

The Director and Staff of the Bibliothèque Nationale, Paris.

The Municipality of Port Louis, Mauritius.

The Librarian and Staff of the Library Association, London.

The University Archivist and Staff of the University of Illinois at Urbana-Champaign.

The Director of the Institut National de Documentation et de Recherche Pèdagogique, Paris.

The Librarian and Staff of the Yale University Library, Connecticut.

Marie Consuelo, my wife for her continuous interest and encouragement.

Mrs. N. Shi Shun who has done an excellent job as manifested in the typescript

# Author's Abstract

This study is an attempt to trace the life of Eugène Morel (1869-1934). It is a critical account of the work of a French librarian who, along the lines of such eminent public library pioneers as Edward Edwards and Melvil Dewey, made a remarkable contribution towards the development of public librarianship in France. Morel was genuinely interested in all facets of librarianship and played a dominant role in molding the development of most of them. His writings on the profession, more particularly his two books, *Bibliothèques: Essai sur le développement des bibliothèques publiques et de la librairie dans lex deux mondes* and *La Librairie Publique,* made a fitting testimony to the life's work of a very active library pioneer. His relationship with the British and American Library Associations helped to bring closer the French professional association of both of these. Morel had an "avant-garde" view on the automation of libraries and was the first to encourage the employment of women in French libraries. It is to be regretted that the work of a true library pioneer has gone unrecognized for such a long time.

There is a bibliography of works consulted as well as a general index. The appendices which precede the index have been included as supplementary to the text.

# The Early Years

The pride of the third arrondissement in Paris is the Quartier du Marais, but by the second half of the 18th Century Le Marais had lost much of its elegance. Its inhabitants were the poorer, but very conservative small nobility.[1] Balzac, a hundred years later, was to describe the district in *Honorine* as one where the "backward bourgeoisie and great nobility of the century (were) forsaken in their deserted and badly kept town-houses."

Around 1869, Le Marais was losing its aristocracy and nobility to its neighboring and more fashionable districts such as Faubourg Saint Germain and Saint Honoré.[2] In spite of this decline, Le Marais started to enjoy the reputation of being an industrialized region of Paris. Even two years earlier, Alphonse Daudet, living in the Hotel Lamoignon of Le Marais (now the Bibliothèque Historique de la Ville de Paris), described it as a "beehive of small workshops and the heart of Parisian manufacture."[3] By 1869, the town of Paris, like an octopus, had already stretched out its tentacles and engulfed all the outlying villages of Montmartre, Batignolles, Belleville, Menilmontant, Reuilly, Les Gobelins and Montrouge.[4] Outhouses, warehouses, workshops and factories of all sorts had smothered the parks which still existed in the first years of the 19th Century.[5] This evolution had started during the Second Empire. The remarkable development of the Industrial structure of Paris was brought to an end by making Le Marais the principal sweatshop of an economy, the products of which were sold in the elegant regions of the West in La Rue Saint Denis.[6] "It was a cottage industry making small articles which were sold by street hawkers to passers-by."[7] The old hotels built in the reign of Henry II and Louis XIII were converted by the modern industry of 1859 into either soda water, bronze or chemical factories.[8] This sudden transformation of Le Marais into an industrialized zone had compelled the *grand bourgeoisie* and the aristocracy to move to private mansions mostly in the areas of the Rue Saint Honoré and the Faubourg Saint Germain, then known as the *beaux quartiers*. "The other social classes tended to mix horizontally and separate themselves vertically, each living according to his station and means on one of the levels of the new blocks of flats put up during the great boom of the '50s and '60s."[9]

Charles Adolphe, Eugène Morel's father, did not live in a private mansion in these *beaux quartiers*, but instead had set up a bronze factory in the Rue Thorigny in Le Marais by 1869.

Like most of the main streets of Le Marais, Rue Thorigny was lined by "typical blocks of rented flats, known as *immeuble de rapport*, where the well-to-do *bourgeois* would live with his family in a large flat with as many as ten rooms on the ground floor or the first floor and above would live an artisan or worker and still higher up, in the attics, the servants."[10]

Charles Adolphe's *immeuble de rapport* stood at No. 4, opposite the Hotel Sale. The hotel was one of these sumptuous buildings, the ground floor of which, fortunately, had escaped the inexorable fate of being converted into a sweatshop and of being let to tradesmen for commercial purposes, like Mme. De Beauvais's hotel, built by Antoine Lepautre[11] in 1650. (Even now the Hotel Sale is still a magnificent building and is restored to house the Costume Museum).[12] Adolphe Morel's workshop also stood at No. 4. It is now occupied by a leather-ware factory, the lettering on the plaque of which can barely be read.[13] It took Charles Adolphe Morel time and hard work to make his business prosper before the birth of his sons, Frederic and Eugène. He had had a checkered career before he could settle down and marry Luisa Salanson. Charles Adolphe was the third of five children of Jean François Morel and Augustine Charbonneaux. When he was born in Reims in 1829, his father had already set up a china shop. At the age of 14, as was often the case of ambitious young men of his time, he wanted to join the family business. Jean François took his son to his shop in Reims and started to teach him the rudiments of the trade. Soon, the boy was helping sell his father's wares. His apprenticeship came abruptly to an end when his father suddenly died in 1846. This also put an end to Charles Adolphe's career, which apparently had been full of promise in Reims, as his father's business collapsed soon after his death. As the business does not seem to have been successful, the shop did not pass to the family but merely served to give Charles Adolphe some grounding in salesmanship. The lure of Paris was great. Using the little knowledge he had acquired in selling china, he decided to find a job in a Parisian china shop to earn a living. From then on it is highly probable that Eugène Morel's father moved from one job to another, for it is known that before his marriage to Louisa Salanson in Paris in 1864 he was earning a good deal of money as a clockmaker.

Louisa Salanson's parents were also engaged in business. Frederic Salanson and his wife, Marie Louise, *née* Feart, had both set up in Old Bond Street before their marriage in a London Roman Catholic Church in 1838; they had a tailor shop and a milliner/dress-maker's shop respectively. They were both born in France but had left their native country to settle in London where the affinity of their profession and the vicinity of their shops brought them together. Two children were born, and they received a sound upper-middle-class education in England. They were later sent to France to complete it. Louisa, Morel's mother, was born in 1839, and Alphonse, her only brother, three years later. After having spent her first fourteen years in England, Louisa was sent to a convent boarding school in France. In her studies, she showed a marked preference for music and became a very good amateur pianist, "almost a virtuoso," as her second son Eugène, was to recall later. While Louisa was interested in music and art, Alphonse showed a marked interest in science. He entered the Ecole Polytechnique, and when he graduated he was admitted to one of the institutions that specialized in a professional training. This was L'Ecole Nationale Supérieure des Mines, which was a state college whose primary aim was to train engineers to be responsible for the services entrusted by the state to the mining industry. It recruited principally those who came from the Ecole Polytechnique. On leaving the *Ecole des mines*, they were employed by the metropolitan or overseas mining industry. Alphonse did not leave France to seek employment in the French colonies but instead made himself a name in the industrial milieu of Paris. He occupied mostly posts of a high administrative nature and became president of La Sociètè des Omnibus de Londres. He was not content with the scope and variety of his activities as president of various companies but moved from one job to another in an administrative capacity. In Orne, he was director of Les Mines de Fer de Saint Remy. He then moved to Anjou as the administrator of a state quarry, Ardoisiè de l'Anjou, and finally went to the west of France to administer another quarry, Les Carrières de l'Ouest.[14]

It was after leaving his clockmaker's shop and becoming more interested in industrial art and then his bronze factory in 1874 that Charles Adolphe Morel was to think of marrying Louisa Salanson. Though Charles Adolphe, during the next five years' hard work, became richer, he and his wife Louisa did not think of leaving the building in No. 4 Rue Thorigny for a more select and private residence in "one of the newly fashionable districts like the Plaine Monceau."[15]

It was at No. 4 Rue Thorigny that Eugène Morel was born on June 21st, 1869, five years after his only brother, Frederic. Like most of the Roman Catholic upper-middle-class families of the time, Charles Adolphe and Louisa waited for a while, in this case fourteen days, before Eugène's godfather took him to be christened. The parish church of Saint-Denys du-Saint Sacrement in Le Marais was chosen, as it was in Rue Turenne, only two minutes' walk from No. 4 Rue Thorigny. Built in 1835, it was to become famous because it contained one of the Delacroix's religious paintings, *La Pieta*.

Charles Adolphe's business activities prospered in Le Marais during Eugène and Frederic Morel's childhood. Soon, his bronze factory was flourishing so much that he had to leave Le Marais very frequently to go on visits to various parts of France to display the *objets d'art* which he was manufacturing. His wife used to keep his accounts and Charles Adolphe soon extended his business activities. He was already employing several skilled workers and later had to delegate his responsibilities to a principal foreman who superintended the factory while he was on business trips.

Charles Adolphe could afford to give both his sons the best education. E. Morel left no diaries of his school days, although the historical records of the family are well-documented. The first years of his education were spent in a boarding school in Sainte Marie de Monceau, which his brother Frederic also attended. Monceau was one of the beaux quartiers where the "rich, well-to-do and titled congregated."[16] The boarding school was run by the Marists, who are Members of the Roman Catholic Society of Mary. He was six when he was admitted to the school, and he very probably had a tutor before this, for he knew how to write before he went to boarding school. In February 1876, when only six and a half years old, Morel was able to write, with only a few mistakes, a very long letter to his uncle Alphonse Salanson, in which he spoke of his early activities at the Marists and his various interests.[17] However, he did not go to the extremes of Montaigne (1533-93), who, as a child, would "eschew all pleasures to read Ovid's Metamorphoses"[18]; the young Eugène had a more plebeian taste in reading. A family anecdote relates how he amused his nanny by reading all the murder stories in the daily newspapers.[19] But he more reliably confirms that he was reading *Les Fleurs de l'Eloquence*.[17] At that time, Eugène and his brother Frederic had been devoting much of their time to collecting stamps, learning piano, and going to Madame Galys's gatherings (*séances*), where they were taught drawing and acting. The *comédies* Morel and his brother did were *Les Aventures de Moitié Poulet, Les 2 voleurs* (sic) and *Les Petit Gourmands Attrapées*. (sic)[17] But Eugène did not enjoy the time he spent at the Marists', as he could not bear life at boarding school. In his book *Les Petits Français* (1889), he later looked back on it as a very bad experience and vehemently criticized the hard times he endured there. Consequently, his parents took him back home at the end of the term and very sensibly sent him to the *Lycée Charlemagne,* where he was happy until the end of his schooldays.

At the Lycée, he had a special liking for languages and literature, and mastered all the classical authors. Among the subjects which he preferred were Latin, Greek, French, German, and English. He not only loved the English language but England itself, as he wrote to his brother in 1882 when he was 13 years old: "I entirely share your feelings of love for the English nation."[20] He showed a remarkable appreciation of history and geography and took an interest in historical places and buildings. He used to spend some of his Sundays visiting French castles, and in 1882, after a visit to Maisons Lafitte where he saw Le Chateau de Maisons, he wrote to his brother who was in London and asked him what Windsor Castle was like.

It is not surprising that with his early interest in literature, history, and geography, E. Morel ranked among the best pupils in these subjects at school. But had his uncle, Alphonse Salanson, succeeded in persuading him to change his course of study from arts to science at the Lycée, France would have lost its first public library pioneer.

In fact, his uncle Alphonse, the *polytechnicien* and a scientist at heart, tried to persuade the young *lycéen* to extend the range of his subjects and succeeded in influencing the young Morel to add a few science subjects such as mathematics, physics, and chemistry, in the hope that this might convert the humanist Morel into a scientist. But fortunately for the French public library world, the new subjects did not appeal to Morel, though he tried hard to take an interest in them. For had he been attracted by science at that time, this would have had an impact on his future career and orientated him towards industrial art, mining, and other technological subjects instead of towards law, and later, librarianship. However, the last years at the Lycée consolidated his keen interest in the humanities, and during this time Morel devoted himself entirely to his philosophy classes. In 1884, he wrote to his brother and advised him to read Schopenhauer, whose works Frederic was not the slightest bit interested in reading,[21] though he knew that "In Russia and Germany, he is devoured and in spite of his pessimism, he is a lion which I would like to go through."

At the age of 15, Eugéne Morel was so imbued with philosophical literature that he tried his hand at a philosophical play. His brother Frederic was outspoken about Eugéne's early literary gift and he also thought that his brother "should be more careful about reading philosophical works, especially Goethe's," as "this sort of creative writing can soon become boring and make one yawn."

In 1885, however, Morel had left the Lycée Charlemagne, and at 16 he passed his *baccalauréat*. Now that he had attained the highest form of general secondary education, his parents thought of sending him to university. That same year, The Faculty of Law, as well as three other faculties, i.e. Arts, Science, and Medicine, acquired legal status. These faculties were later regrouped into universities. These steps were taken by the state to stimulate higher education by giving it more autonomy.[22]

Morel's parents decided on law, and his educational achievements satisfied the Faculté de Droit de Paris. He was accepted for a Licence en Droit. At the University, Morel's interest in art led to his close friendship with Pierre Bonnard (1867-1947), and through him with Edouard Vuillard (1868-1940).

Bonnard was one of the very few painters to be elected a member of the Royal academy (1940). [23] His family forced him to study law, but he soon became bored with it, for like Roussel, Denis, and Vuillard, who were his classmates and friends at the Lycée Condorcet in Paris, his first interest was art. He went to as few classes as possible and started dabbling to take up painting more seriously. In 1889, after taking his law degree, he took his civil service examination but failed. Fortunately, he was more successful with his art, for he was paid several hundred francs by the France Champagne Company for a poster he had submitted to them. His father was delighted and agreed that Bonnard should make art his career. Similarly, Morel's mother made him study law in hope that this would give him ample time to devote himself to a literary career.[19] And she was right. Morel had the opportunity at the Faculté de Droit to try his hand at his first novel. In 1886, in his first year at the Faculté and at the early age of seventeen, his pen was flowing so smoothly that he had completed his novel before he started the second year of his law degree.

*L'Ignorance Acquise* was an impressive first work for a young author still studying law. Whether it was written for sale or not is still uncertain. If it were, it is plausible to suppose that the publication at that time would have involved Morel in some expense. Consequently, the work was not published in 1886, but had to wait three years before it came, by chance, to the notice of Léon Hennique (1851-1935). Hennique was a novelist and dramatist, associated with the Naturalist movement, who came to France as a young man from his birthplace, Guadeloupe. He had been contributing to *Les Soirées de Medan* (1880)[24], which was a volume of naturalistic short stories by Emile Zola and five other authors who were his disciples at the time: Paul Alexis, H. Ceard, Léon Hennique, J.K. Huysmans and Guy de Maupassant. *Les Soirées* derived its name from Zola's country home at Medan, where he entertained his friends.[25] Hennique, who contributed *L'Affaire du Grand 7* to *Les Soirées*, sponsored Morel's work. The book was published on Morel's twentieth birthday.[26]

Morel was still not content with the scope and variety of his cultural activities. He joined *La Revue Moderne*, a literary and dramatic review founded in 1857. He was then in the first year of his law degree. Like most of the reviews of that period, *La Revue Moderne,* which was associated with a particular trend in French literature, provided Morel with ample opportunity to develop his talents as a literary critic.[27] In the same year he became the secretary of the editorial staff. He was initiated into his new form of activity with Seraphin Justin Rosny (1859-1949), called "Rosny jeune," who also made his debut at the *Revue Moderne* in the same year. The Revue gave Morel the opportunity of working very closely with Lucien Descaves (1861-1949), novelist, dramatist, and critic, one of the five authors who broke away from their master, Emile Zola, and issued a manifesto (1867) against *le naturalisme*.[28] Both Rosny jeune and Descaves were to become the first members of the Academie Goncourt in 1903, the literary society founded by a legacy left by Edmond de Goncourt, who died in 1896.[29]

Although he spent the next two years or so, which were of great intellectual and cultural importance in his development, in the company of these budding writers, Morel did not abandon his studies at the Faculté de Droit. In 1889, he took his law degree and passed his two examinations for his License en Droit. Whether he enjoyed his years at the University as a law student or not is debatable. But in spite of his literary and journalistic pursuits, Morel was able to follow his academic training with some success. Yet, his future career as a lawyer, as planned by his mother, who thought that this profession would give her son time to devote himself to his literary pursuits, did not materialize. His mother, who had spent so much time closely watching the intellectual and literary development of her son, who was now well-grounded in law, had every reason to believe that he was destined for a very bright future. Both Morel's parents, but Louisa in particular, had very few doubts that his profession would prove lucrative as well as influential.

After he had graduated from university, Morel now had to earn a living. Though qualified, he was not a fully-fledged lawyer and had to be called to the bar. That same year he joined the *barreau de Paris*.[19] But the young man was not recommended for a post in the judiciary service. He was given his first brief soon, but he lost his first case. The young lawyer did not seem to have acquitted himself well, as his address to the Court was not impressive. Presumably, one can excuse this because of his youth together with his lack of experience. He was only twenty at the time and a very bad orator; what is more, in France a bad orator has little chance of becoming a good lawyer! Because of that incident, the French Parquet lost one of its young members to give the French Library Association one of its most vehement and voluble defenders.

After that failure, he did not resign immediately from the Parquet, but waited until he could find a permanent occupation that could suit his temperament. In the meantime, he became interested in writing more novels.[19] It was perhaps at this time that the influence of his mother made itself felt much more. If he had not been successful in fulfilling his mother's wishes of becoming a good lawyer, at least he took a keen interest in meeting his mother's real ambition for him: a literary career. However, Morel still thought that it might be his fate to spend his life in the world of jurisprudence. He was fortunate in befriending an *avoué*, a friendship that lasted to the beginning of 1882.

During 1890 and 1891, Morel was posted in Amiens for his military service. Amiens, the chief town of the department of the Somme, was 131 kilometers from the capital city. Morel was happy to be away for one year from the Paris of the 1890s, which R. Rudorff, in his preface to his book *Belle Epoque*, recalls as a city where people were "terrorized by bomb-throwing anarchists; where political extremists called upon the army to take power; and a large number of important artists, writers, poets and journalists openly supported anarchist and radical thinkers, calling for the complete transformation of existing society."[30]

Morel enjoyed his first year in Amiens thoroughly, for it was there he met the son of Jules Verne, who introduced him to his father, who had retired to Amiens (where he died in 1905). Jules Verne was one of Morel's favorite authors. Later, at the age of thirty-six, Morel recalled, in an article on Jules Verne in *La Nouvelle Revue*, how "from eight to fifteen in full development," he was very enthusiastic about "the old man's tales."[31] In the same article, Morel described how he came to meet Jules Verne and the meeting itself with the "bitter old man" some time before his death.

> As for myself, I met him 1890. I was a soldier. Amiens, the town in which I was garrisoned, seemed to me to be a very special town when I knew that in that town Jules Verne had retired, and that his son wanted so much to introduce me to him...I saw coming towards me a tall bitter old man... shambling along like a big bird which has its foot caught but tries to get away with big whirs of its wings but in vain.[32]

But much to his regret, Morel did not stay long in Amiens. The duration of his conscription, which normally should have been three years, was curtailed to one year.[19] He benefited from this privilege on account of his elder brother, Frederic, who died as a result of an accident in Le Havre in 1884 when he was on active service in the Fourth Batallion and Company of the 179th Regiment. Frederic was then twenty. Judging from the letters

# THE EARLY YEARS

that Morel received from him in 1884[33], he did not seem to have enjoyed his *service actif* in Le Havre, where he was "growing very disgusted with his 'job.'" Before Frederic was enlisted in military service, following the wish of his father who wanted him to take over the family business, he was sent to London to study sculpture. His teacher was the famous English sculptor, Sir Thomas Brock (1847-1922), who was awarded the Academy Gold Medal in Sculpture for his group, "Hercules strangling Antheus," and was elected the first president of the Royal Society of British Sculptors and "member d'honneur" of the Sociéte des Artistes Français.[34] Brock had been described as the "English representative of the more conservative aspects of French sculpture in the second half of the nineteenth century."[35] Perhaps this was one of the reasons why Frederic Morel was sent to London to be his pupil.

But Eugène Morel as a soldier was much luckier than his elder brother, as he was to come into closer contact with the city's leading intellectual circle, while Frederic lived isolated from the literary and cultural milieu in which his younger brother would revel. This was to reinforce Eugène's early artistic and cultural proclivity, which he had revealed in his letters to his uncle and brother,[36] a proclivity which was to be an important aspect of the personality of one whose mission was to propagate culture—a librarian. By 1890, Morel, like many other ambitious young men with literary aspirations and budding talents, was trying to write poetry. Even earlier, he had succeeded in making himself known in some literary circles for his column in *La Revue Moderne* from 1885-1889 and for writing at least two novels: *L'Ignorance Acquise*, published by Stock in 1890, and *Les Petits Français*. Before the latter was published by Savine in 1890, Morel had the chance of having it appraised by Jules Verne at Amiens. This appraisal was one of the most important in his literary career as he would point out in *La Nouvelle Revue* how he, as a young man of twenty who had read Jules Verne extensively, had discussed *Les Petits Français* with the old man:

> I have just finished a big book which I was sincerely delighted to send to the master. This book could be called the memories of my childhood. I can't deny it because of all the true things I have put into it. Throughout the novel I talked about the education of Les Petits Français (young French students). They were deprived—more than they are today—of air, fields, ballgames, joy and science. They were taught—but only rhetoric.

Morel described as much as he could his tendencies and theories to Jules Verne. At first the old man was skeptical and hostile, but later looked at Morel with more kindness and remarked with an irony full of earnestness: "I doubt that by these means (turning a few lectures into a novel) you would be able to find anyone to read your book." Morel writes, "Then he took pity on me and taught me good-naturedly what literature was all about. 'You see... You must ask at the end of every page what you will put into it so that the reader wants to turn to the next page. Urge him to look for what follows. That's the secret.'"[37] Morel found Verne's attitude to literature "that of a good business man—rather revolting."[37]

Jules Verne not only complimented him in his own way but referred to his early writing, for he believed that Morel had "the strength at least to 'compose' such big works." This strength, coupled with the instructions received from the old man himself, were preparing Morel for his big work in librarianship, which would have an impact on the reading public of France.

It was during this period when he was at Amiens doing his military service that the Grenier Goncourt "opened" its doors to Morel (as he would later point out). It was 1890. One year earlier, Léon Hennique had sponsored the publication of his *L'Ignorance Acquise* by Stock. There is no doubt that he was introduced to the literary Salon des Goncourt by Léon Hennique himself, who was among the earliest members of the Grenier, which was founded by Edmond de Goncourt (1822-1896), brother of Jules (1830-70). The brothers wrote novels but were artists primarily. In 1849 they set out touring France, looking for drawings and watercolors. Their notebooks made them writers as well as artists, and in 1852 they formed a literary partnership.

Morel became the youngest member of the Goncourt literary salon and was admitted there while "wearing the heavy overcoat of the soldier."[38] He was to be a regular visitor when he completed his military service.

It was in this earnest, erudite atmosphere that the young ex-soldier Morel went back to the *avoué* to look for a job that would leave him time to devote himself to his literary pursuits.[19] By the beginning of 1892 Morel was helping the *avoué* as best he could, but before long he lost interest in his new job. It is probable that Morel found that he would never be given the opportunity to rise to a better position and that his future as a jurist did not seem to be very promising. Accordingly, he only stayed in the attorney-at-law's office for a short time and gave it up to apply for a part-time job at the Bibliothèque Nationale, where he was told the number of hours he was required to work would be very low. The thought that he was to be employed on a probationary-basis[19] with ample time on hand to devote to his writing made the prospective job at the Bibliothèque Nationale very attractive. Thus his interest in literature and culture indirectly led him to the Bibliothèque Nationale, and into the world of libraries, which were to absorb him for the rest of his life.[39]

# The Making of a Librarian: 1892-1900

By the beginning of 1892 it was quite clear to the unemployed Morel that the Bibliothèque Nationale could offer him the congenial opportunities he was looking for: a means of earning a modest living, the possibility of cultivating himself, and ample time to devote to his literary pursuits. He lost no time in applying for a post in the library and immediately called upon a well-known personality, Octave Greard (1828-1904), to seek his support and to obtain a letter of recommendation. Greard, pedagogist, member of the French Academy and Vice-Chancellor of the Academie de Paris, had undertaken much work to promote French education. His various pedagogical and didactic writings were collected in his *Education et Instruction*. Morel was very pleased when three days before he sent his application to the Bibliothèque Nationale Octave Greard answered his request and confirmed that he had anticipated Morel's application by writing personally to recommend him to the selection board.[1]

On March 8th, 1892, Morel registered for the entrance examination, which was highly competitive. Only success at this examination could make his appointment to the paid post of *attaché* (beginner) on the French national library's staff possible. To his application he attached a certificate of his law degree and another of good conduct during his military service. He also stated that he was ready to undergo an examination to test his proficiency in German, which was a compulsory subject.

Morel's application was successful. On March 21st of the year 1892, "Eugène Alphonse Morel, licentiate in law, became one of the temporary *attachés* for the preparation of the new catalogue,"[1] the *Catalogue des Imprèmés*, the first volume of which would be completed in 1896.[2]

But Morel's interest in the Salon Goncourt, and in various reviews such as *Mercure de France* (a magazine that did much for poetry in the 1890s)[3] and *La Revue Blanche*—the most brilliant and influential of the city's many artistic and literary reviews which was made a meeting place for the avant-garde by Fenson[4]—did not allow him to take his part-time job at the Bibliothèque Nationale very seriously for at least the first two years. One of the reasons for Morel's apathetic attitude to librarianship was that he probably thought that his literary career, particularly in journalism, could provide him not only with a livelihood but also with an alternative to librarianship. Since

1891, "*La Revue Blanche* was one of the few magazines which could pay its staff and contributors."[4]

Soon after his appointment as *attaché* at the Bibliothèque Nationale, Morel succeeded in finding time to write articles for some minor magazines, as well as for many major ones (such as *La Revue Blanche*). Among the major articles was one on Léon Cladel (1835-1892), author of realistic tales and novels such as *Le Bouscassie* (1869), *Les Va-nu-pieds* (1873A), and *N'a qu'un oeil* (1882), which described the peasant or vagrant life in the district known as Le Querry (chief town Cabors.)[5] The clever and perceptive secretary, Lucien Muhlfeld, who was literary critic from 1891 to 1895, and to whom the magazine owed a great deal of its success, agreed to publish it, but limited Morel to eleven pages.

In 1893, the *Revue Blanche* acquired and incorporated another small magazine, *Le Banquet,* founded by Fernand Gregh, of Maltese origin, and some friends, including the young Marcel Proust, who was beginning to make a name for himself with his articles on Parisian society. This was the beginning of the magazine's greatest period. It continued to accept Morel's articles for some years, and amongst his best was "Pour nos gloires," an article about life in Paris which was published in 1894.[6]

Though Morel's early journalistic and literary activities were a considerable success and could provide a great deal of information for an eventual thesis, the eight subsequent years from 1892-1900, spent at the Bibliothèque Nationale, remain thinly documented. There is no surviving diary of his activities during his first years there, as, for example, in the case of Edward Edwards, the English library pioneer (1812-1869)[7] who kept a diary of his first years at the British Museum.

By the middle of 1892, Morel was still giving little attention to his duties at the Bibliothèque Nationale, for which he was very poorly remunerated. At the time, no reading or event aroused in him a liking for librarianship, as William Oldy's *The British Librarian,* which, "though abortive, had encouraged Edward Edwards to think deeply on the wider aspects of his profession in 1846," and had influenced him to begin in October of the same year "to make notes for an article on Public Libraries in London and Paris."[8]

At the end of the year 1892, the Bibliothèque Nationale was still following in the Decree of June 17th, 1885 with regard to the employment and grading of personnel in its different departments. In order to understand clearly the position Morel held at the Nationale in that year, before he was appointed *stagiaire* (apprentice), it is essential to examine the grading of library staff in all the departments of the French National Library.

A memorandum submitted by the members of the Bureau de l'Association des Bibliothécaires Français (French Library Association) to the Minister of Public Instruction on June 26th, 1907 recalls the staffing conditions at the *Nationale* in 1892:

> According to the Decree of June 17th,1885, one becomes a *stagiaire commissionné* (an apprentice who will be allowed to continue in the service,) after passing an examination; and sub-librarian (*sous-bibliothécaire,*) after one year's probation and success in a competitive examination. An apprentice may be dismissed for incompetence. As a matter of fact, the period of probation... lasts but one year for the *stagiaire commissionné*. However, with regard to the casual daily paid beginner (*attaché payé à la journée*) and non-remunerated beginner (*attaché non-retribué*), the period of probation runs for about four years. (The former was usually employed in the Department of Printed Books, the latter in the Department of Stamps.) The result is that the entrance examination takes place four years after the actual admission and the right to dismiss an apprentice on a charge of incompetence can no longer be applied morally.
>
> The competitive examination, which precedes promotion to the post of sub-librarian, is meaningless; the entrance requirements have not been established.
>
> The examining board for apprentices (*stagiaires*) and for the sub-librarians' competitive examination, has not been determined by any consistent regulations which can be applied to ensure the control of the upper administration and the competence of the examiners.[9]

The same memorandum also gives an idea of the staff structures of the Bibliothèque Nationale in 1892:

> "It should be made up of 64 employees. But if one does not take into consideration the General Director of the Bibliothèque Nationale, the four heads of department (*conservateurs*) and their six deputies for whose employment provision was specifically made in the Decree, this number is reduced to 54 full-time employees (*stagiaires*) with an annual salary of 1800 francs, or as sub-librarians (*sous-bibliothécaires*) graded in four categories, with an annual salary ranging from 2400 to 3300 francs, or as librarians (*bibliothécaires*) graded in six categories with an annual salary ranging from 3600 to 6000 francs.
>
> This brought the hierarch to eleven grades to which, however, should be added a twelfth, which corresponded to that of a beginner or learner (*attaché*). Yet this last grade, which in its own right should not exist, was

included. This sub-division of the hierarchy into 12 grades was evidently out of proportion to the average time spent within each grade which was four years. It would take an apprentice at least 44 years to attain the post of librarian Grade One and at least 50 years full-time service before he could enjoy a pension of 3000 francs."[10]

It was evident that Morel's hopes for regular promotion were indeed thin. This was also the case for many of his colleagues, Babelon Bourel de la Roneière, Cadet de Gassicourt, Gordey, Dacier, Laran, Gruny and Martin who were with him in the twelfth grade also shared the same fate.[11] For in this particular situation at the Bibliothèque Nationale in 1892, the memorandum goes on to emphasize that

only one condition of promotion was provided for by the Decree of 1885, that of the sub-librarian which starts at Grade Four after an apprenticeship and competitive examination. Following the silence of the Decree as far as all grades and responsibilities of employees above the post of sub-librarian is, in its own right, limited to the employees drawing 3300 francs and less, and, that one can become librarian without having been either an apprentice (*stagiaire*) or a sub-librarian, and that one can even be appointed to a higher post, namely that of head of department (*conservateur*) and deputy head of department, without having belonged to the establishment before or undergone any single test of ability.[12]

"One can, in fact deduce that there was no uniform recruiting at the bottom if one gives serious and thorough consideration to the interpretation of the Decree."[12]

The literal interpretation of the Decree of 1885 would be described authoritatively by H. Marcel in 1907, in his Book *Le Bibliothèque Nationale*:

one cannot be promoted sub-librarian without having been an apprentice for at least a year and passed a competitive examination... no provision has been made which enacts conditions for the grades that follow or requires the minister to base his choice on seniority and selection.[13]

Henry Marcel could not be accused of exaggeration as he was a former *conseiller d'Etat*.

In fact this arbitrary system was not what the French Government wanted when the Ministry of Public Instruction issued the Decree on June 17, 1885. For, less than 3 years after its promulgation[14], M. Faye, in submitting a decree to be signed by the President of the Republic regarding the conditions governing the retirement from service said in a preliminary report:[15]

> Libraries and archives have been organized administratively on a real hierarchical system and recent regulations have reserved ALL posts for candidates who can give proof of professional qualifications. (Decree of January 23, 1888)[16]

The study of conditions of employment as recommended by the Decree of 1885, which was still in force at the Bibliothèque Nationale in 1892, had no doubt suggested to Morel that his prospects at the bottom of the hierarchy in the twelfth grade were far from good. His daily work as a remunerated beginner did not entail a great deal of responsibility. But as a qualified lawyer, he was attached to the Department of Printed Books where he worked at odd jobs of cataloguing on a daily basis.[17]

At the beginning of the year 1893, the Bibliothèque Nationale was facing great changes. The staff of the library were henceforth to be concerned primarily with the construction of the *Salle Ovale*, which was originally destined to become a public reading room but in fact never fulfilled its purpose. In 1934, it became the Periodicals Room (Salle des Périodiques).[18] The Bibliothèque Nationale was then headed by a man who was not only one of the greatest archivist-paleographers of all time but also at the height of his power, Leopold Delisle. Delisle was trained at the Ecole de Chartes, one of the *Grandes Ecoles de Paris*, which concentrated on philosophy and history, producing mostly archivist-paleographers, and at the same time offering an elementary training in library administration and librarianship. This had tended to bring a certain change in the directing personnel of libraries and gave archivist-paleographers, instead of librarians, control of all types of libraries.

L. Delisle followed Taschereau in 1874 under whose administration the Salle de Travail, constructed largely in iron by Henri Labrouste, was opened. Taschereau also provided a public reading room and longer study hours. He occupied himself at the end of his administration with the catalogue which, until then, was quite inadequate. He also inspired Delisle to begin the general catalogue of printed books, the preparation of which kept Morel and the other attachés busy for thirty hours a week.[18]

Leopold Dleisle's intellectual life was becoming vigorous but his administration had started to become "too inflexible" and "over-conservative."[19] Yet, the interest that he had taken in the collections of the Nationale led him to consecrate a great part of his time and personal work to study questions relating to the origins and development of typography, to the classification of books and to the organization of libraries. It was typical of the man that he should let nobody but the subordinates of the Institution he was administering benefit from his experience.[20] Thus two years before

E. Morel's appointment to the Bibliothèque Nationale, Delisle had already published two useful handbooks on librarianship. These were *Instrucions pour la redaction d'un inventaire des incunables conserves dans les blibliothèques publiques de France* (Lille: Imp. De L. Danel, 1886) and *Instructions élémentaires et techniques pour la mise et le maintien en ordre des libres d'une bibliothèque.* (Lille: Imp. De L. Danel, 1890.) The former gave instructions for cataloguing incunabulae kept in the public libraries of France; the latter was published under the aegis of the *Direction du Secrétariat et de la Comptabilité* of the Ministry of Public Instruction, and gave elementary and technical instructions for the organization of a library. Maurice Pellisson, one of the pre-Morel moving spirits in the French public library movement, recommended its reprint fifteen years later, around 1906, so that it could be used extensively in all types of libraries, even by people who were running popular libraries.[21]

At the beginning of the year 1894, these books were perhaps the least interesting part of Morel's reading, and during the following months he had to wade through even less stimulating literature. While L. Delisle's two books had something to do with librarianship, the new book Morel was advised to pore over was all about paleography and the organization of archives. It was natural for a superior of the caliber of L. Delisle, a bibliophile and historian whose close study of medieval history, paleography and printing had made him an outstanding archivist-paleographer of the *Bibliothèque Nationale,* not to want even an *attaché* like Morel to sweep aside all the rudimentary principles of a good keeper of archives. He did not want any of his subordinates

> to run the risk of confusing copies of documents made by ordinary scribes with the transcripts, the extracts, the analyses and the simple notes made by experts such as the brothers Dupup, Du Cange, Gaignières, Caluse, Clairamabault, Anselme Le Michel, Mabillon, Martene, etc.[22]

So, he gave Morel the "little book which Le Prince had published on the subject at the end of the Eighteenth Century," and he "constantly recommended it for use in all the departments of the library." Delisle had, himself, found "nothing more useful than this book," and was of the opinion that "every assistant should know the history of the Library thoroughly." L. Delisle was talking of his own experiences for once; he had to procure it, for himself, when he was advised to do so by his superior.[23]

This advice from L. Delisle, the teaching and perusal of Le Prince's little book, must have drawn Morel more towards the work of an archivist-paleographer than of a librarian. For then, Morel no doubt had "to know by whom and for whom manuscripts had been made, from what countries they originally came, at what periods they had been copied, revised or completed."²⁵ In short, he had to know everything about the correct preservation of manuscripts.

By the middle of the year 1894, Morel's immediate concern was to be promoted from a daily paid beginner (*attaché payé à la journée*) to a *stagiaire commissionné*, that is to say, to serve an apprenticeship until he was allowed to continue in the service. But even then, he had not given his resignation at the *Parquet de Paris* (the Paris Bar), and still clung to the thought that a lawyer's career might be an alternative to that of a librarian.

However, in 1894, it is more than probable that Morel was thinking along the same lines as his contemporary, C.V. Langlois, (b. 1863) Professor at the University of Paris and one of the foremost French bibliographers and a historian. Eleven years later, Langlois, when giving serious and thorough consideration to the very grave problem of librarianship in France, wrote two letters in Le Temps for December 27th, 1905 and January 10th, 1906 stating that the prospects of anyone contemplating librarianship as a career left much to be desired. These letters were reprinted in *Bibliothèque de l'Ecole des Chartes* for November-December, 1905, where Langlois emphasized that:

> The calling of librarian is not yet in our country a legally regulated and protected profession with definite duties as the teaching professions have long been. It is not truly a career. Entrance to, and promotion within, its ranks are haphazard and the pay is not always in proportion to the work done.²⁶

> Nowhere, not even in the *Bibliothèque Nationale* nor in the University libraries, does there exist a fixed relation between promotion at will and promotion by seniority. It is an arbitrary system tempered by the justice of the chief librarians who are often enough chosen, as it is well known, from outside the profession, and from persons whom the politician who holds the appointing power at the time when vacancies occur, chooses to, or must, appoint. This circumstance does not of course prevent clear-sighted and fair librarians, for it often happens that these improvised judges of the hierarchy are very good fellow indeed but it cannot but demoralize the subordinates, the real members of the profession, because it sensibly lessens their chances of reaching by merit, the best places which the career offers. Organized vocations differ precisely from those which are not organized, in that those in chief administrative positions must first prove their right to be there.²⁷

If this was the state of librarianship in 1905, it must have been worse for Morel in 1894. Then there was indeed little hope for him to find any real motivation. His remuneration, which was very low indeed, was not an incentive. Life must have been worse for his colleagues of the same status who did not, like him, have a *"rente"* from other activities such as journalism, authorship, or literary criticism. Professor Ch.V. Langlois, again in the same issue of the above journal, described the plight of some library assistants in the Bibliothèque Nationale in 1905, but it was very likely that of Morel and his colleagues in 1894:

> It is not enough to say that library work in general is poorly paid, especially in the lower grades; the statement must be emphasized. In the *Bibliothèque Nationale*, apprentices (*stagiaires*) remain at a salary of 1800 francs. There are now, in this library, a dozen attendants earning this salary, several of whom are over 30 years and have more than six years' service. But the inequality between different libraries is more regrettable still. There are libraries where the staff do not do much, either, because there is really not much to do, or because established tradition prescribes excessive zeal, and the salaries are sometimes higher than in the large libraries where the work is very hard. Maximum and minimum salaries in different libraries are fixed by chance, when occasion arises, without a unified plan or preliminary comparisons, and they are shockingly out of proportion.[28]

Despite these conditions, Morel was forced to take a more practical interest in the work on the *Catalogue des Imprimés* at the Bibliothèque Nationale. By the end of 1894, he was feeling hard-pressed, both financially and emotionally, by his literary and journalistic activities. His literary achievements, in spite of his hard work, were eclipsed by those of writers and journalists like R. Rolland, L. Bloy, J-K. Huysmans, Alphonse Daudet, and E. Zola. There were also those who were taking the place of Rimbaud, Renan, Taine, and Maupassant, who had made the last decade of the nineteenth century a great generation in literature. Therefore, Morel found it quite hard to make ends meet. He decided to think seriously about studying for his examination to be promoted to a permanent post of *stagiaire commissionné*, as this would bring him a regular salary of 1800 francs. This salary would be much more secure than his hard day's wages as an *attaché*.

Morel had then to look for the courses which were offered him to qualify for the post of *stagiaire*. Training, fortunately, was not a problem by the end of the year 1894 for assistants of the Bibliothèque Nationale and the university libraries. A.C. Piper, in an article in *Library World* of 1910, reminded readers that:

> There was before 1893 no systematic training for librarians in France except for appointment to the staff of the *Bibliothèque Nationale* or for university librarians.[29]

Also in 1910, F.M. Glenn, in the *Library Association Record* of the same year, shared the views of A.C. Piper and confirmed that the year, that is, 1894, Morel decided to get some training in librarianship.

> France had commenced to cater for her library assistants by the establishment of lectures in bibliography and library economy at the Sorbonne University, Paris, and an institute in Paris known as the Ecole des Chartes, a department of the college of France, and also affording good instruction in some branches of library work, although not founded expressly for giving courses in librarianship.[31]

> Practical knowledge was gained by the daily handling of the great historical collections at the Ecole des Chartes and the courses were also supplemented with practical work at the Bibliothèque Nationale or the Ste. Geneviève Library.[32]

The professional examination that Morel had to sit then did not differ from that of his colleagues who were working in the university libraries. In fact, as A.C. Piper explained to readers:

> The first professional examination for university librarians took place on October 27th, 1879 at the Bibliothèque de l'Arsenal. The principles had not changed (until 1895) except for a few minor alterations regarding age limit to sit for it. For there was no fixed age limit in 1879, but three years afterwards a rule was in force that candidates must be between the age of twenty-one and thirty-five. The knowledge required covered a very wide field. All candidates were to have an extensive knowledge of bibliography and a general acquaintance with the sciences akin to bibliography... and it was necessary to be familiar with all the methods in the various departments of library work, including the choosing of furniture and fittings.

> Great stress was laid on the practical work, for it was absolutely necessary to have had at least one year's actual library experience. Candidates had also to possess a knowledge of the history of books, while the German language was obligatory and it was intimated that other languages were very useful and an additional qualification. A certificat d'aptitude (efficiency certificate) was granted to all candidates who satisfied the examiners."[33]

At the beginning of 1895, Morel's first thoughts were of his *certificat d'aptitude*. He wanted to pass it quickly and therefore decided to attend as assiduously as possible the courses at the Ecole des Chartes and the Faculté des Lettres at the Sorbonne. Though he was compelled by circumstances to find the courses excellent in 1895, he found them quite inadequate when he started organizing his lectures on librarianship at the Ecole des Hautes

Etudes Sociales in 1910.[34] This series of lectures was designed to promote modern librarianship in France and for the Section des Bibliothèques Modernes.[35] This institution, according to its founder Morel, would:

> one day become if not a true school for training librarians suitable for the profession, at least an institution which would teach them some concepts of librarianship still unknown in France. If anybody should find these lectures useless, let him, to support his opinion, at least make it a point to find out what is being taught elsewhere.[36]

Again in 1910, Morel was to give vent to his anger on the method of training in library administration and librarianship that was prevalent in 1895—a resentment that can be justified by any modern librarian but was repressed by Morel in 1895 when he was an *attaché*.

In sharp contrast to what he had believed to be wholly inadequate concepts of librarianship in 1894 and 1895, he stressed one of his "new unknown theories." "Librarianship," wrote Morel in 1910, "is nowadays taught in France through lectures, excellent on their own, but too specialized and incomplete at the Ecole des Chartes and the Facultè des Lettres. Classification of knowledge, commercial, and industrial bibliography are excluded from all teaching."[37]

Seen in the light of subsequent developments this kind of criticism not only revealed an early innate desire for promoting librarianship, but also foreshadowed Morel's major contribution after World War I in the setting up of the French School of Librarianship with the help of the Americans in 1923.[38]

Although Morel was spending several hours in early 1895 attending lectures at the Ecole de Chartes and the Faculté des Lettres, he was also thinking of devoting himself more and more to his literary career. After contributing some articles to *La Revue Blanche*, he became more interested in writing his second novel, *Artificielle*. The success that had accompanied the publication of *Petits Français*, a novel written when he was only seventeen years old, had provided him with exceptional stimulation for his second novel. "*Petits Français*," wrote Marguerite Gruny, Morel's niece, in an article on Morel's work with children, "deserved to be brought to the notice of educationalists for its *avant-garde* spirit of protest, though it was a violent charge against the education of young bourgeois at the end of the 19th century. Everything is denounced in the novel with a mixture of lucidity and extravagance but it would have delighted those who took part in the French student revolution of 1968."[39]

In his second novel, Morel was investigating a subject of special interest to him, as he was not yet married then. The book was all about "the study of a ruthless and snobbish woman who later falls into ridicule."[39] He was then looking for a publishing house to commission his work, *Artificielle*, a much more ambitious and mature work than *Petits Français*[40], which was published towards the end of 1895.

After the publication of his latest novel, Morel was feeling the pressure and the effects of too much work and intellectual activity. So he decided to take a holiday in a country which he had read and learnt so much about while corresponding with his brother Frederic, who was then studying sculpture in London.[41] For obvious reasons, he chose England and decided to spend some weeks in London. It would have been very difficult for him to have made a better choice, bearing in mind that his ancestors, mother and uncle had formed part of the French colony in London.[1] He was surely recommended by his mother to visit London, where she herself had benefited for more than fourteen years from a British education.

London was to impress Morel to such an extent that it was to have an important place in his professional career later.[1] Though with a certain reserve it could be said that the event that influenced him professionally was more fortuitous than intentional. It was natural that the man should spend some of his time visiting the "old French quarter, of Saint Martin's Lane, two minutes' walk from Trafalgar Square"[42], where his ancestors had lived and worked, and also much of his time visiting places of cultural interest, galleries and museums. But it never occurred to him to visit the "London free public libraries." If Morel was interested in visiting any library, it would have been a national library, in this case the British Museum. It is more probable that he would have done this just to satisfy the curiosity of a library assistant employed at the French national library who was interested in finding out how his English colleagues compared with their *confrères* at the *Bibliothèque Nationale*. There was no reason for Morel to be interested in public libraries then.[43] For if he entertained any opinion about librarianship, it would surely have been the same as, or even much worse than, that which Professor C.V. Langlois was to hold in *Le Temps* ten years later:

> It cannot be denied that the majority of the French public still consider library positions as sinecures, a conviction so widespread that some librarians have, until lately, shared it. The attitude of such librarians has helped not a little to reinforce existing prejudices—prejudices the more deplorable because they are the root of all the ills which afflict our libraries.

Apart from a vague idea that librarians are becoming a profession in their own right, the French public has not sufficiently grasped the eminent role which libraries, general as well as special, scientific as well as popular, are now playing in modern society, and it is because the social value of libraries as instruments of research and education is not clearly seen that their budgets remain so miserably small, even while parliament and local authorities give liberally in other ways to science and education. The libraries of France are very poor; the annual budget of the *Bibliothèque Nationale* and of the great general libraries in Paris[44] is less than a million francs; only 20 libraries in the provinces have more than 10,000 francs annually to spend. The state aids municipal and popular libraries only by grants of books, while the annual sum devoted each year to scientific and literary subscriptions instead of increasing is diminishing little by little.[45]

Also, in view of the extremely unfavorable impression which, from a distance, was left by the French public library scene, and the attitude of his colleagues at different levels of the hierarchy at the Bibliothèque Nationale, Morel probably realized that there was indeed no justification for his visiting public libraries in London.

But his calm, professional indifference was slightly ruffled on a rainy night in London of 1895, when he was forced to "rush into a public library." He described the experience of this "unpremeditated visit," which was to have permanent impact on his future, in his book *La Librairie Publique* fifteen years later:

> I discovered *la librairie publique* (free public library) fifteen years ago in London on a night when it was raining heavily. The one in which luck forced me to take shelter is situated in the old French quarter, Saint Martin's lane, not far from Trafalgar Square. I was a bit astonished to see people standing reading newspapers and very glad to find there *Le Figaro*. I went up to the first floor and had a look at the other rooms. I thought it was a special institution of some sort but was surprised to see there a curious thing which Joanne and Baedeker should have pointed out to us.[46]

It is not difficult to imagine Morel's emotions during that fortuitous visit. His professional life was to be made memorable by a sheer coincidence!

At all events, Morel realized that his visit to London did not refresh him as his two previous journeys had: Germany when he was an adolescent, and Sicily and Italy when a grown-up, even if his visit to the latter was less inspiring professionally than his London visit. In his book, *La Librairie Publique*, he relates his impressions of Italian librarianship:

> In Italy, in a certain town (when one looks for the librarian) one is always bound to find him, not in the library—but always in the café, and when

you ask for his services he will lend you the key to the library so that he might not be disturbed.[47]

The London public library situation which reflected the phenomenal growth of the English public library—an example of which was given by J.J. Ogle in his *The Free Library* (pp.67 et.seq.)—revealed to the *attaché* Morel the backwardness of the public libraries in his country and the little interest France was taking in their development. As soon as he came back to the Bibliothèque Nationale, his first thoughts were to pass his examination to be promoted *stagiaire*, the second stage of his professional career. But he could not remain insensitive to the lethargy of the French. The stimulus of his first London visit, his already keen admiration for the English civic spirit[48], and his newly acquired enthusiasm for the "free public libraries"[49] impelled Morel to reveal to his colleagues at the Bibliothèque Nationale that he happened "to have discovered a true free public library in London."[50] It was obvious that in doing this, Morel wanted to influence his colleagues to draw their attention to his personal experiences in London and the still comparatively underdeveloped nature of French libraries vis-à-vis their English counterparts. Morel thought that if:

> I spoke about it to my colleagues, librarians, heads of department from top to bottom of the hierarchy, I would find at least someone who was aware of this development, at least one who would show some interest in the matter.

But he was disappointed to see that this did not give rise to the stormy controversies he had anticipated. Instead, he was disgusted to hear simply that:

> all of them unanimously agreed that the British Museum had plenty of money, and that abroad one is nicer to the public than in France.[51]

Morel was irked beyond endurance by the apathetic and pessimistic remarks and negative reactions of his colleagues when he related his experience. Thirteen years later, he was to write in his *La Librairie Publique*:

> But at that time (1897) I could not give thorough consideration to the question of knowing if this manner of providing a service in libraries [Morel was referring to the Italian librarian in the café who did not want to be disturbed] was the most appropriate way to develop them and serve the public! For I had to pass my examination to be appointed *stagiaire* (apprentice) in the library (Bibliothèque Nationale) where I had been working for five years and I had to learn the dates of the establishment of printing in the towns of France, the abbreviations of the incunabulae, and other urgent matters.[52]

1897 was far from being a quiet and untroubled year for Morel. Certainly, there was no opportunity for him to do any constructive library pioneering for the time being. He had more "urgent things" to do, and had to secure his *certificat d'aptitude de stagiaire*. In the world in which Morel was living, cramming for examinations was important, and a vast amount of serious preparation before admission to the permanent staff of the library and promotion by seniority carried more weight than the personal research and impressions of an *attaché* (beginner). As an *attaché* with the humble position in the Bibliothèque Nationale, with a poor income and poorer prospects, Morel found it quite difficult to realize that his strong proselytizing influence was brought to bear whenever he talked to his colleagues about a prospective library movement. Up until then, he had received, in spite of the general advice of the Director of the Bibliothèque Nationale, little training that would authorize him to mix with those colleagues of his who were full-fledged librarians. Indeed, Morel had always despised such training, as no part of it was geared towards active librarianship, but only to paleography.[53] This hindered the desired modification of the administrative framework of public libraries, which were mostly under the control of archivist-paleographers. Developments in science rendered such modifications imperative in order to meet the demands of the new age. Though a decree was passed in 1897, it did not result in the necessary adjustments.

The Decree of 1897, did not, in fact, bring about anything essentially new. Apart from a number of additional provisions reflecting a stricter government policy of centralization (a reinforcement of Salvandy's 1839 Ordinance), the legislation divided public libraries into *biliothèques classées* with a preponderance of *government* stocks and *bibliothèques non-classées* with a preponderance of town stocks. The public library had had a dual composition: its original stock and the post-French Revolution government confiscations from religious houses and the personal libraries of *émigrés* for which it acted as the *Fonds d'Etat* (government stocks) and *fonds de ville* (town stocks).

The decree of the central government was binding only on government stocks. In short, the Decree of 1897 made the *Fonds d'Etat* the main object of the legislation. The *Fonds d'Etat* was to remain in the town library, but was to be kept separate, and its administration and use subject to much stricter government control, however difficult this would prove in practice. The Decree also obliged all public libraries to appoint only professionally qualified persons, which meant, for practical purposes,[54] those with a diploma from the *Ecole des Chartes* or the library school of the Bibliothèque Nationale, established by Leopold Delisle.[55]

All this compelled Morel to prepare for his examination with greater enthusiasm. By October of 1897, the preparation became particularly absorbing. He was more eager to pass his examination as he knew that success by November of the same year would mean that at least he would be put on the same footing as many of his colleagues, whose qualification and experience entitled them to make suggestions on any subject. This would also authorize Morel in a way to express his progressive views on the state of libraries in France, to compare them with those abroad, especially with the Anglo-Saxon ones, and to discuss the detrimental influence of paleography on librarianship.[56]

It is not difficult to imagine Morel's feelings during the weeks to come. The result of the examination came, and his success was followed by his appointment to the post of *stagiaire commissionné* (permanent apprentice). This was recommended by the "eminent paleographer," Leopold Delisle, whose "influence on librarianship" Morel would later describe as "very baneful to its development," as he had subjected the Bibliothèque Nationale to the exclusive control of archivist-paleographers. On November 13th, 1897, at the age of twenty-eight, Morel became one of the permanent "library assistants" at an annual salary of 1800 francs. His next step was to resign from the Paris Parquet. He gave up his lawyer's career for good and started on the first stage of his activities as a "librarian," which were to keep him busy until his death in 1934. However, the three years that followed his appointment to a permanent post on the staff of the national library of France were professionally uneventful until his promotion to the post of *sous-bibliothécaire de classe* 4 (sub-librarian of fourth category) in 1900.

Towards the end of 1897, now that he had lost his doubts about the choice of a career, Morel could relax and indulge more in his social and cultural activities. At twenty-eight, he had not lost interest in his childhood passion: the theater.

Should any curious reader open a copy of J. Thoraval's *Les Grandes Etapes de la Civilization Francaise*, he might agree with Thoraval that there was no reason why Morel should have abandoned French playhouses and returned to his early passion, for

> The time was very bright for French drama, not only because of the number of plays produced and the enthusiasm of the public, but also the magnificent efforts of Antoine with his Théâtre Libre. This theater inaugurates a new era of scenic design, asks of its actors a more naturalistic

drama, coordinates the action of a united team and introduces the public to famous foreign playwrights with plays by Hauptmann, Strinberg and Ibsen. Lugne Poe at the *Théâtre de L'Oeuvre* perseveres in the same direction."[57]

The various minor theaters and the Théâtre Antoine which André Antoine (1858-1943), after the failure of his first venture, Le Théâtre Libre in 1894, had renamed after himself when he took it over as Théâtre des Menus Plaisirs, were having an immense cultural influence on the French society of 1897.[58]

Although thirteen years later, Morel stated that in 1897,

"the French librarians, however [were reading and] had already read in English a very remarkable book published in the Garnett Series The Free Library by Ogle,"[59]

he took less and less interest in professional matters. Like many Parisians he was more attracted by the Théâtre Antoine and other theaters where he could see such successes as *Hannele Mattern, Jules Cesar, Hernani, Oeidpe Roi, Othello, L'Honneur Japonais* and *Hamlet,* in which Mounet-Sully (1841-1916), a "famous French tragedian," excelled.[60]

Morel, who had watched Mounet-Sully performing since he was a child, had now become his close friend. Of his admiration for this actor, Morel wrote:

"For the past thirty years I have seen many of them [tragedians] and very famous, too. Among the five or six who, as men, have given me the impression of being really superior beings, I do not hesitate to include Mounet-Sully himself."[61]

He went on to say:

"He [Mounet-Sully] has realized the triumph of Hugo, has given an almost romantic turn to French tragedy, has created *Oedipe Roi,* which has often been described as sublime melodrama. In short, his conception of Hamlet, a role he always had longed to act, was not alien to that of Delacroix, whose lithography he studies..."[62]

Morel would spend some of his evenings listening to Mounet-Sully reading *La Princesse Georges*[63] and other books, poetical works which Morel lent to him, his favorite being Rosny's *Daniel Valgraive.* He enjoyed other evenings visiting the various theaters to watch Mounet-Sully in his performances and meeting him in his dressing room where they would discuss the actor's stage-craft. By 1897, Mounet-Sully had made a great deal of money from the stage and had become an influential member of the

Comité du Théâtre Français. His generosity led him to introduce unknown authors and playwrights to the Comité du Théâtre Fraçais. Among these were Eugène Morel himself and Romain Rolland, who "before that [...] was not known by anyone" but was later awarded the Nobel Prize in Literature for his *Jean Cristophe* (1916) and his pacifist convictions.[64] Later, in 1912, Morel, in his prefatory note to the book, *Bibliothèque, Livres et Librairies*, which includes all the lectures organized by him at the Ecole des Hautes Etudes Sociales for the Section de Bibliothèques Modernes, was to acknowledge the great help Romain Rolland gave him in advertising the founding of the Section which was to give librarians an adequate and modern training in librarianship and library administration.[65]

Mounet-Sully gave Morel all his friendly support and encouraged him to try his hand at playwriting since his second novel was relatively successful.

Accordingly, Morel, who had made very substantial progress since the publication of *Artificielle* two years earlier, assumed that with the contemporary literary situation, "where the general tone was frivolous,"[66] he could anticipate success. In 1897, he therefore devoted some of his spare time to completing two plays, *La Femme Adultère* and *Dans la Nuit*. He also put the finishing touches to a novel, *La Rouille du Sabre*, which he had worked on from 1891 to 1894.[67]

*La Femme Adultère*, his first play about the life of an adulteress, was a subject of actuality and was in keeping with the traditional literary trend of the late 1890s.[66] The play was not published, though it was of considerable interest not only for its subject matter but also as a reflection of Eugène Morel's views about married life at the age of twenty-eight. It did not come up to Morel's expectations and was not a success. It was never produced, but one scene was featured (or read) with the greatest success at one of the matinees at the Sarah Bernhardt Theatre. It was there that Morel was introduced to André de Lorde, who offered to collaborate with him to complete *Dans La Nuit*, which achieved some success. It was staged at the *Théâtre des Escholiere* at the end of 1897. However, some dramatic critics reproached Morel and de Lorde for having imitated Henrik Obsen (1828-1906), whose plays had not yet been translated into French, and Maurice Maeterlinck (1862-1949), whose first play, *La Princesse Maleine*, earned him the praise of Octave Mirabeau, critic of *Figaro*. Fortunately, this criticism was refuted and the accusation of plagiarism was invalidated. It was proved that Morel had written the play eight years earlier[68] than *La Princesse Maleine* which was published in 1890, and Ibsen's *Ghosts* which was first produced in France by André Antoine in 1890 also.[69] This incident did not result in the termination of the de Lorde-Morel partnership. On the contrary, it consolidated their joint efforts to write many other plays for the Comédie Francaise, the Théâtre Antoine, and the Théâtre du Grand Guignol,[70] which "specialized in short plays of violence, murder, rape, ghostly apparitions and suicide, all intended to chill and delight the spectator."[71] In 1898, under their joint authorship, *Loreau est acquitté au L'Affaire Loreau* appeared. This was staged the same year by La Comédie Francaise. Two years later, the publishing house, La Librairie Théâtrale, accepted the work for publication.[72]

Morel's third novel, *La Rouille du Sabre,* which is "a study of military servitude,"[73] was given a great acclaim. It was published by Harvard and had an immediate and favorable reception. Success was assured by *Le Journal* of François Coppée (1842-1908) where the novel was reviewed at length by Coppée himself.[74] Coppée had by then been elected Member of the French Academy and was accepted as a great writer, playwright, novelist and "poet of the humble." Before he became famous, he was an assistant librarian at the Senate (Palais du Luxembourg) and the archivist of the *Théâtre Français.* It was not Coppée's recollection of his humble past as assistant librarian at the Senate that had persuaded him to launch Morel's work. *La Rouille du Sabre* was its own publicity, as much so that it was singled out by Coppée from all the books to be reviewed in his column. The editor-in-chief of *La Revue Blanche*, Félix Fénéon, immediately commissioned Morel to write a novel.

Morel was only too glad to accept the proposal. He was relieved that this could mean a supplementary source of income to offset the unreasonable salary of 150 francs a month paid for the work which was becoming more demanding at the Bibliothèque Nationale, for there was much to do on the *Catalogue des Imprimés.*

By 1897, the general administrator of the Bibliothèque Nationale, L. Delisle, who succeeded A.J.A. Taschereau in 1874, had worked hard during the past twenty-three years to transform "this mob of books into a library."[76] A paper read at the Twentieth Annual Meeting of the Library Association, London, in October of 1897, by John Macfarlane, gives evidence of the untiring industry of L. Delisle and his personnel in bringing about his metamorphosis in the life of the French national library. J. Macfarlane expresses the conviction that:

> The National Library of France has the reputation of being the largest and richest in the world, while the British Museum is universally admitted to be the next in importance[77] but it is more probable that this superiority could not be demonstrated on the basis of printed books alone and that it arises from the extraordinary richness of the MSS collections at Paris.[78]

It could not have been a matter of astonishment to the audience of the 20th Annual Meeting of the Library Association that this was so when considered that the Bibliothèque Nationale had benefited from an earlier enforcement of the Copyright Acts than the British Museum. This Act was *L'Ordonnance de Montpellier* of 1537, founded by François I, which allowed for the deposit of one copy of each French book and the offer for purchase by the Library of every book printed abroad on sale in France.[79]

After that, L. Delisle, according to A. Masson and P. Salvan's book, *Les Bibliothèques*, inspired by the alphabetical author catalogue of the British Museum,[80] had decided to set in motion the general catalogue of printed books, which by August 1897, he had completed and published as *Catalogue Général des Imprimés de la Bibliothèque Nationale* (General Catalogue of Printed Books in the Bibliothèque Nationale).[81] In the 1960s it was still the most important bibliographical inventory in the world.[82]

Since Leopold Delisle had been primarily interested in the progress of his catalogue and had been using every means to reduce its enormous bulk and to speed up its production, he had been employing less of his time and effort to fight for the materialistic interests of his subordinates.[83] E. Gabriel Ledos, one of Morel's colleagues in 1897[1], who together with a group of *chartistes* (namely E. Babelon, H. Bouchet, Charles and Victor Mortet and Ulysse Robert), undertook the important work of organization and cataloguing under the impetus of L. Delisle[84], gives, twenty-seven years later, an account of life at the Bibliothèque Nationale under the administrator general in 1897 and in the following year. G. Ledos, in his article *"Leopold Delisle et la Bibliothèque Nationale,"* in an issue of *La Revue des Bibliothèques* of 1924, tells the story of those subordinates who went to Delisle and complained of their plight, and quotes the answer that Delisle gave in response to each grievance:

> Don't you think that the honor of working for the Bibliothèque Nationale is sufficient?[85]

He emphasizes that:

> In fact he wished that all employees of the *Bibliothèque Nationale*, like him, should be proud to belong to this old and glorious institution and also that all, by their knowledge, technical and professional merit, and by their industry, could honor and enhance the reputation of this institution.[86]

In spite of all the shadows hanging over his future, Morel continued his services for the next six months to the advantage of the Bibliothèque Nationale.

By the middle of 1898, he considered that he had been working for six years, and with a little perseverance, in less than two years he was sure to be promoted to *sous-bibliothécaire* (sub-librarian.) He was conscious that he had to work hard and long before he could offset the setbacks presented by L. Delisle's lack of understanding towards his subordinates. He made a bold start at studying for his third professional examination of sub-librarian with all the old thoroughness of his *"pre-stagiaire"* examination. The lure of a certain increase of 50 francs in his regular monthly salary was greater than the uncertain proceeds from writing, although this brought him relaxation in moments of depression.

In order to add a supplementary income to his *stagiaire's* salary, he used his leisure time to complete the two novels he was committed to produce. Besides the proposal of *La Revue Blanche*, the publisher Ollendorff required of Morel another novel after *Artificielle* (1895).[1] He satisfied the editor-in-chief of *La Revue Blanche*, Félix Fenéon, as quickly as he could. Morel, no doubt was aware, like Andrè Gide, that:

> "There was no painter or writer of worth who had won fame in the 20th century who did not owe a great debt to Natans and to Félix Fénéon[87] who had many connections in the press and in Paris society."[88]

Morel and André Gide could not both have been wrong. R. Rudorff, in his book, Belle Epoque, testified that:

> "had there been no other magazine, newspaper or review in Paris during the 1890s, the *Revue Blanche* alone would have sufficed to give a clear and comprehensive picture of all that was most important and significant in Paris's cultural life."[89]

Morel sent *Terre Promise*, on which he had worked closely from 1896 to 1897[1], to the *Editions de la Revue Blanche* after a careful revision. By the end of 1898, Morel was relieved to notice that his *Terre Promise*, which "is a novel about society and a long poem in prose," was published jointly in *La Revue Blanche* and *Fasquelle*, as *La Revue Blanche* had commissioned Fasquelle to print it for them.[90] Ollendorff was also pleased to receive Morel's new novel *Les Morfondus* (The Disappointed). It seems that the publisher Ollendorff had continued to ask Morel to write about women's infidelity as this had become not only an excessively popular subject with a certain category of readers of Ollendorff's publications, but also a favorite contemporary subject of light fiction. It no doubt only provided light reading. Just like *Artificielle* (Ollendorff, 1895) and his play, *La Femme Adultàre* (The Adulteress), Morel's *Les Morfondus* did not spare the infidelity of women; it related again the story of an adulteress.[91]

1899 and 1900 proved to be two busy years both literarily and professionally. His writings forced him to continue to work extremely hard during his hours of leisure, in particular on the revision of two novels which the publishers, *Mercure de France* and *Flammarion,* had commissioned him to write. But this did not prove to be a source of anxiety, as he had already one or two unedited works tucked away somewhere which he could produce in an emergency! His interest in librarianship and his promotion to the post of sub-librarian at the Bibliothèque Nationale made him more anxious to tackle the hurdle of the sub-librarian's *certificat d'aptitude.*

In 1899, Morel finished the preparation and the production of Les Boers (The Boers), which was published by La Société du Mercure de France. He was criticized for his *souci d'actualité* (main preoccupation with contemporary events)[91], though according to the information given by *Le Bulletin de la Maison de Livre Français,* Morel had been working on it three years before the outbreak of the South African War.[92] The main reason for the criticism stemmed from the fact that in November of 1899, the Boer War broke out after the Boers had repudiated British "Suzerainty," which on August 8, 1881, had restored self-government to them by the Convention of Pretoria on condition that they (the Boers) be subjected to the "Suzerainty" of the Crown.[93]

In that same year, Morel completed his last contribution to *La Revue pour les Jeunes Filles,* which had been publishing his articles from 1897. The journal, as its French name indicates, was a magazine for young girls. The contribution Morel made was his impressions of his travels, visits, and holidays in various parts of the world. The countries he had visited then were Germany, Italy (including Sicily), England, Turkey, and Greece. Some of these articles were titled *Rome, Grèce, Sicile,* and *St. Germain*—the names of the places he had visited.[94]

The following year Morel returned to work, not merely to his daily responsibilities at the Bibliothèque Nationale but to many activities which surely made 1900 one of the busiest and most decisive years of his professional career. He had to devote most of his leisure time to following lectures at the Ecole des Chartes and studying in preparation for his examination to be admitted to the post of sub-librarian. He spent the rest of the time worrying about his promotion and revising and getting ready the novel that was required of him by the publisher, Ernest Flammarion. This must have taken him many evenings from 1896 to 1898, for it was "of all his works the one that he liked best and was entirely written in verse."[95] He submitted his manuscripts of *La Prisonnière*[96] to the publisher, Ernest Flammarion. The novel, according to his handwritten lists of novels, "ran to aout five thousand lines."[97] It was well received and was also serialized in *La Nouvelle Revue* of the same year.[98]

Before March of 1900, promotion in the Bibliothèque Nationale was going very slowly. A 1907 article in *Bulletin de l'Association des Bibliothécaire Français* stated,

> the competitive feat that precedes the appointment to the post of sub-librarian (i.e. of Grade Four) is meaningless; the conditions that are required to be admitted to such examination are not fixed in a uniform way. *[100]*

In the time of Morel and his colleagues this was already being realized. This must have sapped the enthusiasm of any potential apprentice willing to take up librarianship as a career. Many were conscious of this ambiguity even in 1900, but no one had tried to enquire into it.

It may be assumed that Morel did not overlook this irregularity but was more conscious that this should not be an obstacle to his progress.[101] If Morel were to become a qualified sub-librarian, this would not only raise his annual salary from 1800 francs to 2400 francs, but would provide him with much more time to think seriously about agitating for better libraries in France.[102] The future, as far as his livelihood was concerned, was indeed full of hope. But if his writings proved unsuccessful and he could not find new publishers for his works, then he would at least have a reasonable salary to rely upon.

When the examination came before March of 1900, Morel was fully prepared and only too glad to take it. His success was followed by his being recommended to the post of *sous-bibliothécaire de classe 4* (sub-librarian in Grade 4) by the Director of the Bibliothèque Nationale.[103] This recommendation was sent to the Minister of Public Instruction and Fine Arts, Georges Leygues to be ratified. Georges Leygues, who had been Minister of Public Instruction in 1894, was re-elected on November 1st, 1898 to the same Ministry in the third cabinet of Charles Alexandre Dupuy (1851-1923).

After the usual intricate machinery of C.A. Dupuy's Government, the appointment of Morel to the post of sub-librarian in the Bibliothèque Nationale was approved. This involved the *arête* (departmental order) to be signed by Minister G. Leygues, who confirmed Morel's promotion. This was then sent to Louis Liard, who made an attested copy under seal of it.[104]

Finally, "a certified true copy" (*extrait conforme*) was signed by L. Delisle. A few days after this routine business, Morel received a copy of the departmental order endorsed by the Minister of Public Instruction, the

Director of Higher Education and the Chief Librarian. The *arête* was dated March 1, 1900.[105]

At the end of March 1900, Morel was able to collect his 200 francs salary from the Directeur du Secrétariat et de la Comptabilité. But his interest in the world outside librarianship was further stimulated by an essay competition on drama. It was opened by the *Revue d'Art Dramatique* which had as one of its main objectives the promotion of everything that had to do with the theater. The *Revue* gave encouragement to young actors and supported the work of individual playwrights[106] in the same way as Rachilde, the famous female exponent of decadent eroticism in literature, and her husband, the founder of *Mercure de France,* had been doing for poetry in their magazine.[107] The *Revue d'Art Dramatique* especially interested Morel. He started working on an essay entitled *"Project de Théâtres Populaires."* It ran to "about three thousand lines."[108] It was favorably received by the *Revue d'Art Dramatique* and was awarded the first prize. The publisher, Ollendorff, was later to publish it as a 78 page pamphlet, under the same title.[109] Le Congrès de l'Art Théâtral of 1900, which was the first international theater conference held in Paris, made good use of Morel's article in a report on popular drama in France.

Delegates at the Congrés agreed with a part of Morel's report regarding the desirability of having itinerant dramatic companies intended for all classes of people in France. Morel, however, in his article in the *Revue d'Art Dramatique,* September 1900, which described the activities of the conference which he himself had attended, regretted

> That we had no time to discuss in a useful way the question of theatrical companies on tour, for the future of the theater in France is seriously involved here.[110]

The only obstacle to the realization of Morel's project was the French government's refusal of financial help.[111]

Morel's contribution to *La Revue d'Art Dramatique* had played a minor role in the existence of the magazine. But his previous experience in 1886 with *La Revue Moderne,* of which he became the secretary of the editorial staff[112], had been a useful preparation for much greater personal responsibilities with *La Revue d'Art Dramatique,* in the running of which he had started taking an interest. By the end of 1900, Morel became the editor-in-chief of the magazine, a position he retained until 1903. The magazine's function was to take a greater interest in everything vital and original in theater. During his period as editor, he published monthly reports that had a separate pagination and were entitled *L'Art Dramatique et Musical*. These were "a repertory of theatrical works that one would like to possess nowadays."[113]

Although Morel's relationship with journalists, literary circles like le Salon Goncourt and La Societé du Mercure de France, and his absorbing activities as a sub-librarian at the Bibliothèque Nationale were keeping him very busy in 1900, his own reading, as always, was the last of his personal pursuits to suffer through lack of time. Although he read less than in his schooldays, he was still an avid reader and managed to find great enjoyment in a variety of old and new favorites, which included Hugo's *Hernani* and Rosny's *Daniel Valgraive*. Rosny had made his journalistic debut with Morel in *La Revue Moderne*.[114]

But there is considerable evidence that Morel bought all his books or borrowed them from his friends instead of using the services provided by the various types of public library scattered around the arrondissements of Paris. The term "public library" embraces all the *bibliothèque populaires* and *bibliothèques scolaires* (the historical development and importance of which will be treated in the following chapter), and, to a certain extent, the municipal libraries. The latter's development had their origin in a decree of the National Convention during the French Revolution.[115]

Indeed, in 1908, almost eight years after his promotion to sub-librarian, Morel's first published book on library economy, *Les Bibliothèques: Essai sur le développement des bibliothèques publiques et de la Librairie dans les deux mondes*, did not reveal him as a supporter of either of these popular libraries, or of the municipal libraries.[116]

The municipal libraries were driving away the general reader while remaining the center of attraction for a *coterie* of local allied spirits whose talents were as harmful to public library development as their eccentricities. The municipal libraries were concentrating more on conserving their stocks rather than gearing them to public tastes. They had therefore been functioning at less than their potential. Their old-fashioned outlook and closed access were a deterrent to their use. The directing personnel, the archivist-paleographers, themselves highly intellectual, took more interest in the collections than in their readers. This distinction between scholarly librarians and popular libraries reveals the rift between the social classes in the use of libraries. The English public library pioneer, Edward Edwards, seemed to have had this discrimination in mind in 1869:

> The general character impressed on the district libraries partakes much more of charitable gift from richer to poorer than of public provision for a public interest. In this feature lies the salient distinction between the free libraries of England and America and many *Volksbibliotheken* of Germany

on the one hand, and the *bibliothèques populaires* of Paris and many other French towns on the other hand.[117]

This dichotomy was still maintained in 1900, and Morel, in 1910, in his book *La Librairie Publique*, tackled this problem in explicit terms:

> Municipal and popular libraries! This is absurd. It's the distinction, I know, that one would make at the police station in separating out *Les Blouses* (the badly dressed) from *les paletots* (the dressed up) who had been nabbed in merry-making. This discrimination can easily be made at branches and annexes in districts. But there is no need to write it on the door. However, let me point out that it is prejudicial to have two 'carte' hours. In opening as it is the case here, the populaires in the evening and on Sundays only, and *les comme il faut* (libraries for the intellectuals) in the afternoon up to 4 p.m., we deprive readers of all classes of society who are really interested in using libraries from using them properly.[118]

If this point of view was still contested in 1910, the condition for readers must have been worse in Morel's 1900.

Part of *Les Bibliothèques* was directed against the danger that the popular and school libraries stood in the way of the development of "free public libraries," and gave Morel's theoretical plans for building up an adequate French system of public libraries in a way comparable to that in the Anglo-Saxon countries. Most of these popular libraries had been state-supported since 1879, as they were "recognized to be of certain use to the public" *(reconnues d'utilité publique)*[119], and were counter-attracting so many readers from the municipal libraries that it was quite difficult for the French Government and local councils to decide whether they should withdraw their subsidy from the popular libraries and give all their moral and financial support to the municipal libraries. Thus, *les conseils municipaux* (local councils) would be able to run their municipal libraries on the same lines as their counterparts on the other side of the Channel, where the Public Libraries Act, which was passed in the Houses of Commons and Lords on August 14th, 1850 made it possible for "municipal libraries to be fought for in the individual towns."[120] The Report from the Select Committee, London, had revealed earlier that "England was still in want of libraries freely accessible to the Public and would derive great benefit from their establishment."[121] Morel was thinking in these terms for the setting up of French municipal libraries. Local councils would be authorized by a similar library act to set up free public libraries from the proceeds of a levy on the citizens. Thoughts like these presaged the end of the popular libraries and the establishment of "true public libraries"—the free public libraries of which Morel was to be an enthusiastic advocate.[122]

Michel Bouvy, in a review of J. Hassenforder's *Développement compare des bibliothèques publiques en France, en Grande Bretagne et aux Etats Unis dans la seconde moitié du XiXe siècle, 1850-1914*, in *Le Bulletin des Bibliothèques de France* of 1969, made the reader aware of the important problem of the unstable and charitable nature of these popular libraries which suffered from "the appeal to benevolence, lack of security, lack of means, the character of a charitable work of paternalistic nature."[123] On the other hand, M. Bouvy pointed out how Hassenforder had demonstrated that the French municipal libraries born during the French Revolution, which paradoxically served as model institutions to the first English and American libraries around the 1850s had been forced, since their creation by the National Convention, to drag, like a convict, their enormous ball and chain of volumes acquired from confiscations of the monasteries and the personal libraries of noble families. The mass of ancient collections, though invaluable and interesting in themselves, had to be catalogued—a thing which was not yet completed in the 1960s and smelled of midnight oil. They were a matter of magnificent study to a more erudite, rather than professional, librarian. This had relegated the function of the French municipal libraries to the preservation of stocks which had been removed from their traditional repositories during the Revolution and Empire and entrusted to them in 1803. This function had not changed in the 1900s and 1920s.[124] The idea of going beyond it never seems to have occurred to anybody, and the storing of books seems to have been taken by the municipalities as adequate justification for the existence of their libraries. Very few dreamt of retrieving the books for use. No doubt they were discouraged by lofty indifference of the provincial public and its lack of interest in scientific activity. The nature of the stock itself—a legacy from church and monastery containing works on theology, church history, canon law, and related disciplines—limited its clientele and dampened the enthusiasm of those who wished to visit the library. Its origin explains the almost complete absence of modern literary and scientific works. Thus, there was a wide gulf, an almost total lack of relationship between the library's stock and the contemporary orientation towards scientific interest and recreational reading. All this had thrown the municipal libraries open exclusively to a very few erudites—elitist *bourgeois* (nobles, doctors, notaries, ecclesiastics, and judges)—the backbone of the local scholarly classes—and the library personnel themselves, the archivist-paleographers who were making of history and old literary works a hobby in which they took more pride than in their own every day work.[125]

Thus, the library was born only for those who, on account of their social position, could avail themselves exclusively of the municipal advantages and wanted but one thing: to preserve jealously these treasures which the "general reader" was not considered worthy of and was not encouraged to have access to.[126] The municipal libraries were thus to retain, even in Morel's times, this elitist characteristic.

As early as 1833, an effort was made to overcome this tendency in municipal libraries. An extract from a circular issued on November 22nd of the same year by the Minister of Public Instruction, which was quoted by M. Pellisson in his book, *Les Bibliothèques Populaires*[127], then by J. Hassenforder[128], purported to show this:

> The majority of libraries are frequented by a small number of readers. This lack of interest can well come partly from the indifference to self-study. But there is also another reason for it: the lack of agreement between the needs, the spirit of the readers, and the types of works that are offered for recreation and relaxation.

This circular did not bring any improvement to public libraries in France. The French greeted it with less enthusiasm than they did the previous one. Many later circulars were to have the same fate.

Four years after this famous circular of 1833, Edward Edwards, the English library pioneer, paid a visit to Paris. Ten years later he recalled it in an article, "Public Libraries in London and Paris" in the *British Quarterly Review* of 1847, and forecast the snobbish French system of having one library for the intellectual and another for the general public. This had already started to cripple the expansion of public librarianship in France. E. Edwards, in his brief reference to the lamentable catalogue but remarkable service of the Bibliothèque Royale (later Bibliothèque Nationale), apparently felt that

> On the whole, it cannot be doubted, that far more ample provision is made for the student in Paris than in London, even were the *Bibliothèque Royale* the only public library in the former capital...[129]

But Edward Edwards' France of 1837 did not change a great deal in terms of library provision in the next sixty-three years. The public library as an institution legally controlled by the authorities, state or municipal, remained, for the time being, an Anglo-Saxon phenomenon. In France's 1900 it was merely a vague wish. It did not have the necessary vigor to force the authorities to realize that the private sector (popular libraries) could not keep pace with social evolution nor the demands it aroused in adults—demands that the existing libraries, including the municipal library, could not satisfy. For it was evident that many of Morel's contemporaries and colleagues in 1900 who did not know what E. Edwards' term *public library* embraced—a term which Morel understood to be a *free accessible library*[130] supported by the special rate raised for public library service[131]—took their Société Franklin's libraries, popular, school and parish libraries for their public libraries. At that time, people were not aware of the fact that if a public library were to play its essential role, it must be an institution of fairly extensive activities manned by an adequate number of professionally trained *librarians* and not archivist-paleographers. Later in his book, *La Librairie Publique*[132], Morel gave vent to his repressed feelings about the popular libraries and the unhappy state of affairs in the library world of France. In his view,

> A *populaire* (popular library) differs from *la librairie publique* (free public library) as much as the private commercial establishment at the street corner which deals in books, haberdashery, stationery and newspapers differs from the library of the University. The habit of branding every collection of books, which does not concentrate on archeology or literary criticism, with the name of *populaire* explains perhaps the one reason for the backwardness of French libraries. Even the most broadminded people who are au courant with what is going on are behind this confusion.[133]

Morel went on to show that even the administrator general of the Bibliothèque Nationale was far from understanding the term *La Librairie Publique:*

> The former administrator general of the Nationale, M. Leopold Delisle, eminent paleographer, whose influence, according to us (librarians) was very baneful (to library development) complained at the *Congrès des Bibliothèques* (International Conference of Librarians, Paris), held in 1900, that our big libraries and even *La Nationale* tend to become true reading rooms where people come and ask for popular works and current literature...

He proposed that big public libraries should be created and be richly stocked with no more than about a hundred thousand volumes, which would be sufficient, said he, with a certain disgust, "for the research work of scholars."[134]

As far as the popular libraries of the *Société Franklin* are concerned, J. Hassenforder, in an article in *Education et Bibliothèques* in 1963, on the "history of an attempt to promote popular libraries by La Société Franklin," revealed why these institutions had not succeeded in creating the basis for the continuous development of public readership while their counterparts in

# THE MAKING OF A LIBRARIAN

America and England had.[135] He quoted a Report submitted to the General Assembly of La Société Franklin, May 19, 1896, which shows that the *Société* had started to decline, but a few years afterwards it had disappeared completely[136] through lack of funds, lack of understanding for readers and the death of the directing personnel.

Michel Bouvy, in the review of J. Hassenforder's book, is more conclusive about its importance and dissolution and emphasizes that

> after all, La Société Franklin was an illusion; it was but an association of very small and independent libraries. A very small and isolated library is not really a library and it is the opposite of a free public library,[137]

such as the Anglo-Saxon municipal library. For the municipal library in England and the United States in 1900 had rapidly become a fundamental institution. In both countries, laws had been passed since the 1850s that allowed municipalities to levy special rates for the development of their public libraries. This made a public municipal library the work of the local community for the local community.[138]

By their failure and decline in 1896, the school, parish, popular libraries, and La Société Franklin had begun to show Morel that a library which was not properly financially supported was of no use and did not stand a chance of survival. To Morel's mind, these libraries had not only counter-attracted readers from the French municipal libraries but had discredited the notion of *la librairie publique*, that is to say, a free public library, in a milieu where this had taken so deep a root.

It was very difficult for Morel to eradicate the old idea and implant a new concept that was briefly brought to public notice by a French observer in 1895. The latter described the evolution of the concept of the free public library embodied in the Public Libraries Act, 1850, and which London was the slowest of any district in England to adopt, but to which it was won over before 1900:

> If you go over the London constituencies," wrote the observer, "you cannot refrain from noticing on the main roads a certain number of institutions almost new because in 1885, there was not a single one of them bearing this inscription, "free public library." Now they do. The main door overlooking the main road is always open. People come and go without interruption. In the evening, their windows flash with a brighter light than those of the neighboring cabarets, thus inviting the crowd in. When one has crossed the threshold of any one of these libraries, one will find a reading room. On a special desk are arranged all the daily newspapers; on the tables all the journals. In all London libraries, I have come across French magazines or newspapers. The crowd read in silence;

this one reads the advertisements, that one the news, the third his trade or professional journal and so on and so forth... Close to that room is the lending library. It deals only with the loan for home reading... Finally, high above is a reference library, quiet and calm... supplied with desks where the readers can come to consult and use all the reference books that the Library contains...[139]

Accordingly, by the end of 1900, Morel, in his capacity as sub-librarian at the Bibliothèque Nationale, was inspired by his first visit to London five years earlier. He felt that the popular libraries were alienating the state's attention from the municipal libraries. France was therefore already taking the wrong road in maintaining a bastard conception of the public library—a free public library as he understood it to be in England and the United States.

In the 19th century, in both countries, library pioneers tried to define the term "public library." The American Andrew Keogh in *Public Libraries*, in July of 1901, in a comparative study of English and American libraries, wrote thus:

> A library may or may not be supported by taxation. It may or may not be controlled by the municipal or other local authority. But so long as it opens all its departments free of charge to the residents of its district, it is a public library...[140]

However, in a more restrictive way, one understands by the term public library, a library financed by public funds. Yet in the 1840s, the great English library pioneer E. Edwards (1812-1886) laid stress on the degree of accessibility that the library could offer in his definition of a public library:

> I would take it as embracing first of all libraries deriving their support from public funds, either wholly or in part, and I would further extend it to such libraries as are made accessible to the public to a greater extent.[141]

True, the French municipal library was *public* in the sense that it was maintained by the local authorities, and, *theoretically*, was open to all. But its almost exclusively scientific stock and purpose prevented it from complying with the requirements and fulfilling the functions of a public library for all sections of the population. France was therefore without a true public library system, in spite of all the theoretical considerations brought forward in numerous propaganda campaigns and treatises, like A. Chevalley's in 1898 and those of some Catholic personalities who had tried to put forward theoretical plans for a proper public library system based on Anglo-Saxon lines. A. Chevalley worked in that particular direction by writing his monographs and compiling many others on adult education in England for

# THE MAKING OF A LIBRARIAN

the production of his 300 page book entitled, *L'Eductation populaire des adultes en Angleterre* (1896). In 1898, he conducted a press campaign in *Le Temps* and *Le Manuel Général de l'Enseignement primaire* for the establishment of public libraries for all sections of the population.[142] In 1910, Morel wrote:

> Among those [Roman Catholic personalities] who have understood and made themselves supporters of the concept of the public library in France, of the free public library, I mean, open to everybody, come foremost among the fervent Catholics l'Abbé Perreyve and le Père Piolet. [They] have been the first to reveal this social novelty—the *librairie publique* [free public library] and its role in England—a thing that the majority of laymen and politicians know nothing of.[143]

But the campaign of A. Chevalley, l'Abbé Perreyve, and le Père Piolet "did not have constructive results, nor any, in fact. The time was not ripe for such a campaign."[144] It was too moderate and left people in France around the 1900s with the opinion that French public libraries approximated to those of America of 1876.

The actions and endeavors of these library pioneers, however, did little towards the setting up of the free public libraries. It was at this juncture that Morel thought of taking his rightful place in the evolution of libraries and of modeling the French public library according to his ideals. It was then that he also started to work on his ambitious work *Les Bibliothèques*[145], in which he testified to his early vehement propagandist movement:

> I began this book more than ten years ago and many chapters of it have appeared in *Le Mercure de France* and *La Nouvelle Revue*. It was written or rewritten in 1906 and completed in 1907.[145]

From that day, France had found a moving spirit in Morel, who was to be behind the progressive development of the *free public library* and to spend his entire life continuously and fiercely campaigning against the caste system in the municipal libraries and against everything that would spoil the prospects of a modern public library system. His vehemence against all the political developments that had ruined the chances of a sober and calm evolution of the library had been repressed until now. But it would become more definite and conclusive in such criticisms as:

> Before saying a word on popular libraries, let us say: France will have libraries only when she gives up the *populaires* [popular libraries.][146]

Or, in indignant statements like this, which could be justified:

> We have to show that neither in Paris, nor in France, do we truly have libraries...With our term *'populaire'* and *'scolaire'* [popular and school

library] we do not know what a free public library is. As for the municipal libraries which should be accessible to all sections of the population, they are run by archeologists who open them exclusively to those whose main interest is history. They are not accessible to the general public, are impervious to modern concepts of librarianship, have ridiculous budgets, and impossible hours of opening. Not only the public but the librarians themselves do not know the meaning of a free public library.[147]

It was abundantly clear that the pioneering work that awaited Morel was far from easy. He had to work hard and long for success.[148] A new chapter in his profession was beginning.

# Moving Spirits in the French Library Movement

In order to understand the role of Eugène Morel in the development of public libraries in France, it is essential to look back on the history of public libraries in that country, as well as on the achievements of various library pioneers before Morel.

The modern history of French public libraries begins with the French Revolution in 1789, when special attention was first given to the development of public libraries by the Convention Nationale. A decree of the National Assembly (November 2nd, 1789) declared all the possessions of the Church to be National property *(biens nationaux)*.[1] The municipal libraries had their origins in a decree of the Convention Nationale entrusting to the schools the numerous large libraries which had formerly belonged to religious congregations and to noble families, often referred to as aristocratic *émigrés*.[2] Although some early town libraries, for example that of Lyon, date back to 1530, most of the municipal libraries owed their origins to the confiscations of the Revolution. These confiscations were allocated to various municipalities which, according to the concept of equality of the French Revolution, were supposed to be made accessible to one and all so that every citizen could have parity of use. Many collection points were established in Paris and other communes for the purpose of storing these large confiscated stocks of books and manuscripts.[3] The Legislator of Fourth Year of the French Revolution thought—like Mirabeau, Talleyrand and Condorcet—that libraries should fulfill a civilizing role by being accessible and free to all classes of the population. Unfortunately, this democratic ideal of the library promoters of the French Revolution did not become a reality, and the administrations which succeeded the Convention Nationale did nothing to keep these libraries up to date.[4] They retained, even at the beginning of the 20th Century, the characteristics of learned libraries which were merely encyclopedic in nature.[5] Instead of allowing

> all the French without distinction of rank or fortune to develop their intellect in all spheres and to follow up during their life, by voluntary study, their personal education[6]

these libraries met the requirements of a few privileged erudites.[7] However, Maurice Pellisson, in his book, *Les Bibliothèques Populaires à l'Etranger et en France, 1906*, remarked that

> if the Revolution's public readership concept had become a reality, France would have had a network of libraries comparable to that of the Free Town Libraries which England started to organize from 1850 and in which she takes a legitimate pride.[8]

Because of the above factors, public libraries in France were of far less value than their counterparts in Great Britain and the United States and were to persistently lag behind them. Before the appearance of Eugène Morel, there were many French library theorists who tried to overcome the traditional apathy in the development of public libraries and to urge them to fulfill their role of educating people.

The history of public libraries in France is characterized by the repetitive efforts of a very few men or groups of men to promote their cause. Unfortunately, these efforts were too isolated to make any impact. Among these men may be cited Gabriel Naudé (1600-1653), Philipon de la Madelaine (1734-1818),[9] and more particularly, statesmen like François Guizot (1787-1874), François Villemain (1790-1870) and Comte Narcisse-Achille de Salvandy (1787-1856). The last three were closely associated with the Ministry of Public Instruction and devoted themselves to improving all types of library.[10] Each, in his own way, maintained that French libraries should lay stress less on the conservation of the stock which was bequeathed to them and more on making it as available as possible to the general public.

The first to make a plea for a public library accessible to all in quest of knowledge was Gabriel Naudé, a librarian of the 17th century. This he made in the ninth chapter of his book, *Avis Pour Dresser Une Bibliothèque, 1627*, which was the first practical treatise on libraries:

> What purpose could be more noble than to consecrate [the library] to the use of the public, and never to deny it even to the least of men who should wish to consult it.[11]

Gabriel Naudé also made a plea for a public reference library. This was so much in advance of his time that it did not bring immediate fruit.[12] But,

> When, in 1664, he issued a second edition of his treatise, he had the pleasure of seeing a library dedicated to the public growth under his hands, a collection such as his youthful enthusiasm had pictured seventeen years before.[13]

In 1783, Louis Philipon de la Madeleine, a literary man and lawyer who became the librarian of the Ministry of Public Instruction in 1795[14], recommended in his book *Vues Pratiques sur l'education du Peuple, tant des Villes que des Campagnes* (Lyon, 1783) the creation of depots where the poor would find books useful to them. Louis Philipon de la Madeleine went so far as to support the idea of opening libraries in the villages to cater for rural readers. "The popular library as conceived by L. Philipon de la Madeleine," remarked M. Pellisson in his book,

> was no other than a benevolent institution meant only to give people a practical knowledge of things that could be immediately utilized. However, he did not think that it could and should be used to promote general culture and become a civilizing influence.[15]

This concept which P. de la Madeleine had been unable to put into practice was the one which inspired the library promoters of the French Revolution.

François Guizot (1787-1874), who laid before the 1849 Select Committee on Public Libraries of Great Britain the results of his experiences in France in his capacity as Minister of Public Instruction (1832-1836, 1836-1837), succeeded in linking the Municipal Libraries to his department.[16] Until then no control was exercised over them. From 1837 onwards, libraries were regularly inspected and encouraged to improve their collections. They received donations of books and money which came from the state, especially from Guizot's Minsitry of Public Instruction.[17] In 1849, France had 107 public libraries, and unrestricted admission was already in operation.[18] This practice and the stocks of these libraries would be used by Edward Edwards to support his case for the promulgation of the Ewart law and would be cited as an example at the British Parliamentary Committee on Public Libraries, on July 23rd, 1849. Though in 1849 Guizot, in describing the situation of public libraries in France in the pre-1850 period, before the 1849 Select Committee, remarked that "they [the public libraries] are accessible in every way; the library is open to everybody who is a well-known person in the town,"[19] these libraries were left with a worse fate than the British libraries until the move made by Eugène Morel at the beginning of the 20th Century. (It must be noted that the reliability of Guizot's evidence on the flourishing state of public libraries in France is still open to discussion.)

One of the reasons why French libraries did not flourish like their Anglo-American counterparts was the lack of civic spirit and small number of philanthropists.

If there were philanthropists in France, they could be counted on one hand. In Paris, however, there were some examples of private donors who had enriched popular libraries. In 1895, a library in Impasse d'Oran was bequeathed a legacy of 90,000 francs by Mrs. Gustave Tridon, which gave the library a yearly subsidy of 2,331 francs.[20] In 1882, Aimé Samuel Forney made a legacy of 200,000 francs, and four years later, the Bibliothèque d'Art et d'Industrie Forney was established in Rue Titon. This sum was bequeathed at his death in 1879 for the construction of a public municipal library to cater to the working classes of Paris. It yielded a revenue of 7,105 francs, which was used for the maintenance of the building and the building-up of its stock.[21] Generally, the municipal libraries were strongly biased towards the humanities, but the Forney Library developed into one of the most interesting municipal special libraries with a large collection of works on art, technology and science. (This Library is, today, unique in Paris.) Besides these, there were some book donations from M. Groud (1,000 volumes), Léon Coignet (600 volumes), Edelstand du Méril (5,400 volumes in 1892), Mocomble (600 volumes in 1886), Foussier (2,000 volumes in 1885), Parent de Rossan (4,000 volumes in 1895), and Bonnemain (800 volumes in 1903). As Maurice Pellisson pointed out:

> It is possible that in certain parts of the country there could have been donations of this kind, but though one does not have positive information about them, one can confidently deduce that they were very few...From what we know of the popular provincial libraries they receive only books which one would like to get rid of. As regards the little money which they collect, it is the proceeds of school fetes, subscriptions, financial help received from *societés* like *La Ligue de l'Enseignement, La Société Franklin, Le Sou des Bibliothèques,* etc., resources which after all, cannot be other than meager and precarious.[22]

In spite of the successive efforts of these early library theorists, the public library in France never reached the same standard as its firmly established counterparts in England and the United States. France was to discover the public library only after the Second World War. Few public libraries had any specific objectives, and those which had were orientated towards the original function of preservation. The libraries were not supported by fixed taxation levied for the sole purpose of setting them up, as was the case with their Anglo-Saxon counterparts after 1850. Therefore, the development of French libraries remained static until the beginning of the 20th century. Maurice Pellisson, in his book *Les Bibliothèques Populaires à l'Etranger et en France,* was to recommend that, "the financial régime of our libraries be modeled on that which is prevalent in America and in England,"[23] and propounded the idea of launching a referendum in 1906 to see if the Municipalities and the citizens would consent to a levy of rates for the establishment of public libraries.[24] However, this recommendation was not implemented by the central and local governments.

To revert to the work of Guizot and other public library pioneers, it may be pointed out that while Guizot undoubtedly performed useful preparatory work, he did not take the state of the French Library seriously. The spade work was done by Comte Narcisse Achille de Salvandy, Minister of Public Instruction (1837-1839, 1845-1848).[25] It was he who tried to remedy conditions in the Bibliothèque Nationale by putting one person in charge, thus introducing the principle of authority. Salvandy also acted with far more enthusiasm than Guizot in the affairs of city libraries. In his ministerial circular of April 14th, 1838, one year after he took office as Minister of Public Instruction, he invited all municipalities to organize evening classes for artisans on the same lines as those set up by the British Mechanics' Institute, thus trying to cater for the adult education of French citizens. The Municipal libraries were to be a means of furthering their education. To support this, he was instrumental in reorganizing existing libraries and in building new ones.[26] This task was entrusted to J.A. Buchon (1791-1846), journalist and philosopher, and J.G.F. Ravaisson, Chief of the Secrétariat of Public Instruction, in 1837, who was to be appointed General Inspector of Public Libraries on March 15th, 1839.[27] They both had to consider if any benefit could be derived from the depots, which since the Revolution had been neglected.

In order to force departments and municipal authorities to put their affairs in order, Salvandy directed them to submit their catalogues to the central authority. The submission of these catalogues gave him the opportunity to compile a large number of inventories, which give one some idea of the state of the French Municipal Libraries around 1838. These inventories contributed towards the launching of *Le Grand Livre des Bibliothèques Publiques de France*. In 1838, *Le Grand Livre* served a double purpose: the establishment of central control over the French city libraries, and the creation of a central bibliographical aid to scientific research. Thus the idea of centralization in the public library system in Paris was introduced. This, to many library theorists, would be the immediate cause of the backwardness of the French public library system.

Salvandy was responsible for some reorganization in the public library sector. One move which was to be of great future significance was to secure the appointment of full-time city librarians. He also insisted that the city libraries be opened to the public all day. Another step which he took and which was to determine the fortunes of the French library for the rest of the century was the promulgation of L'Ordonnance Royale du 22 février, 1838. Salvandy's Ordinance (as it is usually called) did not refer exclusively to library affairs, but regulated all cultural matters falling under direct jurisdiction of the Ministry of Education. This document was the real charter or constitution of the French library. However, Salvandy was not given unlimited authority over the library. He had control only over those libraries entrusted to his jurisdiction by the government. He had no say over the stocks of the city libraries, but only over those of the Government libraries. The city authority retained full control over its own stock. Salvandy could not personally enforce the Ordinance. He had to leave administrative control in the hands of the city authorities. Finally, he was reduced to recommending that they should treat the Ordinance as a model and follow the same procedure with regard to their holdings as that which he prescribed for the government stock. The improvement that Salvandy brought about with his Ordinance was that he could introduce commissions, under the chairmanship of the mayors, to exercise continuous and efficient control over the activities and fortunes of the local libraries.[28] The Ordinace also provided for the nomination of town librarians by central government. But this encroached on the autonomy of the communes and aroused such fierce antagonism that Salvandy was forced to restore this right to the town councils. This Ordinance concerning libraries might have led to great progress if the city authorities had heeded the government's intentions. Though Salvandy's administrative capacity was revealed in this Ordinance, it is unfortunate that in the library sphere, as in other fields, France has always witnessed a big gap between legislative intention and implementation. Also, the centralization of power in Paris had always thwarted the active moves of the other subordinate library authorities to provide a service similar to that in the Paris libraries. The inertia of Paris was to reflect on other libraries in all parts of France. All the plans which should have been implemented immediately were bogged down in an endless process of delay. One of the advantages that France derived from the Ordinance was the introduction of the Library Local Authority Commission. This Commission strengthened local authority and subjected the library to communal control.[28]

This organization, or rather reorganization of municipal libraries, was an undertaking which could have given appreciable results in the long run. However, it was to benefit urban people only, for the majority of those who were in favor of popular education were willing to act without delay and wanted their action to have an effect on the country as a whole. As this action was always delayed, private bodies tended to create libraries in small communes, and in order to do this immediately, they were forced to formulate projects which were very modest. Projects of this kind were therefore quite considerable in number. It would not be out of place to describe a few of them. Libraries for the people in Paris grew out of small *"cabinets de lecture"* and private libraries based on the idea of François-Marie Delessert, who in 1836, while discussing the budget of the Ministry of Public Instruction, made an appeal that all communes should be provided with popular libraries.[30] In 1837, M. Perdonnet, President of the *Association Polytechnique*, founded a library at the Halles aux Draps for the workmen who followed his courses.[31] By 1850, the Société des Bibliothèques Communales had planned a library for every commune and the Paris arrondissements with a catalogue of 100 books each. This plan never became a reality.

Around the middle of the 19th century, the French Minister of Public Instruction of the Provisional Government of 1848 contemplated a reorganization of the library system in France. He was the son of Lazare Carnot, called *"Le Grand Carnot"* Hippolyte Carnot, who took part in the Revolution of 1830. When the advent of the Republic of 1848 imposed for a short time a democracy upon those who were in power, the government was careful not to forget the question of libraries.[32]

On behalf of the provisional government, Hippolyte Carnot announced a plan.[33] The French government of 1848 was unstable, however, and his plan had no future. His successor, Freslon[34], in the permanent government, was able to implement only the declamatory portions, in the form of a directive to the French prefecture. Carnot's plan had advocated the establishment of public libraries for town and country.[35] It emphasized the importance of the attainment of post-school qualifications by the masses through self-study and reading. But France in the 1850s lacked a philanthropic and civic spirit and could not boast of a powerful organization comparable to the British Mechanics' Institute. The plan failed because the type of literature recommended for such libraries did not meet the requirements of the readers. The plan was far from being an administrative set and contained no concrete suggestions, but approximated to an election manifesto full of unfulfilled promises for the future. If this ephemeral Republic and Carnot's recommendations had survived a little longer, and if Napoleon III had not started to exercise absolute power from 1852-1858, France might have been able to recognize in the plan the first relevant, official move to promote such mass enlightenment as England was witnessing at that time.

On the other hand, Napoleon III, feeling, like all statesmen, vulnerable in his anarchic constitutional position, found it essential for his government to win over the masses. He advised his Minister of Public Instruction, Vicomte Frederic Alfred Pierre de Falloux, to direct his attention to the lowest class of the community. Napoleon III made as many concessions as he could to them. He directed his main attention to the farming population. Falloux succeeded in promulgating the law of freedom of teaching in 1850, for which he had been fighting. Though Napoleon III realized that the urban working class interest in reform was a major threat, he made considerable efforts to include them in his attempt to enhance the popularity of his new regime by a semblance of mass education. His first move was the promulgation of the Falloux Act of 1850, which placed public education and reading matter under the supervision and control of the church. His interest was mainly centered in the rural areas where his proposed libraries could easily be affiliated with two established systems: a generally organized and nation wide school system and a group of parochial libraries. Initially the library promoters saw no disadvantage in the policy and they supported and expanded both the parochial and school systems. Thus, the library was linked to the school, even where it was thrown open to adults. The Decree of June, which came twelve years after the Falloux Act, enforced the setting up of the French school library. So much importance was attached to it that it was expected to function as a public library. Napoleon's plan was put into force by Victor Dury, his liberal-minded minister of Public Instruction from 1863-1869, who achieved reforms in the domain of education.[36] Dury's plan was to establish about 40,000 similar libraries, that is to say, as many libraries as there were schools. By 1872, the government had set up but one third of them. In such a short period, it was a fair achievement.

But the Second Napoleonic Regime was unable to arouse enthusiasm, and Napoleonic conservatism started to decline. The move for mass education seemed to lose its glitter, and public libraries began to wane. Fortunately, at this critical period one of the most prominent figures in liberal progressive circles started pleading earnestly for the general expansion of libaries.[37] He was the famous author Charles Augustin Sainte Beuve[38], who was to find an indefatigable supporter in Ernest Renan, the church historian. In 1866[39], they founded the famous Ligue de L'Enseignement on the suggestion of the French publicist, Jean Mace.[40] This new society strove to divorce the cultural and intellectual sector from ecclesiastical control and served as a powerful instrument for the general secularization of education and schooling. The organization of the Ligue rested with Jean Mace.[41] By the beginning of the 20th century, the Ligue had fully attained its objective, though around 1866 the struggle for power was intensified as two opposing forces, Church and State, were disagreeing on the desecularization of the State and public affairs.[42]

While in its Decree of June 1862 the Napoleonic regime had concentrated its library policy on the provincial and rural areas, with good though one-sided results, the Jules Ferry Decree of 1870 was to divide its attention between the provinces and the capital.

Ferry's plan envisaged the establishment, in every district of Paris, of a public library with free and unrestricted access which was to remain open throughout the day. It was also to operate a lending system. After a slow start, by the turn of the century, Paris had 75 district libraries with a quarter of a million books and a loan circulation of a million and a half. It should be pointed out here that to arrive at these figures one must include not only Jules Ferry's lending libraries but a number of other distinctive types of library. Though Ferry's idea did eventually bear fruit, it was to mark the beginning of the over-development of the Paris library system compared with the rest of France.[43]

The Paris Library system up to this date has always represented a powerful separate force in the overall structure of public librarianship in France. The development of Paris municipal libraries was reflected in 1894 in statistics of loans which, according to tables shown in Maurice Pellisson's *Les Bibliothèques Populaires à L'Etranger et en France*, were 1,609,754.[44] Yet these libraries were to witness a gradual decline in their activities after 1900.

By the 1870s the library system was in such chaos that Jules Ferry's successor, Jules Simon, Minister of Education, ordered a general *enquete* on January 8th, 1873, into the whole of the library ramifications. Communes, associations, and private undertakings had all set up popular libraries in many places. The *enquete* was to ignore no aspect of the town library, the school library and private libraries in existence. The result was the issue of the Decree of January 6th, 1874 based on the enquiry's findings. The Decree was to determine the policy of the library for the next quarter of a century. In the light of French library policy it seemed likely to inaugurate an organized library service. In the decree, the French government, for the first time, distinguished clearly between popular municipal libraries *(bibliothèques populairs municpales)*, usually called the "popular library," which were independent of popular libraries; popular state-aided libraries, which were subjected to state control; and the school library that had been thrown open to adults. The *enquete* revealed that there were 1000 independent libraries[45] and 15,000 school libraries.[46] This *enquete* gives one some idea of how France set about solving the problem of adult education.

The Decree of 1874 was not very effective. The French Decree encouraged but did not compel municipalities to set up local libraries, the grant of a state subsidy being dependent on the acceptance of state supervision. To consolidate state supervision, a commission was instituted to each prefecture. The state sent regular consignments of books selected by the Commission on the basis of the prefecture's recommendations which were based on the nature and extent of the requirements of each library. However, libraries did not receive grants. A sort of censorship was practiced at the governmental level, as a close watch was kept on the trend of the literature provided and on the direction of the post-school development of the masses. From that day, the strict control of the state over public library affairs was centralized in Paris. The British Ewart Law and those that succeeded it in Great Britain tended to give all municipalities virtually complete autonomy to administer the public library service they offered. In France, the centralization was to have far reaching and detrimental effects on the future development of the public library. This was due to the fact that the state determined what was and what was not to be read, leaving local authorities no autonomy to deal with the matter. In 1879, three commissions were set up: one for the public library, one for the school library, and one for the general selection of books.

As has been pointed out earlier, French libraries had been attached to the Ministère de l'Instrucion Publique since 1830. The first library charter was obtained in 1839, when a Royal Commission considered the organization of all types of library. Those holding stock from the Revolution were considered as being, to some extent, controlled by the State. In 1897, they were given the name of *bibliothèques classes*. A third of the librarians' posts were given to archivist-paleographers, who, by attending the Ecole des Chartes, had received some elementary knowledge of bibliography and of library economics.[47] But effective government and control were not achieved. Various modifications continued to be made to the charter until 1919. Charles Mortet, in the September issue of the *Library Association Record*, 1925, gave some information on the government of the "public libraries of France, national, communal, and university" and pointed out that the government of libraries in France was remarkable until World War II for its diffuseness.[48] This system prevailed. The Anglo-Saxon libraries were more associated with the educational movement for the furtherance of adult education. French libraries did little to promote this. For instance, in the United Kingdom, the Education Act of 1870 was indirectly to encourage British municipal libraries to initiate substantial programs of lectures and classes which were to become very popular towards the close of the century.

Some of the British public librarians found it highly desirable to have courses of lectures in connection with public libraries. This is made evident by an article which appeared in *The Library World* of 1899 which emphasized that "they [courses in connection with Public Libraries] are recognized not only as valuable aids in making known the contents of the library on particular subjects, but as tending to foster a closer relationship between the institution and its frequenters."[49]

The whole move behind the development of school libraries began in France with Rouland, Minister of Public Instruction in 1862, after he sent a circular letter to all Prefects on May 31st, 1860, stating that they were to further not only the education of school children, but that of the adult population as well.[50] Rouland's initiative saw the creation of libraries that sprung up like mushrooms. In 1902 there were more than 43,000. However, five years later these school libraries declined as quickly as they had emerged. The acute crises through which they passed were revealed in an inquiry made by Ch.V. Langlois, a member of the staff of the National Education Department, in the *Revue Bleue* of 1907. His article stated that seventy per cent of books provided were valueless for public use. Badly off financially, these school libraries were unable to refresh their stocks, and as a result, "few custodians were enthusiastic about shelving them [the stocks] properly." The dusty, worn out books were far from appealing to the ordinary reader.

The popular libraries set up by private bodies were also instrumental in attracting the majority of the general reading public away from the public municipal libraries. These, as well as school libraries, made some progress around 1860. They were also set up independently of the municipal libraries, the majority of which owed their existence to the philanthropic American society, the Société Franklin. This Society, which tried to encourage the development of popular libraries by conducting research and establishing a system of exchange of personnel, publication of catalogues, and purchase of books, was founded in 1862.[51]

Its utility was recognized by the Government in 1879.[52] It was set up for the purpose of furnishing books free of charge or at reduced prices to libraries of all types and for furthering the development of popular and army libraries. In 1878, it received a gold medal from the Jury International de l'Exposition universelle for its effective work in the domain of popular libraries.[53]

Various personalities, instead of supporting existing municipal libraries, would have nothing to do with them, and instead gave all their moral and financial support to the Society. In 1868, the Executive Committee of the

Society was made up of the following personalities: Boussingnault of the Academie des Sciences was the honorary President; Chasseloup Laubat, Senateur President; Jules Simon, a member of Parliament, Vice-President; A. d'Eichtal, an ex-Member of Parliament, Vice-President; Levies, Maitre des requêtes, sous gouverneur du credit foncier, Secretary. Men like Charton and Laboulays also came to the help of the new society. The support given by these personalities and others was one of the reasons for its rapid development. Benefiting from many Maecenases, it created opportunities for the setting up of libraries which could rival the innumerable number of school libraries that were mushrooming at that period.[54]

One year after the founding of the Société Franklin, in 1862, the favorable climate that was prevailing for the setting up of popular libraries led J. Macé to establish La Société des Bibliothèquess Populaires du Haut Rhin.[55] In a short time, more than 52 popular libraries were created in this department. Before J. Macé set up his society, there were many popular libraries founded by manufacturers for their workers. Among these manufacturers may be quoted M. Trupp, Jean Jacques Bourcart, and Adolphe Japy.[56]

Stress must be laid on the work of La Société Franklin, for if England had many philanthropic societies, France had very few, and these were less generous than their English and American counterparts. The only society which had paved the way for the development of popular libraries was the Société Franklin. However, in encouraging popular libraries to mushroom in different parts of France, the Society was to thwart the work and efforts of Eugène Morel in establishing effective municipal libraries on the lines of the Anglo-Saxon ones. If the popular libraries, which gave a more attractive service to the general public, had not counter-attracted most of the readers, they would have gone instead to the municipal libraries, and therefore the state or local authorities might have given more attention to their development.

The Société Franklin published the first issue of its journal in 1868. Its publication continued until 1880. It contained articles on professional library administration directed at those responsible for the running of a library. Unfortunately, the decline of this publication foreshadowed the decay of a powerful association. The disappearance of this first French professional library journal from circulation was perhaps due to the mentality of the French people, a mentality which lacked a certain civic spirit and solidarity. Its disappearance also anticipated the internal crisis of the popular libraries.

Though the number of popular libraries had increased since 1875, and though in 1902 they recorded 6 million book issues (2,400,000 in Paris, 3,600,000 in the provinces), their growth was beginning to be stifled by shortage of funds, inadequate opening hours, and lack of competent and enthusiastic staff.[57]

The Society remained for long the backbone of the popular library movement in France, from its founding in 1882 to 1904.[58] These small public libraries were not confined to Paris, but were scattered widely all over France. The latest available statistics, those of 1902, report 2,911 tax-supported popular libraries, in addition to 82 in Paris, possessing 4,166,417 volumes.[59]

While provincial, municipal, and popular libraries were being set-up at the turn of the century, the library system of Paris was developing independently and progressing more rapidly. Special reference should be made here to the municipal libraries of Paris, as they represent (even today) a powerful, separate force in the overall structure of public librarianship in France. The centralization of government and population rendered this inevitable, and was to bring about the complete control of all libraries in Paris. By the Revolution, several Paris libraries had flourished and benefited greatly from the decline of others.

In or around 1900, the public libraries in New England and on the other side of the Channel were flourishing more extensively than their French counterparts. This was a different situation to that prevailing in the 1850s, when British libraries were using French libraries as their model. The Anglo-Saxon libraries were providing all day service and offering various services such as reference, lending, libraries for children, as well as some extension activities; French libraries were functioning more as lending libraries and were open only a few hours weekly.[60]

This comparison was described more fully in one of Morel's lectures, "*La Librairie Publique en Angleterre et aux Etats Unis,*" which he gave in a series organized by the French Library Association in 1911.[61] In this lecture, he gave not only an account of public library development in Great Britain but pleaded for the establishment of free public libraries in France based on British and American lines.

In England, the support of public libraries by a specific taxation and appropriations from the municipal council started when the original supervisory authority of the central government was surrendered according to the Law of 1877 to the Local Government Board. This Board became the organ of local government. The British municipalities were free from a centralized supervisory control when taxation or rates were to be levied for the setting up of libraries. They had come a long way from their French counterparts at the beginning of the 20th century. The latter were still stagnating in a pseudo Anglo-Saxon, mid-nineteenth century state.[62] The establishment of a public library by the municipality was dependent upon the enthusiasm of the mayor or the local interest of the citizens, for the French local authority was not more bound than the British to allot to libraries any percentage of their expenditure. A move towards making the government aware of this was made by M. Pellisson, who wanted to influence the French government to model French public libraries on their Anglo-Saxon counterparts.[63]

> Undoubtedly we think it most desirable that the mode of financing our libraries be modeled on that which is in force in America and in England. It is mostly to the levy of a special municipal rate that the libraries of these two countries owe their prosperity. But of what use is it to propose something like this? Are we not aware how meager and inflexible is the budgetary support of our communes to finance our libraries? Can we believe that the French ratepayers will be prepared to impose upon themselves a new charge? However, if there could be found, by chance, any town whose population would agree to impose upon themselves such a sacrifice, could not the municipality by means of a referendum, offer them the opportunity to express their feelings and if the citizens were prepared to be taxed, would the High Judicial Court refuse them authorization to levy such tax?[64]

Maurice Pellisson made it quite clear that this could not be put into practice very quickly, and he contended that the public libraries could survive only if they developed into free public libraries and espoused the cause of culture for all.[65] They concluded that failure to do so would condemn them to lifeless sinecurism. "Public libraries," he remarked, "cannot be included in the French plan,"[66] namely that of using public libraries to support post-school work. For ten years earlier, when the campaign, *ouvres post-scolaires,* opened, the propagandists did not direct their efforts towards the progress that the popular libraries could make, but instead "they thought that the popular libraries could play but a minor role. They talked about them because they had but to expend their efforts on other undertakings. Judging from this, we could say that this campaign, usually noisy and brilliant, to all intents and purposes, was, in short, badly conducted; it is not sufficiently realized that without the library, post-school education cannot have either a good foundation or far-reaching effects."[67]

As was obvious from the move made by Maurice Pellisson, the French government was very slow to pass any specific legislation to compel municipal authorities to provide for better library services. The promulgation of a law as such might have brought about the elimination of many libraries which were too small to be run effectively. In England, in 1919, the Public Libraries Act of the same year enforced the abolition of the penny rate, which liberated the local authorities from the crippling financial restrictions to which they were subjected for the setting up of public libraries that rested mainly on the rate payer's taxation. This Act permitted local authorities to spend whatever amount they thought fit on public library services. With all the support received from the British government, it is not true to say that the service in every British local authority was excellent, but at least it could boast that a British public library at that time and even earlier was better than its French counterpart and far more extensive in its coverage. Even this was pointed out in 1911 by Eugène Morel in his lecture, *La Librairie Publique en Angleterre et aux Etats Unis*, which he gave at the *Ecole des Hautes Etudes Sociales* in Paris.[68] In spite of all this activity to promote the public library, there would not be any further French legislation which would make it statutory for every public library authority to provide an effective library service according to specific standards laid down by the French government.

By the beginning of the 20th century, more precisely in 1908, J.D. Brown, the British library theorist, stressed in his book, *Guide to Librarianship*, that the regions served by public libraries in Great Britain (553 municipal libraries in all) were recording an annual home reading loan of 2.4 books per inhabitant.[69] In France at that time, with the exclusion of Paris, which was better served, though still lagging behind when compared with London and New York, the popular libraries which were serving the French reading public better than the public municipal libraries were lending approximately one volume per ten inhabitants.[70] Even in 1966, Jean Hassenforder, a specialist in French library matters, categorically proved in his book *Développement Comparé des Bibliothèques Publiques en France, en Grande Bretagne et aux Etats Unis dans la Seconde Moitié du XIX Siécle: 1850-1914*, that

> France is definitely out-distanced and considerably lags behind. She has not yet caught up with the level of activities of British public libraries in 1908.[71]

In sharp contrast with public libraries in England, French public libraries had not developed along the lines of popular education like the British ones. Instead, they aimed at preserving the more serious type of books which were suitable for a highly intellectual elitist class, rather than the general public. French municipal libraries did not have this inherent didactic tendency that gave the British public library its remarkable character in organization and policy. This had caused the Britain of the 1910s to busy herself with the implementation of the various Public Libraries Acts from 1850 to 1919, giving a more liberal access to the stock of public libraries stipulated in the acts, with unrestricted access.

The English public libraries were to assume functions which, in France, have always belonged to the realm of education and "popular" cultural institutions, but not to libraries. In England, recreational reading was becoming popular among the general public. The scholastic and encyclopedic nature of French libraries, characterized by the national legacy of ancient records, did not appeal to the masses. This concept of French public librarianship, which tended to persist from 1910 until 1967, was highlighted by the French journalist, Frederic Gaussen, in a series of articles which appeared in the newspaper *Le Monde* in the months of July and August of 1967. Guassen, under the derisive, common title of *"Des Bibliothèques sans Lecteurs,"* laid stress on the precarious and static state of public libraries in 1967.[72] As was pointed out earlier, this was also emphasized by Jean Hassenforder, Director of the *Institut Pédagogique National.* One can appreciate the precarious state of public libraries when Morel started to campaign for their development. It is obvious that it did not lie in the nature of the public library in Morel's time to spread its field of activity over the whole area of France, as was the case in England. England, unlike France, had the privilege of having legislation. The Public Library Act of 1892, for instance, consolidated the confusion of laws and regulations and permitted even the smaller cities, towns, and parishes to be defined as library districts, and smaller districts to combine to form larger ones. It was evident that the policy of library provision in 1908, and even in 1969, was more widespread in England than in France. The Anglo-Saxons were more conscious than the French that a library provision was not a privilege for the community, but a right.

By the 1910s it was absolutely necessary to activate the French service and to meet the requirements of a rapidly growing public whose reading tastes were cultivated by the Société Franklin's popular libraries. However, in France, there were very few municipal libraries that were active, and those that were active were concentrated in Paris. Morel stressed the need for establishing proper libraries which, he advocated, should give the reader the books he needed, with browsing facilities and open access, and he stressed the need to offer informative assistance to all readers without exception. This crystallized what Morel thought the philosophy of the public library in France should be.

Popular readership could have increased in France from 1900 to 1910 if the Municipal authority had been given standards to measure the efficiency of the library service or had been compelled by legislation to establish an effective library service. But public libraries had, in Morel's early campaign period, lacked the didactic mission of the Anglo-Saxon libraries, which was expressed in a more refined advisory service, in cooperation with both lower and higher schools, in their close link with literacy and educational institutions and, above all, in full participation in the adult higher education movement of working men. If there was any move made at doing some educational good for the working classes in France it was expressed earlier than Morel's movement in Samuel Forney's unique benevolence[73] and M. A. Chevalley's appeal for the development of public libraries as a powerful organ of popular education.[74]

M.A. Chevalley, a prolific writer of monographs on adult education in England, the best of which was *L'Education Populaire des Adultes en Angleterre* (1896), believed that in public libraries the opportunity for self-teaching could be provided to the working classes. According to Ch.V. Langlois, in an article titled *"Programme du Bulletin,"* published in 1906 in *Bulletin des Bibliothèques Populaires*[75], M. A. Chevalley conducted a press campaign for the promotion of public libraries in the newspapers *Le Temps* and *Mánuel Général de L'Enseignement Primaire* that he thought could help the development of adult education. He started this campaign after a trip to England. There he studied the administration of institutions for adult education, and was determined to make known in France the achievements that had been made in the domain of public libraries. In an issue of the *Manuel Général de l'Enséignement Primaire* of October 29th, 1898, he leveled vehement criticism at the bad organization of the unattractive popular municipal libraries, which, he pointed out, should be improved to attract more people from the working classes.[76]

It was quite evident that the structure of French public librarianship was not completely suited to the situation, and the network set up before 1906 was obviously inadequate.

This crisis in 1906 did not escape public attention which was awakened in that very year by the founding of the French Library Association (L'Association des Bibliothécaires Français). The Association made the general public aware of the considerable difference between France and England. Those who encouraged the development of public readership were its presidents. For example, for four years, Eugène Morel organized lectures on libraries, and more particularly on the problems of public library under-development at L'Ecole des Hautes Etudes Sociales; M.

Henriot, who successfully activated the libraries of Paris arrondissements; Henri Lemaitre, whose role in the development of libraries was very important in and outside of France and under whose initiative the Congrés International de la Lecture Publique was organized in Alger in 1931, under the auspices of the French Library Association. However, from the outset, members were not very interested in the problem of the Association which, according to Pellisson, in a footnote in his book[77], was made up of librarians of scholarly libraries and of archivist-paleographers. M. Pellisson was to remark also that there was much to gain if the French Library Association could take after its American and English counterparts and open its doors to librarians of popular libraries. He also felt that the members should consider it a duty to take an interest in the future of these modest depots.[78]

In spite of this spirit of discord and conflict between archivists and librarians that prevailed within the organization, the movement undertook a reshuffle of activities and acted as a forum for the exchange of ideas. Despite its shortcomings, the association, strengthened by library theorists and famous librarians like Eugène Morel, A. Vidier, Ch. Mortet, J. Denniker, E. Coyecque, L. Garrau-Dihigo, Pol Neveu and Gabriel Henriot[79], performed a useful role in the expansion of public librarianship itself.

From its creation in 1906, the Association des Bibliothécaires Français helped to put the profession on a firmer footing. In 1907, a professional journal started to publish studies on the techniques of librarianship and gave an account of the activities of the profession. This bulletin, in fact, was to constitute the principal source of reference on the Association. It was, and still is, called *Bulletin de l'Association des Bibliothécaires Français,* and was to grow very rapidly. In 1910, the Association had more than 250 members. Among the insuperable problems which it was to solve was that of the recruitment and status of librarians. However, it was generally the large scholarly libraries which were given most consideration. The municipal libraries were also given a certain amount of attention, but they lacked the vitality to put representatives in the association to support them. The popular libraries were hardly represented at all. However, some moving spirits, like Charles Sustrac, librarian of Sainte Genevieve, Henri Michel, librarian of Amiens, and, later, Eugène Morel, communicated to their colleagues the problems which beset the development of public libraries in France.

At the beginning of the 20th century, the municipal libraries still had their old characteristics—encyclopedic, scholarly, and literary depots—characteristics they had had since 1850. Some, no doubt, were more frequented and used than others, but their image had not changed. Henri

Michel, a well-known librarian of the 1910s, gave a very uncomplimentary picture of the library of this time. He wrote,

> In France, in the busiest towns, and, more so, in dormant towns, the Library is usually a somewhat secretive place, a reserved place, shadowy and silent, which the noise of life reaches only in a deadened and distant form. It induces one to think of the past more than of the present or the future.[80]

The critical state of municipal libraries was made evident from the studies undertaken about them at that time. Most of the libraries had very old and unsuitable rooms to house their stock. The richness of the old stock contrasted strongly with the poorness of the yearly acquisitions. The staff was badly paid and the opening hours were usually inadequate. "Among the 400 municipal libraries that existed in 1912, excluding those of Paris, more than 200 were open but only a few hours per week, had no funds, or were popular libraries without any means to provide high culture. Only forty of them were worth the name of great libraries..." and furthermore "except in towns with a university, the issues average 20 to 40 readers a day. The reason can be attributed to the unsuitable hours of opening."[81]

Even if one takes into consideration the various categories of library as a whole, concrete efforts for their improvement remained very limited, and immense task awaited library pioneers and theorists at the beginning of the 20th century.

In spite of the incredible number of libraries in France in 1902, which, according to Hassenforder in his book, *Développement Comparé des Bibliothèques Publiques en France, en Grande Bretagne et aux Etats Unis dans la seconde moitié du XiXe siècle, (1850-1914)*, totaled 3,000, Morel was to remark that there was a complete disinterest in the services that the libraries could give and that France had not witnessed the growth of public and professional interest in the affairs of the public libraries. In his plea for the reorganization of the public library service, he recommended that French public library authorities model their services after those in Great Britain.

Could this indifference be ascribed to a disinterest in study itself? Surely not. But probably more to another reason, namely the lack of harmony between the recreational and educational needs of the readers, and shortage of the appropriate kind of reading matter. But the biggest stumbling block was the almost complete absence of "newsrooms" and reference services, even in large libraries. It was at the time when the French public library service was at its most critical and precarious state that Eugène Morel's intervention was decisive.

Of all the members of the newly created library association, he was the only one to question openly and vehemently the objectives of public libraries in France, their structure, which was the symbol of passive "conservatism"—an anachronistic concept for a modern readership—and, finally, to grapple, in spite of strong opposition, with the insuperable problems that prevented the development of public libraries.

# Morel and Library Education

Before Eugène Morel started his pioneering to promote professional education in France in 1910, there had already been, in the latter part of the nineteenth century, moves made to ensure that librarians possessed a professional qualification.[1] The subject of training for librarians was discussed in France back in 1846 in a decree which was not properly enforced. The Decree of June 30th, 1869 was passed to modify the Decree of 1846, and it required the Ecole des Chartes, which was founded in 1821 and moved to the Sorbonne in 1879, to hold regular courses in bibliography and classification for librarians and archivists. But the Ecole des Chartes was not really effectively geared to turning out efficient librarians. Its main aim was to produce scholars, paleographers, and archivists to work with source materials on the history of France.[2] The core of the syllabus was theoretical. It was only in 1880 that these theoretical courses were supplemented by the practical training, which was made available not at the Ecole des Chartes, but in one of the main encyclopedic libraries, the Bibliothèque Sainte Geneviève.[3]

However, in 1897, a ministerial decision required mayors to appoint only professionally qualified persons to run their libraries in the cities. This meant that only those with a diploma of the Ecole des Chartes were entitled to run the municipal libraries. According to some historians, this was done not only to put an end to amateurism and, to a certain extent, to sinecurism in the different types of libraries, but also to authorize all the vacancies for municipal chief librarians to be filled by "chartists," who were mostly archivist-paleographers. This virtually gave the Ecole des Chartes control of the municipal libraries.

These municipal librarians, in turn, were against the progress of modern librarianship as they preferred to use the resources of their libraries to do research for their own scholarly advancement. This gave them no time to adapt their libraries to cater for the general public.

In many French municipal libraries, the concern to preserve the collections and the preoccupation with historical considerations overrode the concern for efficiency. In this climate, therefore, attempts at reform were not likely to succeed.

When Morel envisaged the establishment of a proper training in modern librarianship in 1910, it was evident from the state of affairs above that this would be difficult. Morel had to fight a preconceived resistance against any library education movement, even if this movement came from the Ecole des Chartes. He had to try to diversify the teaching of librarianship, which was based on a "conservationist" library practice.

When one compares the work of Morel as an educationalist with that of the American library education promoter Melvil Dewey, it is evident that Morel's task was more difficult, as he did not occupy an administrative post in the Bibliothèque Nationale. Dewey, on the other hand, was the librarian of the University of Columbia and succeeded in using his influential position to open and direct the first library school in the United States in 1887.[4] Similarly, Morel's superior at the French National Library, Léopold Delisle, used his influence at the end of the nineteenth century to start lectures in librarianship at the Bibliothèque Nationale, and to define the technical character of the professional training of the librarian.[5] When one considers the unfavorable circumstances in which Morel was working and his low position in the National Library, one must agree that his efforts and achievement in the promotion of library education are among his most successful activities. Then, in 1911, Morel was promoted. The *Bulletin de l'Association des Bibliothécaires Français* of 1912[6] states that Morel and a certain Dieudonné, also employed at the National Library, were both promoted by a decree of July 13th, 1911 from third to second class librarian.[7] However, it was not before 1919 that Morel was promoted to first class librarian.[8]

In spite of these disadvantages, his activities regarding library education in France were highly praised by the French Library Association. In the above *Bulletin de l'Association des Bibliothécaires Français*[9], the Association's secretary, M. Gautier, in a reported speech, could not help extolling the very good work that Morel had been doing regarding library education when the latter contemplated the setting up of courses of lectures in 1910, which he would preside over.

That Morel was genuinely interested in promoting library education can be seen from the large part of his time, between 1910 and 1926, which was entirely devoted to the establishment of proper library training with the help of the French Library Association, the British Library Association, and the Americans. His influence had also been instrumental in making French libraries and library education known abroad. Some foreign professional journals seem to have been aware of his activities. For example, an article written by him on French municipal libraries, *"Les Bibliothèques municipals de France,"* which appeared in an issue of *Le Matin* of 1911, was translated into English and published in *The Library World* of the same year.[10]

It is probable that Morel was greatly influenced by what the British Library Association was doing in the 1910s in the field of professional education when he envisaged a course of lectures to be set up in France. His main preoccupation at that time was to establish a course based on the lines of these held in Britain. C. Wuhlenfeld, in an article about the library schools of the continent printed in the *Library Assistant* in 1913, gave the following information on the training of librarians in France in 1910:

> In France, there is training for the future university librarian and the librarians of large municipal libraries. For workers in popular libraries, the Association of French librarians in 1910, for the first time, opened a course based on the lines of those held by the British Library Association.[11]

C. Muhlenfeld did not make any mention of E. Morel's initiative in promoting a course of lectures to train librarians in 1910. However, a newsletter of the same year, which appeared in an issue of the French Library Association's professional journal, the *Bulletin de l'Association des Bibliothécaires Français*, on the *Conférences sur les Bibliothèques Modernes*, mentions Morel's efforts to promote library education in France. The newsletter gives the reader to understand that Morel had contacted the French Library Association and persuaded them to consider backing his proposal to the *Ecole des Hautes Etudes Sociales* to start a course of lectures on modern librarianship for the benefit of the directing personnel of public libraries. According to the newsletter, Morel's attempt met with success:

> The Committee of our association to whom the general plan of these lectures, which we publish hereunder, was submitted, has unanimously decided to give their entire patronage to this undertaking. M. Eugène Morel has agreed to be the general secretary of the organization. He urges us to make an appeal to all French librarians to take keen interest in this scheme.[12]

From now on, all suggestions regarding the course were addressed to Eugène Morel. The "chronique" of the French Library Association Bulletin gives the general plan of the lectures. During the course, instruction was to be given in:

| | |
|---|---|
| I. Book Knowledge: | kinds of paper and ink, binding, illustrations and editions, copyright, periodicals. |
| II. Classification: | Bibliography, the use which may be made of a library; its resources; bibliographical repertoires; documentation of a subject; |

| | |
|---|---|
| | bibliographical systems; special bibliographies; contemporary history; sociology, science; commerce and industry; catalogues; indexing of books and periodicals. |
| III. Libraries: | |
| (a) | The Large libraries: Bibliothèque Nationale, British Museum; French and foreign university libraries; budgets; special scientific libraries. |
| (b) | The Public Library in England, America and Australia; Ewart's Act; lending and reference libraries and newsrooms; *Bucherhalles* in Germany; *Les Populaires* in France; libraries and teaching; school libraries and children's libraries. |
| (c) | The profession of librarian; management of the library; administration; statistics; professional examinations; career; librarians from a social point of view.[13] |

On November 11th, 1910, E. Morel's plans became a reality. He succeeded in instituting the first series of modern courses on librarianship in France, which lasted for more than 3 years.[14] Morel gave the name Section des Bibliothèques Modernes to these courses of lectures which were intended to instill into those responsible for the organization of libraries a new concept of modern librarianship like that prevalent in Anglo-Saxon countries (Section III(b) of the above general plan). Those who gave Morel their cooperation in instituting the Section des Bibliothèques Modernes were French personalities like M. Croiset, the eminent Dean of the Faculty of Arts, president of the school, Miss Dick May, the Secretary; M. Fournière, who was kind enough to accept the proposal of Eugène Morel and Romain Rolland and Pierre Marcel, who were kind enough to present the Section des Bibliothèques.[15]

Before describing the few lectures which E. Morel personally gave at the Ecole des Hautes Etudes Sociales during the period 1910 and 1911, it would be interesting to note how foreign professional journals had viewed Morel's initiative in expanding professional education in France during the above period. An issue of *Library World* of 1911[16] very sympathetically describes the

LIBRARY EDUCATION                                                        67

active work Morel had been doing towards the organization of the courses between 1910 and 1911, and reports on Morel's achievements:

> It will interest British librarians to learn that a strong endeavor is being made to rouse France, and particularly Paris, to the need for public libraries on Anglo-Saxon lines. Belgium, Holland, and the Scandinavian countries are already stirring in this matter, and France seems likely to follow at an early date. M. Eugène Morel, of the National Library of France, and author of several books on popular libraries, has organized a very interesting and comprehensive course of lectures at the *Ecole des Hautes Etudes Sociales*, of which the following program will give an idea. The lectures were under the patronage of the *Association des Bibliothécaires Français* and other bodies and extended from November 11th, 1910 to April 7th, 1911: -

*Les Bibliothèques Modernes*
   Les vendredis à 5h 1/2
1. Les Bibliothèques et le public (11 novembre)
   HENRY MARTIN, administrateur de la Bibliothèque de l'Arsenal, president de l'Association des Bibliothécaires Français.
2. Comment se server des Bibliothèques (18 novembre)
   SUSTRAC, bibliothécaire à la Bibliothèque Sainte Geneviève.
3. Ces Grandes Bibliothèques de Paris (25 novembre)
   ALEXANDRE VIDIEE, bibliothécaire à la Bibliothèque National.
4. L'Oeuvre de l'Institut International de bibliographie et la Coopération, en matière bibliographique (2 décembre) LA FONTAINE, senateur de Belgique, secrétaire de l'Institut International de Bibliographie.
5. L'avenir de la Bibliographie (9 décembre)
   PAUL OTLET, Secrétaire de l'Institut International de Bibliographie.
6. La Classification Decimale et la Bibliographie Scientifique (16 décembre)
   E. SAUVAGE, professeur à l'Ecole des Mines et au Conservatoire des Arts et Métiers.
7. L'usage pratique de la classification (23 décembre) MICHEL SVILOKOSSITCH.
8. Les Bibliothèques scientifiques (13 janvier)
   DENIKER, bibliothécaire en chef du Museum d'Histoire Naturelle.
9. Les Bibliothèques de Droit et de Science Sociales (20 janvier)
   JEAN GAUTHIER, sous-bibliothécaire de la Faculté de Droit.

10. La Librairie Publique en Angleterre et aux Etats Unis (27 janvier) EUGENE MOREL, bibliothécaire à la Bibliothèque Nationale.
11. Les Bibliothèques de Province. Bibliothèque municpales. (3 février) HENRI MICHEL, conservateur de la Bibliothèque d'Amiens.
12. Les Bibliothèques commerciales. (10 février) F. THEODORE-VIBERT, conseiller du commerce extérieur.
13. Le Prét entre bibliothèques (17 février) CAMILLE BLOCH, inspecteur general des Bibliothèques.
14. La librairie classique et le livre d'enseignement. (24 février) BOUREELIER, éditeur, directeur de la librairie A. Colih.
15. L'Edition littéraire du XIXe siècle, (3 mars) HUMBLOT, éditeur directeur de la librairie Ollendorff.
16. Les transformations du livre. Le Dictionnaire des contemporains. (10 mars) MAURICE TOURNEAUX.
17. Histoire économique de l'imprimerie et de la librairie au XIXe siècle. (17 mars) PAUL MELLOTTEE, impimeur-éditeur.
18. Les procédés artistiques de reproduction. (24 mars) MARTY.
19. Histoire du depot legal jusqu'à la loi de 1881. HENRI LEMAITRE, sous-bibliothécaire à la Bibliothèque Nationale.
20. Le régime actuel. Les reformes necessaires. (2 avril) MAURICE VITRAC, bibliothécaire à la Bibliothèque Nationale."[17]

At the end of the first series of lectures, Morel edited them and was responsible for publishing them in 1912.[18] They were published by Michel Rivière in one volume entitled, *Bibliothèques, Livres et Librairies: Conférences faites à l'Ecole des Hautes Etudes Sociales sous le patronage de l'Association des Bibliothécaires Français.*[19] A free copy was distributed to the members of the association.

In this first volume of the *Bibliothèques, Livres et Librairies, 1912,* Morel had collected 28 lectures by specialists who had given their valuable collaboration to this first attempt made in France to inform librarians, students, and the general public about the various aspects of modern librarianship as conceived by Eugène Morel himself.[20]

A preface which E. Morel wrote for *Bibliothèques, Livres et Librairies,* Volume $I$[21] provides useful information about the aim of these lectures which were meant for the following three categories of people:

> First, to the general public: in spite of the recent movement, the public is still unaware of the benefits which it can derive from libraries in all respects, be they technical or scientific, and also of the advantages regarding up-to-date information and even recreation. The public does not know to which particular library it should apply for these benefits, and

even if it does know, it does not know where to go to find what the library holds and what it is looking for. For these reasons, in a country where public opinion prevails over everything, money is given parsimoniously when it is meant to finance libraries. Public authority does not show any interest in libraries.

Secondly, to students: Students have not only to study in libraries but to do serious research. A smattering of bibliography is becoming more and more indispensable for them before they can carry out their research properly. And if the modern paraphernalia of cards and reference works puts some of them off, it is because either they have not been taught the method of carrying out bibliographical research or they have not been given the proper advice in this direction... May I remind you that in countries other than France, not only students working on a thesis but also school children of the smallest secondary schools are educated in the use of libraries by librarians themselves. Pupils learn how to use the catalogues and choose their books.

Thirdly, to librarians: Our lectures have had this primary result, namely the establishment of direct contact among librarians so that they may have the opportunity to exchange professional ideas. Cataloguing, classification, library buildings and furniture, binding, loan and interavailability of tickets, all the progress which is likely to be made by the profession has been able to be studied and discussed—things we could have looked for in vain except in foreign professional journals.

Another aim of the lectures is to give a professional education to librarians: today librarians and the general public recommend that the position of librarian should be reserved for professionals and that professional knowledge is required of anybody who starts his career as librarian. It is unfortunate that this professional education is not given everywhere, except as a complement to special studies. Of these many branches of activities, namely law, science, industry, commerce, etc. do not form part of librarianship. The creation of a true professional training and education as well as the expansion of examinations and diplomas is imperative and with these lectures we have made a first step.

We would also have liked to give those thousands of library employees in charge of libraries of a popular character the indispensable notions of librarianship in these lectures. The majority of them are occupied elsewhere all day; their libraries keep them busy even in the evening, with the result that they cannot attend our lectures. However, the foundation of an elementary education in librarianship is of capital importance. It is a means of educating the masses. Fortunately in this respect our lectures have been very successful.[22]

> Lavallois-Perret, a municipality with a population of 61,000 has asked the students who attend our lectures if they could reorganize the catalogue of its library which holds around 20,000 books. It has approved the funds to carry out the work. If this example is followed, we can, in addition to our lectures, organize a series of practical exercises for which the students could earn a small remuneration. This can gradually transform these libraries which are treated with disgust by those who see them just as they are now but ignore the many services they should offer.[23]

In spite of all the obstacles set up by the conservative spirit of many French colleagues, Morel's efforts towards democratizing library education, which started in 1910, were to be given full recognition by Ernest Coyecque (1869-1954),[24] chief of the *Direction des Bibliothèques Municipales et des Bibliothèques administratives de Paris et et de la Seine* in 1913 and general inspector of the libraries of Paris and of the Seine from 1916 to 1924.[35] They were also praised by G. de Grolier, editor of *La Revue du Livre* in 1934.[26] The Groliers, husband and wife, in a joint article which appeared in the April issue of *La Revue du Livre,* 1934, in which a posthumous article by E. Morel, "On the Aid Machines can bring to Bibliography," was also published, spoke of "everything that Eugène Morel had done for the promotion of the library profession and professional education."[27]

Ernest Coyecque, who, in his capacity as General Inspector of Paris libraries, was inspired by Morel's prolific works on modern librarianship to reorganize French libraries, confirmed in an obituary on Morel that the library pioneer's efforts, since the beginning of the course in 1910 until it was to run to its third series, was an enormous success:

> "Ten years later [i.e. after 1910] [Morel] had the joy of seeing this concept of modern library education taken up and realized by the American Committee who donated to France the Library of La Rue Fessart in the Hotel de la Rue de l'Elysée. It all began with a double elementary course, normal and abridged. Then, a library school was created. To all these various undertakings, Morel brought his collaboration which became indispensable. He, himself, delivered lectures and invited lecturers to talk on topics of library economy in which they had specialized. He brought a truly sympathetic spirit to this seminar, in which everybody was interested. I am sure that this school would have survived, or, at least, would not have disappeared so quickly, if his advice and instructions had been taken into consideration and followed by those who were at the school: he wanted to limit the field of activities of the school to France only and wanted it to be concerned with the idea of satisfying the educational needs of the personnel of the various types of French library.

However, Morel would have surely experienced a legitimate satisfaction if he had witnessed the creation [in 1932] at the Ecole des Chartes, of a course which trains library officers for a new librarian's technical diploma."[28]

In fact, E. Morel later lectured at the Ecole Internationale des Bibliothécaires, a library school which was opened at the end of 1925 by the American Library Association.[29] His undated *curriculum vitae*, relating to his activities concerning libraries and kept at the Bibliothèque Nationale[30], shows that he was delivering lectures in bibliography of the sciences at this school. Also, according to this *curriculum vitae*, Morel was partly responsible for the creation of this library school:

> By his sustained efforts from 1910 to 1925, E. Morel had been largely the initiator and the active collaborator of the movement to which France owes the creation of an international school of librarianship which has rendered undisputed services to the libraries of France and raised France in the eyes of the public abroad.[31]

As for the lectures given at the Ecole des Hautes Etudes Sociales, these were begun in 1910 and given between 1910 and 1911. They were continued in 1911-1912. This second series of lectures was also collected and published in 1913 by Morel, who was helped by the secretary of the French Library Association, J. Gautier. The second volume, which contained the second series of lectures for 1911-1912, came out under the common title of *Bibliothèque, Livres et Librairies*.[32] It is superfluous to point out the interest librarians took in these volumes, which were offered free to all members of the French Library Association. However, it is imperative to cite here a few lectures given by those who helped Morel to carry on with his Ecole des Bibliothèques Modernes.

For instance, there were those of M. Capet on the British Museum; Jules Lemaitre on the Library of Congress of Washington and the Library of New York; that of M. Canryoke on Dutch University Libraries; and Eugène Morel's on *La Bibliothèque Royale de Berlin*.[33]

In his preface to the second volume of *Bibliothèques, Livres et Librairies*, Morel again outlined the work followed by his course of lectures, which was an educational work for the general public and a work aiming at giving a proper training to librarians.[34] A. Vidier, secretary of the French Library Association, while presenting a report to the general assembly of the French Library Association, held on March 30th, 1913, also gave a brief account of Morel's work for the year of 1911-1912:

> E. Morel enumerates in this book all the lectures which were delivered and which for various reasons have not been able to find a place in this collection. A thing which the modesty of M. Morel has not allowed him to say is all the trouble he has taken to organize these lectures, all the arrangements he had been making so that he might obtain the collaboration of interested people...[35]

Vidier followed this account with an expression of his deepest gratitude to Morel and of the gratitude of those present.

Morel's lecture in this series of 1911-1912 was delivered on December 13th, 1911. This lecture, *La Bibliothèque Royale de Berlin: le prêt et le bureau de renseignements*, gives an interesting description of the lending and information service of the Royal library of Berlin. [36]

The third series of lectures in 1912 was competently carried out under the supervision of Morel. This is confirmed b the December issue of *The Library Journal* of that year. It mentions, among Morel's successful activities, his competent running of the course of lectures. These were given under the aegis of some important French professional bodies. *The Library Journal* wrote that:

> "The section of modern libraries at the Ecole des Hautes Etudes Sociales, organized by Eugène Morel, librarian at the Bibliothèque Nationale, under the direction of the French Librarians' Association and the help of the Institut International de Bibliographie, and the Cercle de la Librairie announces the following course for 1912-1913: The Library of the Sorbonne by Barrau-Dihigo, the French Books in Switzerland by Cordey...the French books in France: Statistics by Eugène Morel— Publishing and publicity by A. Vitrac."[37]

The fourth series of lectures was successful, but the fifth series encountered some problems, as the *Bulletin de l'Association des Bibliothécaires Français* of 1914[38] explains. This series, for the year 1914-1915, was postponed until 1915.[39] But, in fact, Henri Michel, Chairman of the French Library Association, in his speech at the general meeting held on Sunday, April 11th, 1915 at the Hotel des Sociétés Savantes, informed the members that:

> the extreme difficulty of communication has not allowed us to hold in December (1914) our quarterly meeting. The same reasons have forced the *Ecole des Hautes Etudes Sociales* to postpone until next year the fifth series of lectures organized by our colleague M. Morel under the patronage of the association.[40]

France, in fact, was entirely indebted to Morel for having given her the chance to show to the other European countries that she could also train her librarians. Thanks to the goodwill of the Ecole des Hautes Etudes Sociales and the zeal of Morel, all the series of lectures which started in 1910 and ended in 1915 were a success and were published. They are now a mine of information for historians of French library history.[41]

In order to promote library education in France, Morel made many contacts with foreign library associations. His activities were to go beyond France and across the Channel. Morel had some connections in the 1910s with the British Librarians, and tried to promote study tours in France. He was also to arrange for study tours by French colleagues to Great Britain. Though O. Muhlenfeld, in his article on the Library Schools of the Continent in the *Library Assistant* of 1913[42], in giving a brief account of training in librarianship in France in 1910[43], did not make any mention of Morel's relationship with the British Library Association, it is evident from the information given in British professional journals that Morel had contacts with the British for the interchange of educational ideas. A reporter in *Library Assistant* of May 1923[44] made a detailed description of a visit that a party of British librarians paid to the National French Library on Easter, 1923, and declared that Morel had taken an active interest in entering into definite relations with the British Library Association in the 1910s:

> We shall not soon forget M. Morel's delightful little speech in which he referred to our previous visit in 1912 and to the events that had taken place since that time. Very touching was his reference to our colleagues who visited the Library in 1921.[45]

Quite recently, Michael Ramsden, in a section of his *History of the Association of Assistant Librarians*, (1895-1945) gave a brief account of the Holiday School organized by the British librarians in Paris in 1912, and the participation which Morel took in its organization. The account gives the following details of the 1912 visit to Paris:

> This morning, a Friday will be devoted to a visit to the Bibliothèque Nationale, by invitation of its principal librarian, and under the direction of the well-known authority of French libraries, M. Eugène Morel.[46]

Michael Ramsden also gives recognition to foreign librarians like Otlet[47], Director of the Institut International de Bibliographie at Brussels[48], and Morel, who had helped the British Library Association to promote the organization of its holiday schools:

The success of the first school clearly owed a great deal to Otlet who stepped in to deliver the lectures at quite a late stage; it would appear that in respect of the 1912 School, the Association felt considerably indebted to M. Eugène Morel. After the 1911 School, Otlet was made an Honorary Fellow of the Association, and after the 1912 School the same honor was bestowed on M. Morel.[49]

At a meeting of the Library Assistants' Association, on May 22nd, 1912,

> it was moved by the President Henry T. Coutts that M. Eugéne Morel, sub-librarian of the Bibliothèque Nationale be elected an Honorary Fellow of the Association. Mr. Thorne seconded and it was carried unanimously.[50]

In fact a certificate testifying Morel's honorary fellowship of the Library Assistants' Association, dated December 16th, 1913, reads that:

> Mr. Eugène Morel was, by unanimous vote of the Council, elected an Honorary Fellow of the Library Assistants' Association for distinguished professional service in promoting cordial relations between British Library Assistants and the Libraries of France, and for his consistent advocacy of public libraries.[51]

After he had improved his relations with the British in order to promote study tours in Great Britain and France for librarians, Morel became involved with the Americans. In post World War I France, Morel tried to further as much as he could the professional advancement of librarians. He was particularly interested in adopting a method of library education used in America. Consequently he became involved with a Summer Training School for librarians in Paris. This school was established under the auspices of the American Committee for Devastated France and a library was also set up by the Americans. Miss Sarah C.N. Bogle in an article on "Library Development in France" in *Library Occurent*, 1924, described it as one which was "organized to war time needs and was trying to meet the demands of a country aroused to public library needs, enquiries of a people interested in America and wanting information about it." However, the staff of the library, willing as it was, was totally inadequate to carry on the work according to the best standards defined for American libraries.[52]

Maria V. Leavitt who gave a short description of "some French Libraries as seen as by a goodwill delegate" in her article bearing the same title, made the following remark about Miss. Sarah C.N. Bogle and the Summer Library School which was under her responsibility:

> Under the able direction of Miss Sarah C.N. Bogle of the American Library Association, the Library Summer School was a success. This is the

first class for public library training in France in the teaching and interpreting of American methods of library administration and work, though there is a course in the Sorbonne for handling public documents.[53]

This description of the Summer Training School by Maria V. Leavitt is indicative of the efforts made to provide training to French librarians in Paris. She points out that:

> the linking together the work of French and American libraries and librarians on such a foundation is a proof of an international bond established for all time.[54]

The course was conducted at the American Library in Paris, 10 Rue de l'Elysée. It was directed by Sarah C.N. Bogle, and Morel maintained closest cooperation with her.[55]

The reason for the establishment of the course in Paris and the active participation of Eugène Morel in running the lectures was given by Sarah C.N. Bogle in the above-mentioned article of the *Library Occurent* of 1924:

> With the growth of the library idea [mainly American libraries set up by the American Committee in France], the necessity for the training in the country itself [France] of librarians, and the American Committee through Miss Carson, established this summer a six weeks' library training course. It was anticipated that ten or fifteen students would enroll. Fifty were accepted...The course on reference work was conducted by Monsieur Morel, *Bibliothécaire à la Bibliothèque Nationale*. He called to his aid other authorities in special subjects. I question whether any library school has ever had a more illustrious group of interested instructors.[56]

One of Morel's enthusiastic admirers,[57] Ernest Coyecque, Inspecteur Génénal des Bibliothèques Municipales et de la Seine, was together with Morel among the patrons of the school, who contributed much to its success.[58]

When the library course began, Eugène Morel was to be among the "first illustrious librarians" to address the course. Miss Sarah C.N. Bogle made an appeal to a number of libraries in America for contributions of illustrative materials. Dr. W. Dawson Johnstone, the Librarian of the American Library in Paris contributed everything he had and was at the service of the director of the course. The French collaborators were Eugène Morel and Ernest Coyecque. A room in the American Library in Paris was given over by Dr. Johnstone for the exhibits he had contributed.[59] Whether Morel personally used these materials to illustrate his lectures cannot be ascertained but he might have. For, eleven years earlier, in 1912, during a meeting of the French Library Association of April 14th, he illustrated a talk on libraries by using a set of illustrative materials which he called *"bibliophote"*.[60] The *"bibliophote"* would continue to be mentioned very often in the Bulletin of the French Library Association whenever library training was discussed. This was reported by Gabriel Henriot, the Chairman of the French Library Association, in an article in the Bulletin of the French Library Association of 1926, when he was describing the first twenty-six years of the French Library Association.[61]

The opening lecture of the Summer Training School was delivered before June 1923 by M. Firmin-Roz, assistant director of the National Office of French Universities and schools. His subject was "what constitutes a book of literature." This was followed by lectures on *"Littérature Etrangère."* Together with Eugène Morel there were several well-known American librarians in France who addressed the school. Among them were Miss Theresa Hitchler of Brooklyn, Miss Mary Parsons of Morristown, and Misses Mary Davis, Mabel Williams, and Alice K. O'Connor of the New York Public Library. Among the students enrolled were French, Belgians, Swiss, and Russians.[62]

Twenty nine students out of the fifty mentioned above who were accepted for the course were awarded a certificate at the end. An Alumni Association was formed, which committed itself to the task of encouraging the spread of the public library as it is "conceived in America."[63]

Thus, just as the United States had founded two model American type libraries in France, one at Soissons to replace the one destroyed during World War I and one in Paris, with the same practical motives the Alumni Association founded a summer library school in Paris to initiate France into the American system.

This summer school, as Ernest Coyecque pointed out in an article on the activities of a dynamic American librarian, Jessie Carson, would anticipate the creation of an American Library School, in La Rue de l'Elysée in Paris. This school would find in Miss Carson its leading spirit.[64]

But before the opening of the American School of Librarianship in Paris in June 1923, Morel was using his influence with the Americans to try to secure from the American Committee for Devastated France scholarships for French women to be trained in the United States so that they might takeover from the Americans when they bequeathed the French all the libraries they had created in the Aisne.[65] In a report written by Miss Jessie Carson to the above Committee on its activities for the period of April 1920 to January of 1921, it is pointed out that Morel had expressed a desire to help the committee to find these women to be sent to the United States.[66]

An example of these libraries was described by Sarah C.N. Bogle, assistant secretary of the American Library Association, in the *Library Occurent* of 1924:

> In Paris, on the Rue Féssart, in the old Apache neighborhood, in response to the demand of the people, there is a public library serving its patrons as we are accustomed to see the best type of our libraries serve its constituency. And now, too, this library has been taken over, and on January 1st, 1924, will become a municipal library.[67]

The first French woman who, through help of Eugène Morel, was to have an American scholarship to further her library education in the United States was Mlle. Lydie Duproix. It was apparent that Morel was also instrumental in promoting the professional education of two other women who were sent to the United States of America after they had, like Lydie Duproix, an apprenticeship at the American Library of Soissons. An article in *L'Oeuvre* of November 11th, 1924, a daily that had a wide circulation, gave not only relevant information on the creation of the Bibliothèque Féssart by the Americans in their plan of reconstructing post war France of the 1920s, but also ample details about the three women who were backed by E. Morel for a scholarship for library training in America. They were "three of the right kind of French women," whom E. Morel and Mr. Roz of the International Scholarship Department of the Sorbonne were interested in having trained. This wish, as expressed by Eugène Morel before 1920, was reported by Miss Jessie Carson in her "Report of the American Committee for Devastated France."[68]

Though no sources could help the reader ascertain who the two women mentioned above were, it can be deduced from the information extracted from *L'Oeuvre*, November 11th, 1924, that they might have been a certain Miss Baudry and Miss Lacoste. When Mlle. Lydie Duproix became the chief librarian of the Bibliothèque Féssart-Belleville, she was aided in her duties by the Misses Baudry and Lacoste, who also did special studies in librarianship in America.[69] But it was quite unfortunate, as points out Miss Marguerite Gruny, who is the niece of Eugène Morel and still living, that neither of the two assistant librarians who benefited from the American scholarship made a career of librarianship. A third woman student, Miss Quiri, who also received training in America and who later became Mrs. Alianon, continued her career.[70]

The plan for the offer of scholarships to French women was presumably suggested around the middle of 1921. In that year, Dr. Julien J. Champenois returned to France from America, where he represented the

*Office National des Universités Françaises.* He outlined a plan of cooperation between the American Committee and the *Office National* for the selection of French women for library training in America and the sharing of the expenses of this training.[71]

Before a detailed description is given on Miss Lydie Duproix's training in America, which will give an idea of the training prevailing at that time for French women in the United States, it would be useful if Julien J. Champenois's plan could be examined closely. This was as follows:

> The Committee of the Office National making the selection of the French students to be sent to America was composed of two women, Mary Finn and Virginia Newcomb, who had been doing this work for three or four years and had a wide knowledge of a large number of French men and women eligible for teaching or library positions. Most of the students selected by this committee were those who had already spent one year or longer in American Universities and had good records for such work but who were still without a permanent job in France. A group of students were recommended for trial in the Committee libraries for three or four months. Those who proved to be best suited for library training, both as to qualifications and inclinations, were selected for training in American Library Schools.[72]

The first time, not more than six French women students were selected in 1922. The *Office National* paid for the "transportation" of these students to and from America, and in America. It took charge of any expenses due to sickness and gave, when necessary, pocket money, not exceeding 12 dollars a month to each student. The American Library school waived all tuition fees and in some cases was in a position to add to the fund for food and lodging, which amounted approximately to 1,000 dollars a year for each student.

A special committee was formed, which was a sub-committee of the Council of Education in Washington, District of Columbia, to raise funds for food and lodging for those students. It was also responsible for supervising their training and arranging to give them all round experience in America. The Chairman of the sub-committee was Dr. Edwin H. Anderson, and the other members were Alice S. Tyler, representing training; Annie Carroll Moore, representing library work with children; and Anna Morgan, representing the American Committee. Dr. S.T. Capen and Dr. Stephen Duggan were members of the Council of Education.[73]

In 1922, Annie Carroll Moore, in a report of the sub-committee on children's work to the American Library Association that was published in the *Bulletin of the American Library Association* of the same year, gave the following details about Miss Lydie Duproix, the first French woman to benefit from the scholarship provided by the American Committee for Devastated France:

> Melle. Duproix, who had shown exceptional qualifications for library work during four months practical experience at Soissons, entered the Library school of the New York Public Library in September and received a special certificate in June. The generous terms of this scholarship and of Melle. Duproix's admission to the library school and practice field of the New York Public Library made it possible for her to visit libraries and library schools in Cleveland, Pittsburgh, Albany, Boston, and Washington, and also to have a representative experience of American life and institutions.[74]

About Miss Lydie Duproix's activities in France after her return from America, A.C. Moore wrote:

> Melle. Duproix returned to France in July [1922] to assist Miss Carson in the further development of the library work in Paris and in the *Devastée*. So far as I know she is the first French woman to take American Library Training and experience back to France. She combined, to an unusual degree, appreciation of the spirit and purpose of the modern library, understanding of children and grown people, and a fine heritage of French and English Literature. I may add that I watched the initiation of Melle. Duproix into library work at Soissons under Alice O'Connor, and it has been of very great interest to see that her practical work in New York, whether in an East Side Branch Library or in the central children's room, has been characterized by the same clear-sighted grasp of what should be done and the same charm and ease in adjustment to work with people in a strange environment.[75]

For Morel and Miss Jessie Carson, who were responsible for the setting up of American libraries in the Devastated Regions, it was important to preserve and further develop the existing cooperation in library education between France and America. Special provisions were included in the scheme of scholarships granted to French students to receive their education in American library schools. But this would not completely solve the problem, as Miss Jessie Carson said in a report to the American Committee for Devastated France in 1922:

> It stands to reason that all French librarians cannot be trained in America. Consequently, every effort possible will be made to start a training class next fall in the American Library in Paris. This class, if realized, will begin in the simplest way, using certain of the present members of the staff of the

American Library in Paris and the Library Department of the American Committee.[76]

This statement anticipated the creation of the American School of Librarianship in Paris. Morel made good use of his contacts with the Americans and with Miss Carson. The American training school in France was different to most of the training schemes set up locally, which emphasized a knowledge of handling documents.

In June 1923, the dream of Miss Jessie Carson became a reality. In an article on Miss Jessie Carson in *Revue des Bibliothèques*, 1924, E. Coyecque, General Inspector of Libraries, writes about her work in the establishment of the school and how it was conceived. He also gives a brief account of her activities regarding the creation of American libraries in Aisne and Paris, and her future plans regarding the education of librarians in France:

> Furthermore, the directrix of the American Committee for the development of libraries in the devastated regions of France did not limit her indefatigable activity and remarkable dedication to the libraries in Aisne and Paris. Miss Jessie Carson had been struck by the poor condition of libraries of secondary importance, especially those that we call, improperly, 'popular.' They were lacking in competent and suitable personnel. She could not help comparing the French and American library organization: she came to the conclusion that she must consider sending to the United States some young French women who would be carefully chosen. They should possess a good cultural background and have a thorough knowledge of the English language.[77]... From America, they would come back to France fully qualified and would be capable of administering usefully the libraries of a certain category which we have planned to set up, and in turn, they would train good students.[78]

Thus, the training of French librarians in America was carried out for two consecutive years, with the enlightened collaboration of the *Office National des Universités Françaises* abroad.

> Then, to this first formula, the application of which was to remain strictly limited to a very small number who benefited from it, Miss Carson thought of substituting a professional course for training librarians, which could be organized in Paris with a collaboration of the Americans, French, and Belgians. This will start with a six-week elementary course aimed at people who would like to be initiated to the work of a librarian as well as to experienced and self-taught librarians who are already employed.

> The plan was realized in June and July of 1923. The success of the project was so encouraging that Miss Carson did not hesitate to envisage a more widespread organization. She sought all the necessary collaborators to run

the course. The American Committee was on the eve of its dissolution; the American Library Association, therefore, took the whole undertaking in hand; an important donation which would last two years was entrusted to Miss Sarah Bogle, Deputy Secretary of the American Library Association and the Secretary for the Comité d'Instruction pour la formation de bibliothécaires assisted by Miss Parsons.

The School of Librarianship thus created has its seat at the Bibliothèque Americaine de la Rue de L'Elysée; the name of Miss Carson will indissolubly remain associated with it.[79]

The reason why Morel came to associate himself with the Paris American School of La Rue de l'Elysée and Jessie Carson was twofold. First of all, Morel had always had a keen enthusiasm for the establishment in France of an American library system. This was made quite clear in the 1910s. His lecture of 1911, *La Librairie Publique en Angleterre et aux Etats Unis*, the text of which appeared in the book, *Bibliothèques, Livres et Librairies*, volume one[80] and a chapter in his book *La Librairie Publique*, entitled *Aux Etats Unis*, showed how enthusiastic he was to establish in France a modern American library system and to ensure that French librarians should have a proper training in the teaching and interpreting of American methods of library administration and work.

Secondly, the school, which was to contribute from 1923 to 1929 to the popular library movement in France, came up to E. Morel's expectations—it was a movement of which Morel had been a primary champion since the 1910s.

But according to Gabriel Henriot, librarian of the Bibliothèque Municipale d'Art et d'Industrie, Société des Amis de Fornay, Paris,

> The school... was never identified with [the movement] ... since from 1926 on, it was an international school.[81]

But Gabriel Henriot was to recognize the importance of the school as being "the outgrowth of the course of French public librarians which was given in Paris in the summer of 1923 by the American Library Association at the request of the American Committee for Devastated France."

During the five years of its existence, the Paris Library School, with faculty and lecturers drawn from twelve countries, trained students of twenty-five nationalities, many of whom were experienced librarians sent officially by institutions, who returned to positions of leadership in libraries of their countries.[82]

Gabriel Henriot gave this additional information about the school:

When the American Library Association completed its five year demonstration period in 1929 on the eve of the financial crisis, no university or institution was found which could take over the school on a permanent basis. The Alumni Association, wishing to hold the school together in some way until a more favorable time, has been caring for the school library in a room lent by the American Library in Paris, and for four years it has, through volunteer work on the part of its members, maintained regular office hours, attended to correspondence and placement and has furnished technical information about library methods to numerous enquiries, including among others, the author of a French handbook on the organization of popular libraries.[83]

The school of librarianship which influenced the development of modern library education in France was inspired by three people who were advocates of public library education. They were the American, Miss Jessie Carson, and the two French library pioneers Eugène Morel and Ernest Coyecque.

Morel's contacts with the Americans, which started before the 1920s, were to progress on the Easter day of 1921, at the inauguration of one of the most important libraries built by the American Committee for Devastated Regions of France at Soissons. Eugène Morel, who for years had attracted the sympathy of the Americans by his appreciation of their great achievements, was invited by the Americans to this inauguration.[84] Morel was accompanied by Ernest Coyecque, who, appointed as Inspector of Libraries in 1916, was to remain in this office until 1924. About the activities of these dynamic library pioneers in France, Miss Marguerite Gruny, Morel's niece, would add in an article on the library pioneer E. Coyecque, in the Bulletin of the French Library Association in 1954 that:

> The two librarians, Morel and Coyecque, and the American Librarian, Miss Jessie Carson, who had faith that the new libraries in the department of the Aisne might inspire the creation of other libraries, were not without worries for the future: when the time comes, to whom could the reorganization or the creation of certain libraries based on the new models be entrusted?[85]

This common worry lead to the formation of a school of librarians which opened in Paris in 1923 and went on functioning for six years thanks to the subsidies received from the Comité des Régions Devastées, and the American Library Association.[86]

Miss Marguerite Gruny, like Odette Dourver (1904-1970), also "entered the famous American school of librarianship for the training of librarians from where all the pioneers of the public library movement came."[87] She made the following statement regarding its efficiency:

> Those of us who benefited from the teaching there, still remember with emotion: It opened a broad perspective on the world of libraries, present and future, and inculcated this principal thought: 'One becomes master in a field on condition that one undergoes a long practical work sustained by daily efforts.' And, above all, it was enveloped in an invigorating atmosphere of conviction and hope created by the joy of the American who shared their success and that of the two French pioneers [that is to say, Morel and Coyecque] and of their friends who saw the result of their efforts realized.[88]

Not only would Miss Marguerite Gruny, in 1954, give recognition to the remarkable work done by the American Library School of Paris, but Morel, in a 1927 monograph[89], testified to the significant role the school had played in the educational life of French librarians.

In 1927, E. Morel would compare in his monograph, *L'enseignement post-scolaire; La Bibliothèque Moderne*[90], the courses given at his Ecole des Hautes Etudes *Sociales* during 1910 with those of the American School of Librarianship, which was often called La Nouvelle Ecole des Bibliothécaires. In this monograph, Morel not only expressed his conception of education as something which is continuous throughout life, but argued that libraries should be indispensable to complete the education given in school. He also gave a very broad idea of the interest that librarians were taking in the courses run by the new school of librarianship:

> Now that the French Library Association has increased its membership from 60 to 400, now that from the four points of France—Lyon, Nantes, Perigueux, Rouen, Montbrisson, etc.—comes the news that new efforts are being made towards the creation of branch libraries, the filling of library posts by qualified librarians, the building up of classified catalogues, a School of Librarianship is created in Paris, 10, Rue de l'Elysée, with the help of our American colleagues. If, then, we [i.e. Morel and the French Library Association at the Ecole des Hautes Etudes, 1910-1915] had not been able to find two regular students for our courses, we [Morel and the American Library School] are now receiving 140 applications for 20 places. A town in France has sent for 'training' for one year a librarian already appointed to a chief position. Those who want to benefit from these courses are students from various nations.[91]

But E. Coyecque noted, on the other hand, that the vast majority of students who benefited from the courses were not foreign students but French. Many librarians seemed to have followed the course run by the

Ecole de L'Elysée. Ernest Coyecque pointed out in 1928 in La Revue des Bibliothèques[92] that the commune of Issy-les-Moulineau, which had taken over a library maintained by a private organization, insisted on having a woman librarian trained at the Ecole des Bibliothécaires de Paris. The municipality of Glichy also sent its librarian to follow an intensive course at the Ecole de la Rue de L'Elysée as "he very badly needed an apprenticeship for this job."[93] Finally, Henri F. Raux, in a 1950 article in a *Festschrift Eugène Strollveither,* edited by Fritz Rodenbacher, concerning Morel's work as a pioneer of public libraries, made special mention of Morel's activities regarding the education of French librarians at the American Schools:

> Later he [Morel] would also participate in the administration of the Ecole des Bibliothécaires created in Paris with the help of our colleagues from the United States.[94]

# Morel and Children's Libraries

Morel did not only concentrate his efforts on the development of libraries for adults, but was also concerned with those catering for young readers.

The importance of primary education was emphasized in France by Jules Ferry (1832-1893), who served as premier as well as in other key posts in the Cabinet during most of the period 1880-1885. His school laws and decrees during 1880-1881 made primary education free, compulsory and secular, and he enforced his anti-clerical measures by replacing religious teaching in public schools by civic education.[1] Earlier in 1815, Lazare Carnot (1753-1823), who was Member of the Comité du Salut Public and was exiled by La Restauration as a regicide, founded La Société Pour l'Instruction Elémentaire, which aimed at giving to the children of Paris a kind of primary education. He achieved his aims relatively well.[2]

In 1927, Clair Nuchet, Librarian of the Children's Library, L'Heure Joyeuse of 3 Rue Boutebrie, in the 5th arrondissement of Paris, revealed that, "France was the first country to think about libraries for children."[3] But it is unfortunate that there has never been legislation concerning the establishment of children's libraries in France. However, attempts at providing a book service for children were made originally in a decree of June 1st, 1862, issued by Rouland, Minister of Public Instruction, according to which each primary school was to establish a library for its pupils which had the additional task of lending books to former pupils and to the children's parents.[4] But more often than not, these school libraries, interesting in principle, did not meet the needs of children. "School library" usually meant "bookcase under lock and key. They also lacked professional management."[5] From 1862, school libraries were to increase rapidly. There were more than 43,000 in 1902, and they were lending in that year more than 8,000,000 books.[6] In 1907, Ch.V. Langlois, member of the Direction de l'Enseignement Primaire, who conducted a survey among school teachers, reported in *Revue Bleue* of August 3, 1907 that,

> Statistics are lies. Figures are not very reliable. The great majority of these school libraries which appeared in the survey are in fact, fictitious, dead... or are worthless. The misappropriation of funds causes disinterest. It is not enough to emphasize that there should be books in a library; it is much

more important that these books should be readable. Yet, more than three quarters of the books found in these school libraries are not readable.[7]

Unfortunately, by 1906, Maurice Pellisson, in his *Bibliothèque Populaires à l'Etranger et en France*[8], reveals that these school libraries were in crisis. As they had limited funds and resources, they were very small and operated only a lending service. They had, in most cases, neither reading rooms nor qualified staff to run them. They offered book stocks which were replenished,[9] and they were declining in importance. Though initially intended to serve the masses as well as the pupils, the libraries continued increasingly to cater very inadequately for the needs of children.[10] In 1968, Ingeborg Heintze, a Swedish observer of French public libraries, remarked that,

> the school library, which was established for its pupils, former pupils and their parents, was not a successful experiment, and in 1947, only half of the original 45,800 libraries were partly accessible to other than the pupils.[11]

It is evident that the initial experiment of providing reading materials for children ended in failure, as the organization was inadequate. Though views may differ as to the reason for the decline of the school libraries, another observer of the French public library system, Frédéric Gaussen, a French journalist, reported in 1967 in *Le Monde* that "they deteriorated gradually and had practically disappeared by the beginning of the 1914-1918 War."[12]

E. Morel used his mandate as chairman of the French Library Association during 1918-1919, aided by Ernest Coyecque, General Inspector of Libraries, who took over from him as chairman from 1919 to 1920[13], to try and provide an effective children's library system to make up for the deficiencies of the school library system.

It is in his writings, his speeches, and his contacts with the Americans and Library promoters in England, and in his capacity as Chairman of the French Library Association, Vice-President of the Société des Gens de Lettres, Vice-President of the Comité de la Bibliothèque Moderne, and Rapporteur at the two Congrès du livre held in 1917 and 1921[14] that one can trace Morel's influence in the development of children's libraries in France. This influence is also reflected in the general character of the French public library service today, and in the arrangements made by Morel to provide French women with training in library work with children.

Though Morel's long service as librarian at the Bibliothèque Nationale from 1892-1934 qualified him more as a special librarian rather than one concerned with public library matters, he showed an intense interest in all branches of library work with children. As early as 1908, he advocated developments in all branches of librarianship, more particularly in library work with children, by offering a proper library education to people engaged in library work. Maurice Gaillet, Librarian of the Municipal Library of Toulouse, wrote in 1957:

> We are fortunately beyond this stage [namely that anybody could be a librarian] and not at the time [it was in 1908] when Eugène Morel was shouting vehemently and with a trace of injustice: 'The trade of the librarian is not properly learnt in France'.[15]

Some of the developments in the children's library service would be achieved in the 1930s. Marguerite Gruny, Morel's niece, who attended the course of lecture given by E. Morel at the Ecole des Hautes Etudes Sociales in 1910, was among the first to reorganize the important work Morel did for the development of children's libraries in France. In *Bulletin d'Analyses de Livres pour Enfants* of 1969, a review which promoted children's libraries and literature, she wrote that,

> in a review dedicated to books and libraries for children, it is most interesting to recall some observations and ideas of this pioneer on these matters and...to give a more complete view of his work.[16]

> Since his adolescence Morel was interested in the problems of young people. His interest is embodied in his work *Petite Français*, published in his adolescence, which deserves to be called to the attention of educationalists because of its precocious spirit of rebellion. It was a violent criticism of the education of the young people who were suffering from lack of leisure, physical, and sexual education, the segregation of boys from girls in school. All this is denounced with a mixture of exaggeration and lucidity which would have pleased our revolted youth of 1968, who, though, have had the benefit of more than a century of progress.[17]

In order to understand Morel's activities to promote the children's library service, one must go back to the beginning of the 20th century, when Morel, still a young librarian at the Bibliothèque Nationale, realized the inadequacy of the children's library service in comparison with other countries. Ernest Coyecque, his collaborator, remarked in his article on Morel, *"Un grand bibliothécaire français: Eugène Morel,"* in *La Revue du Livre* of 1934, that most of the libraries catering for children's needs were

> providing a small number of subjects which were alien to an active and modern way of life, to the evolution of ideas, achievements, and the needs of modern life. They were bogged down in obsolete formulas and

insupportable customs, and were impatiently awaiting indispensable reforms.[18]

To counteract these obsolete concepts, Eugène Morel introduced the concept of the Free Public Library,

> which was found everywhere in the United States and England, with its services for home reading, accommodation for 'on the spot' reference work, the newsrooms with periodicals—and the children's library—an institution which is well known and imitated now but which was unknown to the majority of French librarians in 1908.[19]

Reading for pleasure did not leave Morel indifferent. However, it was the place that libraries occupied in the United States in the education of children which seemed most to have retained his attention.[20] In the United States, it was at the end of the 19th century that the children's libraries came to swell the number of other departments: lending, reference, and newspaper and reading rooms.[21] While in England, the children's sections were beginning to develop around 1894, and the public libraries were beginning a school library service. Around 1900, less than 50 English libraries had juvenile departments, and only two or three were as effective as their American counterparts.[22]

As early as 1910, Morel described in his book, *La Librairie Publique*, the method utilized in the sections reserved for children in American libraries and the reflections that this method suggested to him:[23]

> Education through the library, has, during the last ten years in America assumed capital importance. It has caused a change in the educational system still greater than the suppression of the *baccalauréat*…or latin, would cause in France. Everywhere the free public library has a section for young readers—children and school-children do not have a school library, but provision is made for them in a special room in the same library as their elders: the use of libraries is part of education.[24]

> Libraries are required to teach two things: firstly, to go deeply into the study of a subject, to follow quietly, progressively, and completely a chosen path, and secondly to choose for oneself; the faults that are committed by the child will be profitable to him; he must form the habit not only to rely on anybody. Rather than confine the child to one book, the unique book, the breviary which the State imposes on the teacher so that he in his turn should impose it on the child, the Americans apply a method called *'séminaire'* (seminar) which consists of presenting to the child various books which he has to compare with a view to extracting for himself an opinion that he thinks right.

All sorts of measures are taken to instill in the child the habit of finding for himself the book that he should read."25

To this effect Morel quotes a communication of Mary Wright Plummer, who enumerated these measures at the Congrès des Bibliothèques in 1910:

1.) Collective visits to the library.
2.) Special loan to teachers of batches of books which will remain one month in the class.
3.) Purchase of books which serve as complement to courses which are on loan for 3 months to schools.
4.) Visits of the librarian to schools.
5.) Books which relate to certain courses are bought in duplicate or withdrawn from public use for a certain period.
6.) Exhibition in the library of engravings and documents illustrating the courses.
7.) Special loan for summer holidays.
8.) Compilation of booklists for homework and for school debates.
9.) Picture books lent to nursery schools (kindergartens)
10.) Some library shelves are spoken of as the private property of a particular teacher who places on it the books that he recommends for reading."26

Morel went on to criticize the French school education system, which was not conducive to the development of children's libraries in France:

> The abuse of the book in general is baneful, and our system of education is rotten. Those who expect to find here a panegyric of the book itself are applying to the wrong author. I am convinced that botany would be better taught in the woods, agriculture in the fields, medicine at the hospital, history by visiting monuments, living languages by talking and literature... by reading and re-reading.27

> It never occurs to anybody that where it exists, the Public Library (sic) can give a bookish knowledge which replaces experience. It is the contrary. It multiplies experiences. It brings facts and more facts into everyday experience. It gives information on everything and it is up-to-date. Does it inform? Not at all. One must go to it, one must make an effort. It gives one the means to inform oneself.28

Morel particularly commends the value of the open access public children's library in the education of the pupils, and recommends that this should receive more attention:

> Literature itself can become a lesson of experience and not just bookish knowledge, provided that the pupil is free to choose and read the entire book so that he might say what he, and not what somebody else, had read.[29]... the child who wants to read should go to the public library like his father, or should go to school. When we founded our libraries, we seem to have wished to discredit them by using offending words like these: *scolaires, populaires*. It is not 'schoolish'—the need of the child who is reading liberates himself from his master and teaches himself.[30]

Morel felt that the system of education in France was at the root of the underdevelopment of children's libraries. The system of education was scholastic; the use of the school libraries was apt to be restricted by all kinds of red tape, and often these two factors did not help children to use libraries properly. The teachers' lectures were confined to the text and did not stimulate the pupils to do their own research. Morel describes his personal experience at secondary school level:

> I refer to the years I spent at the lycée and these words: read surreptitiously, make me dream. Yes, in all the classes, we used to read surreptitiously. Yes, there were two kinds of pupils, those who read surreptitiously and learnt something, and the others who did not learn anything. One year at the lycée, I had this exceptional teacher, Mr. Ernest Dupuy, whose class consisted of ransacking our bags for books which, of course, were hidden expressly in such a way so that he could find them and give a talk on them, but not on those which were in the curriculum. I do not know if when he became Inspector of Public Instruction he applied this method. But I know that he had to modify it once M. Eugène Manuel, the one who has a status and wrote very bad verses, paid a visit to our lycèe. He gave us dictation and we wrote a course of Greek, Latin and French literature, in ten lessons...[31]

Morel was very critical of the conservative mode of teaching prevalent in France. He believed that children should be encouraged to do personal research which would prepare them for self-instruction in the future:

> The word 'lecture' [*cours*] should be banned from all secondary school teaching and a greater part of academic teaching. The class is already filled with experiences, explanations on the blackboard, and exercises: If somebody has to give a lecture, it is not the teacher who should give it, but the pupil himself. A good lecture is beneficial to the one who gives it. Even

here the method is important. This consists of sending pupils to study in public libraries and to ask them to lecture one after another.[32]

He propounded the idea which today is widely accepted by contemporary librarians—namely that knowing how to use the library is a vital part of education and that children's librarians should instill in young readers the habit of doing personal research.

> But one must learn how to use books. One must inculcate in pupils this desire to look things up for themselves. This does not require any explanation when there are good guides. Furthermore, there is the need for the pupils to know how to read these guides...[33]

> At a very young age, the child should be taught how to go through a catalogue, to choose his books...History should be taught in a way that the child should look up facts relating to this or that monument, costume or object, as seen during a walk. If there is a physics or chemistry experiment to be made, the pupil is invited to do it himself. But an explanation should not be given beforehand. He will look it up for himself in books. And it is he who will have to formulate as much as he can the law which governs this experiment which impressed him so much in the last lesson. This is, to say the least, the guiding principle. It gets its inspiration from a very simple truth. No human being can boast to have a memory which equals an encyclopedia. One must condemn intellectual cramming. It is not important to know everything, but you should be able to learn everything...[34]

Morel stressed that children's libraries in France should be recognized, as in America, as a social and educational instrument for encouraging the citizens of tomorrow to undertake self-instruction.

> Instruction nowadays must essentially consist of knowing how to find means to instruct oneself...[35]

> The use of libraries by children from a very early age in America is a 'school of decision'.[36]

> Research should be undertaken freely, either in systematic catalogues or in various encyclopedias, or on the spot... We are raising here a serious question which has been widely debated abroad. In France, one laughs at the mere thought of allowing people, I mean, children, to rummage in the book stacks. Instead of laughing, let us rather learn from this. There are more than one thousand libraries in the world in which this system is operated to the satisfaction of everyone. This system, the open shelf (sic), cannot be applied everywhere... but it is the standard thing. It is one of the major conditions of self-instruction through books...[37]

Morel was insistent that the effective use that children could make of this method depended on the choice of books to be found on the shelves and the extension work that could be done by women to encourage them to borrow books and to consider the library not as an educational institution but as a home:

> It is women who, in fact, contributed most towards the educational extension of libraries, especially for very young children...[38]

> The special activity of librarians for young people is to know how to choose books. They should have the necessary control over the choice of books and provide the necessary guidance. This is a case on which people have written a lot. France herself is greatly involved in quarrels over this subject. There is a need for considerable tolerance and concessions in order to set up a system which would be accepted by the great majority. We are getting there nevertheless. It is women who have made the impact on these libraries for the young, but one must concede that their influence has been constantly exercised in making available sound literature, which is simple in expression, natural and opposed to 'sensationalism'...[39]

> ...the 'juvenile' (sic) section has the duty to teach the child to consider the library as a home which, during his whole life, he will visit to learn, to enjoy himself, and to perfect his skills...[40]

Finally, in order to be successful, E. Morel recommended, it was essential that children's libraries should be provided with open-access facilities:

> The great utility of libraries for education, we have not said it before and we shall say it by way of conclusion, is to allow the child to browse freely among books. It is in doing this that he has a better chance to decide intelligently on his vocation...[41]

In fact, this is what Eugène Morel wrote at the beginning of the twentieth century about his concept of the children's library, which was encouraged by some and at times had to endure the indifference, skepticism, and sarcasm of others. Morel had to wait until the 1920s before he could see this concept accepted in France and adopted by some municipal authorities. This was officially implemented when the Americans started to rehabilitate the devastated areas after the Great War, 1914-1918, and to create American-type libraries. Morel collaborated in setting up these libraries. He succeeded in instilling in the French a new interest in children's libraries.

By his continued efforts between 1910 and 1925, Morel had earned the reputation of being the principal initiator and active collaborator of the children's library movement in France. He collaborated very closely in the creation of the library for children called "L'Heure Joyeuse."[42]

However, it is important to point out here that the French children's library movement of post-World War I was under direct American influence. Morel's contact with the Americans was motivated by his great admiration for the American library system. This had taken him to the United States, and as early as 1910 he gave a description of children's libraries in the United States and in the United Kingdom. He wanted similar libraries to be set up in France. Morel's dream became a reality in November of 1924, when L'Heure Joyeuse was set up; not, however, without opposition. Victor Chapot, the sub-librarian of Saint Geneviève, wrote in 1910 in an article, "*L'Organisation des Bibliothèques,*" in *Revue de Synthèse Historique* of the same year,

> As for the Juvenile Room (sic) as recommended by M. Morel, let us suppress it. It will be more advantageously replaced by small school libraries...[43]

It is interesting to point out at this stage that L'Heure Joyeuse, in 3 Rue de Boutebrie in the fifth arrondissement of Paris, is the first public library for children in France as it was the first institution that was recognized by the municipal authority. There was, before the creation of L'Heure Joyeuse in 1924, a move made by the American Committee for Devastated Areas to establish children's libraries in France. This occurred between 1917 and 1924, and was promoted by the Book Committee of the American Art War Relief Association, which sent three American women whose many years of experience as children's librarians in America were put to the test when they were called to serve France in promoting library work with children. This committee, under the direction of Miss Jessie Carson, devoted itself to the rehabilitation of four *cantons* of the devastated "department" of the Aisne, and she had two other helpers in Marion Greene and Alice O'Connor. It included in its reconstruction program not only houses and institutions, but also the reorganization of a modern social service which comprises five public libraries open to children. Initially, the scheme did not provide separate rooms for children. The libraries contained small collections of books placed in the baraques and circulated to both children and adults on an average of once a week, and several of the village schools were also supplied with books. This library movement was promoted at Soissons and Anizy[44] by Miss Jessie Carson, chief librarian of children's libraries of four cantons, and was to train young French women to adopt American methods of librarianship.[45]

When W.C. Berwick-Sayers was on his "Paris Pilgrimage" in 1923, he admired the great achievement accomplished by Miss Jessie Carson in

France.[46] For before 1924, he had visited in La Rue de La Paille at Brussels, the beautiful little model library for children, L'Heure Joyeuse, and "was curious to know what the American work amounted to which was being done in France."[47] The Belgian L'Heure Joyeuse was founded by another American body—the American Committee on Children's Libraries. After having compared the two institutions of L'Heure Joyeuse in Belgium and in France, W.C. Berwick-Sayers had to admire the work performed by these three American Ladies[48], for "the children's library movement in France was worthy of the best traditions of library work for children in America."[49]

However, these children's libraries, which were built by the American Committee for Devastated Regions, were not geared to serve young readers exclusively, and were shared by their parents as well. This was made quite clear by C.N. Sarah Bogle, in an article on "Library Development in France," which appeared in the *Library Occurrent* of 1924:

> These libraries became the community centres. Children came to them first, and where they came, the elders soon followed.[50]

Two years after the inauguration of one of the five libraries of the department of the Aisne, that of Belleville, in November 1924, in similar conditions to those laid down by the American Committee for Devastated Regions, the Book Committee on Children's Libraries of New York, over which presided Mrs. J.L. Griffiths, offered the City of Paris its first children's library.[51]

It was largely due to E. Morel and E. Coyecque, the General Inspector of Municipal libraries in Paris, wrote Jules Lemaitre in 1925, that this first children's library called L'Heure Joyeuse became a reality. In describing *La Bibliothèque Enfantine de la Rue Boutebrie: L'Heure Joyeuse* (The Children's Library of La Rue Boutebrie: L'Heure Joyeuse) in *Revue des Bibliothèques* of 1925, Jules Lemaitre not only related on how it came to be accommodated in a big separate room at number 3, La Rue Boutebrie in the fifth arrondissement, in order "to be more accessible to all the three large schools of La Rue Parcheminerie," but he also referred to Morel's speech to single out all those who had participated in and supported the project.

M. Firmin Roz, the publisher, was the first to be interested in the scheme. He called on E. Morel and E. Coyecque, who worked for two years on the development of the project and sorted out all the problems that beset the new institution. M. Paul Gaell, who succeeded[52] E. Coyecque, continued the work of the latter and inaugurated the library.

The above information is taken from the speech which Morel, as vice-president of the Société des Gens de Lettres de France, delivered on the inaugural day of L'Heure Joyeuse. Morel's speech is quoted in full by Jules Lemaitre in his article, in which he pointed out that

> Eugène Morel was applauded when he gave a full account of the aims and meaning of the new institution. We are more than happy to be able to give his speech here which, of those delivered, was the only one not to be published in the *Bulletin Municipal*.[53]

This speech by Morel can be regarded as a major plea for the concept of free public libraries for children, and reveals how far-sighted he had been. It also shows that much of what had been achieved was the result directly or indirectly of his efforts and example. In order that the children's library could make an impact in France, Morel emphasized that it should have the following aims:

> The first one is to instruct the child. This we have already said. The other is much more important: to instruct the adults, especially those who would otherwise never come to the library.[54]

In his speech, he deplored the great lack of children's libraries in France and argued that:

> The truth about children's libraries is that we did not have them. To no degree can we say that we have any. We can even say that they were prohibited.[55]

But he concluded that he was happy to see at La Rue Boutebrie that for which he had been striving. The children's library they had inaugurated would have an incalculable influence not only on the development of other children's libraries, but also on adult libraries:

> Many who scorned the children's libraries are now interested in them. Now that they see that the children's libraries have started to develop, we have asked the children: Go in front of the grown ups, show them the new library, the library adorned with flowers, beautiful pictures, and even the library where the Story Hours exist... explain to these old people who do not want to understand. They will listen, but do not tell them that it is a library, for upon hearing this word they will start turning up their nose. Say, "This is L'Heure Joyeuse. The children's library is progressing. It will give a true picture of the library for everybody which France is waiting for, which France will get. Children, we will follow you.[56]

Morel would have been pleased had he lived to see the substantial progress that Paris alone has made in the provision of children's libraries to her citizens:

> Paris possesses only four libraries reserved for young people,

... emphasized Violette Coeytaux in *Bulletin de Bibliothèques de France,* 1966.

> The first one, L'Heure Joyeuse, situated in Quartier Latin, 3 Rue Boutebrie and faithful to its educational mission, tries to develop the taste for culture and encourages young readers to do personal research. The library also remains a place where they can come for recreation. It tries to fulfill these aims by working in close collaboration with the teaching profession which is very anxious to reach the same aims in order to help children progress in their reading, by organizing cultural activities which are related to books, and, finally, by the acquisition of new books which are not only attractive to the users but meet their educational needs.
>
> The second library is situated in 17 Rue Sorbier, in the heart of Menilmontant...the third, new born, is at 109, Boulevard Mortier... and La Bibliothèque de la Rue Féssart in the 19th arrondissement provides for young readers a very nice room situated on the first floor, beautifully furnished... welcoming and brightly lit...[57]

It cannot be proved whether a certain Professor Hollebeque had any connection with Morel and the Americans. But his theory that the French should model their children's libraries on the American type seems to tally with that of Morel. In fact, Morel elaborated his theory in 1910 in his book, *La Librairie Publique,* while Professor Hollebeque's article appeared in 1919. Even if one cannot prove that he was influenced by Morel's writing, Professor Hollebeque wrote in his *Education thru books according to American methods in Public Libraries* of 1919,

> To succeed, then, it becomes necessary to establish a library modeled after the American public library, but the immediate objection brought forward against this project would be the expense it would incur. France, in her present impoverished condition, could not find at one effort adequate financial support to maintain an institution of this importance. Why should we not begin then to establish a single organ, which, as its resources were increased would hasten the others? But what shall this first organ be?
>
> We are at a period in the life of our country where, in order to recuperate the losses occasioned during the war, and that each individual force should be productive, the effort of the nation should bear upon its education. The safeguarding of our children is one of our most important duties. To have an influence upon the young, it is necessary that all should bear a share in the sports, in manual labor and through the aid of books.
>
> A library should be equipped, therefore, with a section for the children.
>
> All French children take a deep interest in reading. Nevertheless, far from favoring (sic) their tastes, it seems that many things occur to interfere with them. The editors, always willing to publish successful books, are in accord

> in their discrimination to put out books of interest to children; nor is there any classification permitted to guide the parents or schoolmasters in the choice of subject of reading for the children, and nothing either to encourage composition of value from the writers of stories which would appeal to the imagination of the young children.
>
> Why not risk a first experience in organizing in a great city like Paris a library for the children according to the American type of pattern, having a personnel qualified with a knowledge of choosing books according to their intellectual and artistic value, and then classify them by their subjects, age, intellectual qualities, influences, and thereby aid the young readers; whilst some one skilled in the telling of stories would endeavor to capture and hold the attention of the very youthful. Desirous of profiting by the long experience of our American friends in these matters and by their familiarity with methods of library system and routine, we would be glad to undertake this fruitful work. Untiring, since they have been in France, they have worked to save the lives of our children, and assure the future of our race. They are too idealistic not to admit that it is also necessary to develop and elevate the mind. A project such as this, the creation of a library organized for children, cannot but appeal to their sympathy. Moreover at this time, when the instruction of the English language is becoming obligatory in the French schools, these libraries, by containing a selection of American and English books, would become the centers of union between these countries. By these means, through the children, would grow the firm bonds of affection which we wish, and closer acquaintanceship during earliest childhood.[59]

Finally, an aspect of children's work about which Eugène Morel felt very strongly was the importance of a trained librarian in the children's library. This view was indeed uncommon in the French library world of Morel's time. Miss Marguerite Gruny, Morel's niece, wrote in 1969 how she was impressed by Morel's insistence on the need for training facilities for librarians to be in charge of children's library work.[60]

> The training of specialist librarians, was there anything done in this respect in France? No, as far as this is concerned, we had to wait for Morel. As early as 1910, Morel had organized at the Ecole des Hautes Etudes Sociales a course of lectures for people who would be in charge of children's library work. He had organized in 1923, when the American School of librarianship was created in Paris, a program in which were included lectures on children's libraries and literature, and no soon had L'Heure Joyeuse been founded that it set up a similar course.[61]

In spite of the pioneering efforts of Morel, it was evident, wrote Miss M. Gruny, that "that need was not met adequately,"[62] until, thanks to Jules

Cain, an official certificate in children's librarianship was granted in 1953. However this was only meant for the lower echelons of the profession. It is only recently (1968) that the problems of children's libraries have been discussed in the higher courses of librarianship.

Two female librarians who benefited considerably from Morel in their training were Claire Huchet and Marguerite Gruny. Morel's influence on them was considerable. His contact with Mrs. John L. Griffiths, chairman of the American Book Committee of the Art War Relief Association[63], and with W.C. Berwick Sayers, the librarian of Croydon, whose influence and writings on children's libraries in England were invaluable[64], had been instrumental in providing a proper training for these two ladies. Miss Marguerite Gruny wrote:

> Miss Huchet was attached to Croydon Public Library under the children's library pioneer, W.C. Berwick Sayers. She was there for four months, in 1923, during which period she was given the chance to acquire a thorough grasp of library work with children and young people. She spent the school year 1921-1922 in a London private school as a French teacher. Her knowledge of current English permitted her to read and study books on librarianship. [At this time, most of the books of librarianship, especially on public modern librarianship were in English.] In 1923, she was able to benefit from the summer course run by the Ecole des Bibliothécaires, founded by the Committee for Devastated Regions at the Rue de L'Elysée in Paris. In 1924, she was a student at the school of librarianship at University College of London, where she passed her examination.[65]

Miss Gruny herself was not attached to Croydon Library, though the Annual Report of Croydon Public Libraries for 1925[66] reveals that

> the library continues to attract visitors both from the British Isles and overseas [and] amongst them was Miss M. Gruny of *L'Heure Joyeuse*, Library, Paris.[67]

But in 1923 she spent more than a month in Bruxelles at the first L'Heure Joyeuse set up by the Americans in Europe. There, she studied the rudiments of library work with children.[68]

The primary motive behind sending these two women to acquire an insight into what was being done in children's libraries in other countries was to give them the chance, when they had received proper training, to take over from the Americans. They would organize L'Heure Joyeuse together. Miss Huchet remained the *directrix* of L' Heure Joyeuse from 1924 to December 1928, when she left France for America after her marriage to an American, Frank Bishop. She became interested in reviewing children's books, in children's books in general, and in writing books for children. Among those written by her are the following: *The Five Chinese Brothers, Blue Spring Farm, The Big Loop, The Trifle Pig,* and *Toto's Triumph.*[69]

Miss Gruny took over from Miss Huchet. Before the opening of L'Heure Joyeuse in Paris, both Miss Huchet and Miss Gruny, future *animatrices* of L'Heure Joyeuse, had already pioneered in holding story hours in many town halls and parks and they had become experts in the art of telling stories to children. Henri Lemaitre, in his article on L'Heure Joyeuse in *Revue des Bibliothèques* of 1925, reproduces as documentary evidence one of the posters inviting children from the twelfth and fourteenth arrondissements to one of their story hours. The poster reads as follows:

---

VILLE DE PARIS

AUX ENFANTS

DES

XIIIe ET XIVe ARRONDISSEMENTS

Les Mercredis 18 et 25 juin

À 16 heures et demie très précises

AU PARC DU CONTE

De jolis contes amusants, racontés

aux enfants qui les aiment, par

Mesdemoiselles HUCHET et GRUNY[70]

---

The efforts of these two dynamic ladies were also concentrated on preparing French children in the twentieth arrondissement of Paris, as well as those of the eighth arrondissement, to accept the concept of the children's library modeled on the American one.[71]

Work with children in libraries has indeed come a long way since 1908 when Morel started local authorities to realize its importance.

# Advocacy of Public Libraries

To more than one generation of librarians, not only in France but throughout the United States, and to some extent in the United Kingdom, the name of Eugène Morel was synonymous with that of a pioneer of public libraries in France. His advocacy for free public libraries started as early as his debut at the Bibliothèque Nationale in 1910. For twenty-five years he struggled to realize his concept, and this makes him one of the first to have advocated the system of *"la lecture publique"* in France, i.e. free public libraries for everybody.[1]

His efforts were mainly directed towards developing the librarian's capacity to respond to social, cultural, scientific, and industrial needs. He saw the librarian as a purveyor of information, and not merely as a "conservator" of books. Morel was the leading figure in the library movement, and his influence as a protector of the ideals, applications and principles of a system of modern librarianship cannot be underestimated. Many are the tributes that have been paid to his gift for inspiring students and aspiring librarians who had the good fortune to pass through his hands. Miss Marguerite Gruny, his niece, who followed the lectures given by him at the Ecole des Hautes Etudes Sociales, wrote:

> He was forever expatiating on the initiative of the staff [of British and American libraries], whose enthusiasm did not run in neutral gear in an old-fashioned spirit as in France, where everything is hampered by administration.[2]

E. Morel found in the French Library Association the most suitable medium for expressing and developing the many ideas and plans his fertile and active mind generated.[3] Though his professional career was spent entirely in the French national library, most of his thoughts and energy were directed towards the development of free public libraries. His concept of modern librarianship transcended the narrow limits of his day-to-day work, as he had the breadth of vision to see the needs of the public library service in all its facets and the ability to criticize virulently all its defects for the benefit of the French reading public as a whole.

Fortune brought him into contact with another dynamic library pioneer, Ernest Coyecque[4], and with the French Library Association. This happened in 1918, at a critical period in the Association's history, when it needed as president somebody with a good knowledge of the English language, who could foster a rapprochement with the American Library Association. Morel not only had a sound knowledge of the French public library system, but was thoroughly acquainted with the progressive Anglo-Saxon library service.[5]

While Morel was advocating procedures to ensure the development of the public library, the questions that most concerned him were why public libraries had developed more in the United States and England than in France, and what he needed to do to influence the proper authorities to make French libraries on a par with those in other countries. Morel made this quite clear as early as 1911 in an article in *The Library World* on Municipal Libraries for France, which was a translation of the article which had appeared in French in *Le Matin*, and in which he emphasized that:

> For twenty years in England and the United States, the public library has provided new customs, really taught one how to teach oneself and to keep in touch with the times and one's trade. Scotland, Canada, Australia, Germany, Japan are establishing Public Libraries. Is it not time that something was done in France?[6]

But another article in *The Library World* of 1911 shows that the pioneering work of E. Morel had already started as early as that:

> It will interest British librarians to learn that a strong endeavor is being made to rouse France, and more particularly, Paris, to the need for Public Libraries on Anglo-American lines. Belgium, Holland and the Scandinavian countries are already stirring in this matter.[7]

In order to publicize this concept, E. Morel had organized a very interesting and comprehensive course of lectures at the Ecole des Hautes Etudes Sociales.[8]

Morel's pioneering efforts for the expansion of the concept of *La Lecture Publique*, which the Anglo-Saxon library promoters translate as the Free Public Library, were first made known in the publication of his remarkably comprehensive book on libraries: *Bibliothèques* in 1908. His efforts were to continue until his death in 1934.

Quite recently, in 1950, when public libraries were undergoing rapid development in France—something which many specialists on French library matters had remained skeptical about for quite a long time—Henry F. Raux, a writer, pointed out the important role that Morel had played in the development of the free public library in France:

> Perhaps it would not be without interest to recall the memory of one of those to whom it [*la lecture publique*] owes most, one of the first to

understand the importance of *la lecture publique* and help it to get away from the impasse into which, led by pedants and humanitarians, it had gone astray.[9]

One of Morel's first steps in his advocacy of free public libraries was to ensure that everyone had equal access to the services available in the public libraries. Because of his democratic outlook, Morel could not accept that an elitist class be privileged and that the masses be given a second class service.

This democratic ideal led him to criticize the specialization of libraries which provided preferential treatment to some readers. These libraries would usually take into account the social circle in which their readers moved. Thus, he wrote in 1910:

> To insist in maintaining a dichotomy between municipal and popular libraries is utterly absurd. This can be compared to the kind of distinction which I personally know is made at the police station between vagrants and non-vagrants who are arrested on the same festive days. This distinction prevails also in branches or sub-offices set up in the wards of the town. There is no need to write it on the door. Above all, it is annoying to see that there are two castes as far as hours are concerned.
>
> It is the custom in France to open the popular libraries in the evenings only or on Sundays. The scholarly libraries reserved for *comme il faut* (gentlemanly readers) are open up to 4 in the afternoon, which prevents people from all classes of society who are most interested in reading from doing so. First of all, one deprives the skilled workers who work during the day, and who are keen to study, of the use of the library. For these the evening popular libraries are of no use. But are these people vagrants? Surely not. However, they are considered to be so because they are only skilled workers. For those whose intention it is to use the library for research—be they tradesmen, office employees, educated youths, people with a future, rich or poor—for them the libraries are closed because these libraries have impossible opening hours. Even skilled workers are deprived of library facilities.[10]

Commenting on the opening hours of public libraries in 1915, Ernest Coyecque, the close collaborator of Morel in the expansion of public libraries and Inspector of the Municipal Libraries of Paris, remarked that they were still inadequate seven years after Morel's criticism of 1908:

> The great tragedy of our French libraries as our colleague, Eugène Morel, has said somewhere, is that they are always closed. Out of the 82 libraries of Paris, there are 14 which open two and a half months yearly; 87 others open one and a half months yearly; only one library, that of the eleventh arrondissement, and the oldest of them all, the creation of which dates

back to the Second Empire (1852-1870), operates about 3 months yearly. Please note that the first 14 are open for two hours a day and the other 87 for one hour a day; the Library of La Place Voltaire, on the contrary is open from 11:00am to 5:00pm and from 8:00pm to 10:00pm.[11]

When Morel launched his campaign for the setting up of free public libraries that would be open all day, to judge from Ernest Coyecque's statements above, he had to face the antagonism of those who were against his opening libraries from early morning to 10:00pm. Ernest Coyecque compared the libraries advocated by Morel with the existing municipal libraries of 1915:

> If with the Ideal Library, with the Library of Tomorrow... one compares the present state of the municipal libraries of Paris, one would unfortunately notice that the difference is a very large one. Library specialists have been commenting on it for a long time. Eugène Morel particularly mentions it in his book, *La Librairie Publique*, which one should make a point of reading if one is interested in library affairs.[12]

As far as the advocacy of Free Public Libraries in France is concerned, the real value of what Morel intended to do can be assessed by an analysis of the text of a lecture which he gave in 1910 at the *Ecole des Hautes Etudes Sociales*. This lecture was entitled *La Librairie Publique en Angleterre et aux Etats Unis*, and appeared in the book, *Bibliothèques, Livres et Librairies*, published by Marcel Rivière in 1912. A survey of the most outstanding points of this text illustrates the pioneering nature of Morel's advocacy of free public libraries. In the final paragraph of this lecture, Morel asks the reader:

> to think of this institution for which we are making a plea to be set up in France as one which represents moral and practical benefits that will accrue to the community. The benefits will be those of an institution of conciliation and temperance, that will rival cafés and public houses.[13]

In this lecture, Morel referred to his attempts to spread the idea of establishing "Free Public Libraries" in France and explained why he still felt that they should be modeled on Anglo-Saxon libraries. Then he started explaining the reasons for giving his lecture:

> Under this title—*La Librairie Publique en Angleterre et aux Etats Unis*—I want to talk to you not about the *bibliothèques* or *librairies* (libraries or bookshops) of these countries, but about something more important which, frankly, does not exist in our country: the organization of free public libraries"[14]

He went on to say:

> The free public libraries (sic) are not libraries? To tell the truth, I believe that it is important that we should coin a new word to describe them. We do not have these institutions in France. Germany did not have them. She is going to now. I have just visited in Berlin a Buckerhalle quite similar to libraries in England. Now there are at least 27 of them in Berlin. Germany has created the words *Buckerhalle, Lesehalle*, reserving the word *Bibliothek* for the big depots which are meant to preserve books. Are we going to coin a new word when we already have a very clear cut word in French, which was once used as the right word to describe depots of books and which translated almost letter by letter the word we need to translate? For Library and *Bibliothèque* it is *librairie ordinaire* [ordinary public library] without distorting the meaning of the word by adding to it a quality, that of being accessible to the public and at times (not necessarily) that of being free...People continue to give to booksellers the name of hirers of books [*loueuses de volumes*]. We have gone to a great deal of trouble to find this simple word. We believe that it is high time that France should try to get up such an institution which renders so many services abroad. At least she should attempt to make it known! We appeal to all men of goodwill to find a word, and if somebody finds a simpler, clearer, easier word to remember, better fitted to designate this new thing that we would like to see adopted in France, a word which sounds more French, I beg him not to let us look for it any longer."[15]

In the following extract from his lecture, Morel emphasized the need for the creation of public libraries:

> However, I believe that if we really want to give our attention to having free public libraries in France, we will have to achieve good results, to organize the reading public in the country, to another France in reading palaces as nice, lively as the Café de la Grand Place, to do what has been done in England, America, Australia, South Africa, and soon in Germany, Japan...perhaps this is possible in France, we do not know yet. Those who deny it are naïve, for their denial is surely sterile. Anyone who makes an effort, however powerless, has more chance of achieving something.[16]

This is the reason why Morel made the following recommendation:

> It is not time that France started thinking about the development of these libraries...Librarians you who have at heart the improvement of your materialistic and moral position have here a field of enormous activity"[17]

Strongly influenced by the development of the American and British public library systems, Morel led the way in propagating the concept of the free public library, which is epitomized in the following paragraphs:

> Who can deny that during the past few years the state of libraries has been changing, that the general public is showing a keen interest in them? One person tells me it is not so and believes that he is teaching me something. I know better than he that it is not so. For several years I have been writing papers, mounting exhibitions, and even giving lectures for the benefit of the public...[18]

Morel laid down his strategy to implement his concept and, in this case he compared the library situation in Germany and France:

> Unfortunately, we neither have free public libraries—not even outside Paris—nor intellectual centers which can compare with the network of centers for the advancement of higher education set up by Germany. Germans travel, know the free public libraries (sic) of America and England, and admire them. They, therefore, have already set some up in their country.[19]

He goes on to explain the importance of attracting sympathy to public libraries:

> To start with, we must win over everybody. Gradually, municipal councilors, mayors, teachers, town clerks... the public in general must know that there exist *Libraries* or *Bibliothèques* which are useful to, and convenient for, everybody and that France should make it a duty to establish them. One must concede that people who visit England and pay a visit to libraries there. Let us stop asking scholarly libraries to provide services which they cannot afford without falling short of their role. It is in the interest of everybody to think in this way; namely that before founding a special library it will be most economical and interesting for this library to provide the following: A central stock of books which are conveniently classified; an all day service; lending postal and telephone services; and above all a librarian who is a professional. Societies, trade unions, newspapers, groups of every kind who need books must immediately think of this when they want to set up a special library and must not inflict upon someone the pompous title of 'librarian,' especially when that librarian will be without salary and at the head of a library without funds.[20]

Morel was aware that there was a big problem to overcome, and he felt the solution lay in his volumes, *Bibliothèques* and *La Librairie Publique*.[21]

His books advocated the setting up of certain types of libraries which were a novelty in France. The type of library which Morel borrowed from the Anglo-Saxon countries to use as a model in France was the *Free Public Library*.[22]

In *Bibliothèques*, Morel discussed the system of free public libraries he was trying to introduce in France. In 1910, he published a small volume through which he wanted to reach a bigger audience. *La Librairie Publique* was a more popular work and its tone more objective. Polemics played but a minor role and all the problems related to the free public library were tackled in this new book.[23]

*La Librairie Publique* was the first handbook in France to deal with the Free Public Library rather than the scholarly library.[24] In the title *La Librairie Publique* Morel played on an old Anglicism on the word "*librairie*." He wanted to make *librairie* synonymous with library, but *librairie* was used by the French to describe the book trade. Morel brought to the notice of the reader who used his book *La Librairie Publique* that the French had, therefore, been wrong from the start to make a distinction between scholarly and public libraries. They had chosen the wrong word *bibliothèque* to translate to *library*, leaving the French word *librairie* to the English to describe the free public library. This is made clear in Morel's work, *La Librairie Publique*, which bears the following epigram:

> What pedant invented the word *bibliothèque* and left the French word *librairie* to the English?[25]

With these words, Morel summarized his whole philosophy. By describing the essence of *La Lecture Publique* and questioning what other countries had done to develop their public libraries, he tried to bring home to the French what they lacked. He also wrote:

> We do not have to invent a word to describe this essential tool of Anglo-Saxon civilization. Its name is French and we will write it in French: *Librairie Publique*.[26]

In *La Librairie Publique,* Morel studied in detail the various aspects—moral, technical, financial and social—of the public library. Free public libraries abroad are analyzed and compared with French libraries. If his two volumes on *Bibliothèques* are a group of concepts mixed with an enormous mass of documentation and some remarkable intuition, on the other hand, *La Librairie Publique* presents all these data clearly. In it, Morel aimed at promoting his concepts and succeeded in doing so.

His work on librarianship is not filled with school discussions, disputes of literary concepts, and academic controversies, but abounds in facts, examples, figures and a striking picture of the experiences from abroad which could be used to improve the French library system. Most of his experiences of library systems were acquired from foreign travel, especially from visits made to libraries in England and to the United States, in Germany, India and even the East.[27]

This enormous amount of documentation brought its contribution to the old controversy, which had not yet subsided, between those who favored the expansion of libraries which should cater for the general public and those who were partisans of specialized libraries. It was in favor of the former that Morel took up the cudgels. However, he recognized that in each region there should be a general library where one could find all the publications of this region and a specialized library to cater not only for history but for science as well.[28] Thus, Morel presented a reasonable solution which prevails today in the most highly civilized countries and had begun to emerge in France at the beginning of the 20th century.[29]

But Morel's main objectives were to solve the problems that had made France backward in providing a free public library service. He was preoccupied with the need, which later became an obsession, to show how the *bibliothèques populaires* had not resolved the problem of catering for the general public. Morel could not immediately solve the problem of the *populaires* because they sprang from a conception which was adverse to the promotion of public libraries. They were born from a grave sociological heresy.

In *Bibliothèques* and *La Librairie Publique,* Morel described his conception of librarianship as something which should be militant and part of every French library employee's philosophy. His books denounced the backwardness of the French library. He supported this denunciation by a remarkable statistical documentation on the whole library system of France. He offered various suggestions on library organization, and, most of all, revealed to France the public libraries (which Morel in all his writings in France termed *free public libraries*) which France did not have. Both books, *Bibliothèques* and *La Librairie Publique,* were enthusiastic appeals for the creation of free public libraries in France. He inveighed strongly against the conservationist library tradition which had laid stress on the preservation of books on history in most municipal libraries, and against the rift between public libraries termed *scholarly* (catering for the intellectual elite of society) and those termed *popular* (catering for the general public only). He criticized the inefficiency and wastage in these libraries. This work, as well as others that would be a sequel to his *Bibliothèques,* would give rise to controversies among his colleagues, the press, and groups of writers. Besides antagonists, however, he also found many supporters.

In order to appreciate fully the importance of E. Morel's *Bibliothèques* and *La Librairie Publique* in the development of public libraries, one must be aware of the state of libraries in France at the beginning of the 20th century. One of the authorities on the library history of France, Jean Hassenforder, gives the reader a realistic picture of the state of public libraries between 1850 and 1914 in his book, *Développment Comparides Bibliothèques Publiques en France, Grande Bretagne et aux Etats Unis dans la seconde moitié du XIXe siècle: 1850-1914*. This is reviewed by Michel Bouvy in *Bulletin de Documentation Bibliographique* of September, 1969. The review reveals not only the early work of young Eugène Morel in advocating the reform of public libraries in France, but also the critical situation of various types of libraries. This is supported by many references from Jean Hassenforder, who gives a significant picture of the situation of the French library profession before 1914.[30]

> Jean Hassenforder," wrote Michel Bouvy,"helps us to discover another reason why our French public libraries have not been discussed in public for fifty years when he compares the history of our public libraries with that of their English and American counterparts. Paradoxically, it would seem that the author has attempted to write the history of an institution which did not exist in France before 1914—the date at which the author sets a limit to the history—and which hardly exists fifty years later.
>
> It is a fact that this is one of the merits of this study, namely that of reminding us that the basic concept of the free public library had already had, before the First World War, remarkable advocates who had understood from that very time that France was going astray from library development by maintaining a bastard conception of the library. It is convenient here to point out that one should remember the name of Eugène Morel, whose concept of free public library, entitled *La Librairie Publique*, has not become obsolete and the present champions of the free public library could almost take it up again to defend the cause of the expansion of public libraries.[31]

Michel Bouvy goes on to give more details of Jean Hassenforder's study of public libraries:

> The French municipal libraries, created at the period of the Revolution and which, paradoxically, were used as models for the establishment of the first English and American libraries had unfortunately been forced since their creation, to carry like a prisoner, a huge millstone round their neck made up of the books confiscated from the Revolution.
>
> The majority of these old books (the value of which is not to be questioned) had to be catalogued—a thing which has not yet been completed up to now (1967)—constituted valuable matter for scholastic study for an erudite as well as a professional librarian. This has led our municipal libraries to concentrate more on the past and abandoned the libraries to those who had made the study of history a hobby. These were

the elitist class of bourgeoisie, the leading citizens, doctors, notaries, ecclesiastics and magistrates, the pillars of the country's scholarly circles.

Thus was born the library for the few, especially for those who, because they held a good position in society, had at their disposal the municipal 'manna' and expressed only one wish: to keep themselves treasures which the common people were not worthy of sharing. This state of affairs would not have been very serious had it not been behind the concept of municipal libraries which, a hundred years later, were about to disappear."[32]

A circular in 1833 revealed that most of the libraries were used only by a small number of readers. This lack of interest in libraries[33] could have been partly the result of an indifference for study itself. But there could be another explanation, namely the lack of correlation between the readers' needs and the concept of reading and the type of books which were offered for home reading. This circular knew the same fate as many others. It was ignored, as the municipal libraries of the 19th century were entrusted most of the time to indifferent amateur librarians appointed to the posts and who lived isolated in their town without having any contact with the profession. One could say that the 'profession' virtually did not exist.[34]

However, one could have witnessed in France a parallel development of popular libraries as in England, which would have gradually transformed into public libraries. But then it would have been necessary for the state itself to set up a special network of popular libraries. But one could not ask each of the thousands of communes to 'think' about the library problem and maintain the different library systems. It was quite natural that one of these should suffer. However, before 1914, men like Henri Michel, chief librarian at the library of Amiens, and Eugène Morel had already gone to the core of the problem.

As the French librarian was a keeper who preferred to preserve books, rather to encourage people to use them, he was not interested in improving his methods of organization. He would have only done so if it helped him to preserve his collection better. Therefore, it is not surprising how backward French libraries are when compared to the Anglo-Saxon ones. They are slow to develop and reluctant to introduce open access.[35]

Morel criticized this attitude in 1910 in his book, *La Libairie Publique*.[36] Morel must, indeed have had a strong personality if, despite his lowly position, he was able to influence as many librarians and even the French authorities.

Between 1910 and 1920, there was neither a public library which could serve as an effective prototype on which France could model her public libraries, nor a detailed report published by any authority which could have influenced the public to take more interest in public libraries in France. If one were to cite any publications which could have influenced the general public and the authorities, one would cite those of Morel.[37] In both his books, *Bibliothèques* (1908) and *La Librairie Publique* (1910), Morel stressed the hestitating phases through which his advocacy for public libraries had passed. Henri F. Raux, in 1950 in his article, "Morel as an initiator of free public libraries," summed up the phases through which this concept had to go:

> Firstly, the present regime is absurd and cannot last longer; secondly, what can be done to better the regime and improve the state of librarianship in France; thirdly, a better system exists; this is the reason why one has to study it and apply it in France.[38]

It was in his books, *Bibliothèques* and *La Librairie Publique*, that Morel urged the reader to become aware of it.

A summary for two pages of his book *Bibliothèques*, which is taken here as an example, gives the following details:

> On one hand, there are the big scholarly libraries, with the *Bibliothèque Nationale* at the top, faithful to their tradition but not adapted to cater for readers with a modern outlook, specially for the needs of those who are doing scientific research; on the other hand, the university libraries, most of them newly created, have limited resources which do not allow them to be au courant with what is published abroad. A survey conducted by La Revue Scientifique of 1905 had revealed the deficiencies of the French university library stocks. As for the general public, its needs were supposedly catered for by the municipal libraries. But these could not meet its needs, as they were often rich in precious old stocks from the collections of the Church during the Revolution. The stock of books was not renewed, as the municipal libraries were doomed by such ridiculously small budgets that they had vegetated without any hope of being salvaged. There were also other 'public libraries,' which were usually called 'popular libraries.' These were born from a wonderful élan of 1848 and were consolidated after the Third Republic. After having reached their peak development around 1896, they declined through lack of support and in 1909 were struggling for survival.[39]

The pages of this book, *Bibliothèques*[40], are filled with indignation at the backwardness of French public libraries, compared with their Anglo-Saxon equivalents. But the deficiencies of the French libraries, which were accepted as a matter of course by the authorities and the French government, did nothing to improve them. In this book, Morel maintains that it was imperative that the education of librarians be entirely reformed:

> The time has come, after half a century of efforts which triumph today in England and in America, to conceive public libraries as a public service, a municipal public service like refuse-collecting, health, light and fuel and gas service and body hygiene.[41]

Finally, *Bibliothèques* also gives enthusiastic reports on library development, especially when Morel deals with what could have been done for the improvement of public libraries in France and compared the work that had been done abroad with that in France. His book impressed the readers by its passionate plea for the establishment of public libraries modeled on the Anglo-American type. Though the book was often quoted to convince library promoters of what had to be done to overcome the backwardness of the French library system, his antagonists often questioned the accuracy of his detailed documentation. Though Morel was very hard on his opponents, the inveterate "conservators" and archivist-paleographers who had converted all public libraries into sluggish and ineffective museum pieces, his aim was to find a way of arousing the authorities and public opinion to the backwardness of the French public libraries. It is fortunate that in spite of this relative antagonism, Morel succeeded through his books, in creating the impact he wanted on the public. The publication of the two volumes of *Bibliothèques* created a scandal among professional circles and "shocked" everybody when he flung at the head of his colleagues (according to the words of one of them) these two voluminous works.[42]

Reactions to Morel's work varied. Lucien Maury, one of his contemporaries, in *La Revue Politique et Littéraire* of 1910[43], was enthusiastic. On the other hand, Emile Chatelain, librarian of the Sorbonne Library, in an article of *La Revue des Bibliothèques* of 1909, was clearly antagonistic.[44]

These articles represent the two extremes of feelings present. Many writers took sides. Even the general public was shocked by the first volume of *Bibliothèques*. Accordingly, Morel realized that the second volume should be published without delay. Hence, the origin of *Bibliothèques: Essai sur le development des Bibliothèques publiques et de la librairie dans les deux mondes* (1908) in two volumes. These were recognized up to 1950 as the most original and complete books on library economy ever published in France. They contain the results of a significant survey of libraries in France, studies on the great national libraries of the world, and the organization of public readership throughout the world, as well as a vast synthesis of the problems of *La Bibliothèque Libre* (free public library)[45] as it existed in the Anglo-Saxon countries in 1908 and began to appear in German with the establishment of *Buckerhallas*.[46]

Finally, Morel wrote copiously on the concept of *La Lecture Publique* (The Free Public Library) as mentioned by Henry F. Raux, as well as on the method which should be implemented in order that this concept could spread all over France. On the international level, the concept of E. Morel seemed to lean towards that of the great Anglo-Saxon library pioneers: the American Melvil Dewey and the English Edward Edwards.

Just like Melvil Dewey and Edward Edwards, E. Morel, writer, library critic, playwright, and controversialist in analyzing the needs of a modern world, also criticized the efficiency of the administration of libraries in early 1908:

> An immense amount of work keeps libraries busy—starting from the cataloguing of books to stock staking which is done very carefully—all this requires time—in spite of everything libraries do not attract readers. If one can go through all the specialist journals, reports and proceedings of congresses, one notices that there is not a single mention that libraries are set up to offer reading facilities to readers.[47]

While Michel Bouvy's review of Jean Hassenforder's book, *Dévelopment Comparé des Bibliothèques Publiques en France, Grande Bretagne et aux Etats Unis dans la Seconde Moitié du XIXe Siècle* (1850-1914), and Maurice Pellisson's book, *Les bibliothèques populaires à l'étranger et en France* (Paris: Imp. Nationale, 1906. 220p) were revealing the profound and desperate crises of public libraries in France at the beginning of the twentieth century, a French journalist, Frédéric Gaussen, in an issue of *Le Monde* of July 30th, 1967, was emphasizing that the state of public libraries had not changed significantly in the 1960s. To illustrate this, Gaussen quoted a primary school inspector from Morbihan of 1909, who stated that books provided by the French State Library Directorate of 1967 to libraries were of no interest to their readers:

> Three quarters of the books which are found in our libraries cannot be read...the majority of them which are donated by the Ministry comprise *History Choisies de Tite Live, La Marine des Anciens, Les Irrigations dans le Var...* All this occupies quite a considerable space in a library, helps very little and just lies on the shelves; this remark of the inspector of a primary school of Morbihan of 1907 is still with us...[48]

In the opening years of the 20th century, the seriousness of the situation became very obvious. The "erudite" municipal libraries had developed little, as one competent librarian, Jean Laude, wrote in his book, *Les Bibliothèques Publiques*:[49]

> They were housed in old buildings, lacking all conveniences and with inadequate reading rooms, badly equipped and cramped administrative quarters, too little reserve storage space...[50]

Because of lack of funds, the book collections were not renewed for years on end. The municipal libraries "contain the almost complete treasures of the verities acquired by man up to the end of the eighteenth century, but...since then, their additions to these treasures have been significant. In these libraries, the intellectual movement of the nineteenth century... and the great rebirth of science which that century witnessed...were to all intents and purposes not represented."[51] The situation in other categories of library catering for the general public was scarcely better.[52]

It is quite clear from all that has been said that at the beginning of the 20th century, the French public libraries were in a lethargic state and had little hope of advancement. It was in this climate, therefore, that E. Morel started his campaign for the establishment of effective, free public libraries in France to be run on the models set up by the Anglo-Saxon countries. In vitality and stature, Eugène Morel was the equal of the great British and American pioneers, Edward Edwards and Melvil Dewey, and it was Morel who introduced into France the principles of modern librarianship. Like all pioneers, Morel was destined to meet with opposition. A quotation by Lucien Febvre in the preface of his book, *Combats pour l'Histoire* (1965), may be used here to remind the reader of the vicissitudes of the pioneering efforts of Morel:

> The lot of the pioneer is misleading. Either his generation approves his pioneering efforts immediately and absorbs in one big collective effort his isolated endeavor of investigation or it resists it and leaves future generations to nurture the seeds of pioneering which had prematurely been sown in the drills. This is the reason why the long-delayed success of certain books or certain articles stuns their author, because they will find an audience (a true audience) only ten, fifteen years after their publication.[53]

Before dealing with Morel's attempts at reform, it would be interesting to summarize the factors that affected Morel's endeavor to promote public libraries, and to compare English and French attitudes regarding library development. This may explain why Morel's pioneering efforts had a slow impact on the French mentality.

At the end of the 19th century, France, unlike England, was, relatively speaking, a divided society:

> Most churchmen and many army officers still favored a return to monarchy. The republicans wished to destroy the political power of both groups. The prestige of the government was weakened, however, by the disclosure in 1892 that the French company engaged in building the Panama Canal had gone bankrupt. This was followed in 1894 by the Alfred Dreyfus scandal, in which the army captain, a Jew, was convicted of espionage. When it was learned five years later that the evidence had been forged by a monarchist, army influence was shattered and the republicans gained new strength.[54]

The above factors were bound to adversely affect any reform movement. Pioneering efforts came first from sectarian quarters rather than from the public sector. Etienne Vidier, in his book *L'église et les oeuvres socials en 1900*[55], reveals that the Roman Catholic Church in France was running more than 30,000 popular libraries. But these only catered for a group who professed the Roman Catholic religion. The movement did not result in the setting up of free public libraries. There were very few isolated library promoters and E. Morel recognized as early as 1910 the efforts of these Catholic personalities who directed their attention to this end:

> Among those who were the first to have understood and made themselves the propagators of the concept of 'free public libraries' in France are fervent catholics. L'Abbé Perreyve and Father Piolet have been the first to reveal this social novelty, the free public library and its role in England, a thing which the majority of laymen and politicians are ignorant of.[56]

This impetus by the Roman Catholic Church was dampened, perhaps because in 1905 Roman Catholicism was abolished as the country's official religion.[57]

The backwardness of these and other public libraries reflected to some extent the persistence of certain conditions whose prevalence in the past Jean Hassenforder has brilliantly examined in his *Développement Comparé...1850-1914*. These conditions were namely the limited opportunities for continuing education, the centralization of power in Paris, the traditional scholastic methods which gave little encouragement to the development of free personal enquiry, individualism, bureaucratic rigidity, and the excessive importance attached by certain parties to the conservation function of libraries. In fact, the personal aspiration for culture was less strong in France than in England, and the efforts exerted on behalf of adult education less intensive. France lacked the corporate spirit and local initiative of a British Mechanics' Institute. Finally, the lines on which the French library was conceived initially influenced its subsequent success or failure; the expansion of public libraries in the United States and the United Kingdom from 1850 onwards was due in no small part to the quality of the prototype library set up in these countries. From the outset, the services offered in Great Britain and the United States were varied enough to interest the whole community, and each library was sufficiently large to be able to operate efficiently and accommodate effectively these services. In the Anglo-Saxon countries, the libraries were institutions intended for the entire population. In France, on the contrary, as we have seen, there was a clear-cut distinction between popular libraries destined for the general public and municipal libraries frequented by a scholarly elite.[58]

The parallel progress of public libraries in the United Kingdom and the United States was accompanied by the establishment of very close relations between those working in the field of librarianship on either side of the ocean. For example, *The Library Journal*, founded in 1876, was initially a forum for both the American and British Library Associations to exchange their views on library methods. The development of free public libraries in these English-speaking countries was to inspire Morel in the early 20th century. He was to cite constantly the rapid development of Anglo-Saxon public libraries in support of his advocacy of public libraries in France.

Morel was to follow the same procedure adopted by Edward Edwards, the English library pioneer, in Great Britain. As early as 1846, Edwards began to assemble important statistical information on libraries of Europe and America in order to write, in 1847 and 1848, articles on the subject laying emphasis on the backwardness of English libraries. When the English library system was compared with the French library system, the backwardness of the English system emerged from a statistical study in which Edward Edwards had assembled statistical data on public libraries in Great Britain, France, Germany, the United States, and other countries.[59] By following the same procedure in his book, *Bibliothèques: Essai sur le développement des Bibliothèques Publiques et de la Librairie dans les Deux Mondes*, 1908, Morel was able to demonstrate his country's backwardness in the development of public libraries. He contrived, thereby, to awaken public interest in the matter and secure the help of the newly created French Library Association in 1908. At the conferences and periodical meetings which the French Library Association had organized and the proceedings of which had been published in the *Bulletin de L'Association des Bibliothécaires Français* since 1907, the Association had discussed most of the problems raised by the reform of the libraries and the progressive improvement of the profession.[60]

Morel's role in the expansion of American prototype public libraries in France, on which France could model her future public libraries, was very important. He advocated the development of libraries which would respond to the social needs of the ratepayers. Impressed by the need for cultural provision in some unprivileged areas of France, Morel undertook the reorganization of the Levallois-Perret Library, that of Meudon, and the municipal libraries of Paris when the authorities concerned decided to reorganize them. These were pilot projects which became a reality due to the help of the Americans after 1918.[61]

As for the development of the Levallois-Perret Library, Morel was wholly responsible for it. It all started in 1910[62], when Morel began to organize his course of lectures set up at the Ecole des Hautes Etudes Sociales, and a decision was taken by the Municipal Council of Levallois-Perret to entrust to Morel the reorganization of its municipal library. The library had then a stock of 15,000 volumes, and there was the need to furnish it with new additions.[63] The Levallois-Perret Library was a popular library, but the staff was deprived of the most elementary technical knowledge of librarianship.[64] In accepting the responsibility of reorganizing the Levallois-Perret Library, Morel had to seek the help of all his pupils and colleagues from the Section des Bibliothèques of the Ecole des Hautes Etudes Sociales which he was directing.[65] This provided Morel with the opportunity of applying all his theories and techniques of modern librarianship to this municipal library.[66] In 1911, Morel took over the reorganization of the library of the town which had a population of 50,000. He immediately gave his attention to the establishment of effective lending and reference services, and was anxious to build up the catalogue of the library.[67]

In 1913, he succeeded in publishing a catalogue which was to be cited many times as an example in the professional sector because he applied, for the first time in France, the Dewey Decimal Classification to organize the subjects in his catalogue.[68] The catalogue, which is known as *Le Catalogue de la Bibliothèque de Levallois-Perret, publié sous la direction d'Eugène Morel*, was recognized as a first attempt in France at setting up an important classified catalogue supported by an alphabetical subject index. A general alphabetical index by author's name and titles of books by anonymous authors rounded off the catalogue. Its preparation took Morel three years, and the first edition came out in 1913. Of the 1913 catalogue:

Appearing at the end of 1913, the *Catalogue* was almost sold out. 2,000 copies were printed, but this was not sufficient. There were so few left that by July 1914 the experiment would have stopped even if there had not been war. We had no copies from which to reprint. Fortunately, in 1920, the Germans returned to us those copies which had been lent for the *Exposition du Livre*, which opened in Leipzig in the summer of 1914.[69]

It was not long before the library grew into a complete active lending library. During his stay in office as Chef Bibliothécaire de la Ville de Levallois Perret he was seconded for duty there from the Bibliothèque Nationale.[70]

The second edition of the catalogue came out in 1925.[71] This edition was republished by Morel and is preceded by a preface, where he once again propounded his concept of modern librarianship and expressed joy that the idea of *la lecture publique* had progressed a great deal since the time he produced the first catalogue of Levallois-Perret in 1913.[72] The preface of the 1925 catalogue also reveals Morel's modesty:

> that he did not think of appropriating to himself this merit, but was certain that many other elements had contributed towards the success of the pilot scheme at Levallois-Perret, and that other theoreticians of modern librarianship, other enthusiasts of the profession, had participated in boosting his concept. However, it is evident and recognized that Morel was the first to have drawn up the major plan on which the modern library should be based in France.[73]

The experiment at Levallois Perret, where Morel stayed in office as chief librarian during its period of reorganization[74], was very successful, and undoubtedly left its impact on the reorganization of the municipal libraries of Paris when Morel's fellow library pioneer, Ernest Coyecque, the General Inspector of the Paris municipal libraries, undertook to reorganize them as early as 1913.[75]

Morel also associated adult education with free public libraries. It should be appreciated that all the activities and institutions Morel mentioned as early as 1910—namely free public libraries, social meetings, debating rooms in libraries, lectures—were in those days very new devices to promote adult education. What was also a novelty in France was Morel's grasp of the whole concept of self-instruction, more particularly that of adult education.

Morel emphasized that the public library had a tremendous role to play in the promotion of self-instruction of the people:

> The public library has the aim and means to educate people. I would go so far as to say that it should be the place where self-instruction (sic) can

be carried out. If the library has its origins as part of school, I emphasize that it should be as important as school itself.[76]

In order to achieve all the reforms he had in mind, he had to level criticism at the deficiencies of all types of library. He criticized popular and school libraries which had counter-attracted potential readers who would normally have used the municipal public libraries.

He also bitterly criticized the tendency for archivist-paleographers to occupy key positions in the municipal libraries instead of qualified librarians:

> With our label populaire and scolaire that we stuck on libraries we do not know what a free public library means...the municipal libraries which should be made accessible to everybody are led astray by archivist-paleographers who led them towards pure historical curiosity; they are closed to the general public, to modern ways of thinking and have ridiculously limited budgets and impossible opening hours...[77]

It is to be remembered that in England, the British pioneer of public libraries, Edward Edwards, had also met a great deal of opposition when he campaigned for the promulgating of a Public Libraries Act (1855).[78] One could recall that Edwards had based himself mostly on statistical evidence when he conducted a survey in 1848 of what he believed to be the vastly better public library service provided abroad. E. Edwards's detailed documentation, before the British Parliamentary Committee, on the public library services in France and other countries had impressed the Committees in 1849. That year, E. Edwards revealed the backwardness in the library activities of Great Britain compared with France, yet half a century later Morel could see that there had been a rapid development of public libraries in England, and the progressive French type of libraries referred to by E. Edwards in 1849 had remained in a state of underdevelopment, and were still stagnating in the 20th century.

Paradoxically, E. Morel's entire advocacy of public libraries was inspired by the Anglo-Saxon examples:

> In London, in 1902, there were eighty libraries which are not like ours. First of all, they all have a very big newsroom where newspapers and magazines are put at the disposal of readers, and lending and reference sections where documents can be consulted on the spot. They are open not only for two hours in the evening but everyday from 8:00am or 9:00am to 10:00pm. I would like to point out that there the opening hours are uninterrupted.[79]

Just like the British library pioneer, E. Morel used abundant statistical evidence to show not only how inadequate French public libraries were, but also how far the French library services lagged behind those of Great Britain and the United States. All this he had made quite clear in his books, *Bibliothèques* and *La Librairie Publique*.

Though Morel's books are at times polemical and written in a style which is a trifle involved in some places, they reveal a scientific mind in his way of producing statistical documentation to back up his theories and philosophy. To quote a typical example Morel wrote in 1908 in volume one of *Bibliothèques*:

> The Libraries of Greater London lend books at the rate of two books per head of population, while the outskirts of Paris do not reach even half a book per head.[80]

Morel has not only left his mark on modern librarianship in France by his writings, but also by his continuous efforts advocating the need for free public libraries. These efforts were directed towards, firstly, the analysis of the needs of the general public, secondly, organization of library work, and thirdly, assessment of results.

His pioneering work made a big impact during his lifetime in the 1930s, but his actions were to have, according to library development observers, more considerable repercussions after the Second World War.[81] If the French Library Association supported every aspect of his campaign and provided him with many partisans for his movement, Morel also met vigorous opposition from a clique who thought that libraries should exist only for an elitist class and not be open to all without discrimination. Morel's concept of modern librarianship, which he felt should serve the general public with a view to developing the reader's desire for self-instruction, as mentioned earlier, was in conflict with a "caste spirit" deeply imbedded in French customs. These customs were linked with a typically French national tradition. The antagonism of librarians was reflected in the reaction of Victor Chapot, who was licentiate, doctor of law, and a cultural man and sub-librarian of the Ste. Genevieve Library.[82] It is surprising that Victor Chapot, with all these qualities and qualifications, should have denied the necessity of reform at a time when French libraries needed it very badly.

Victor Chapot saw in the public library as advocated by the reformer Morel:

> A combination which is extremely suitable for providing materials to cater for light reading and culminates in a reference library and an information bureau for practical life:

> This will do for an Anglo-Saxon ideal. One is an anglo-maniac or one is not. Mr. Morel is one, and much good may it do him.[83]

Victor Chapot's blatant skepticism of Morel's move to establish public libraries modeled on British and American lines is shown in these remarks:

> In the United States, railways have only one class, in England the third class brings together the wretched, the skilled workers and the bourgeois. In public libraries, people from all walks of life hobnob without embarrassment. I can hardly see this situation prevailing in France in the near future. We still need for the different classes different books and separate premises.[84]

Victor Chapot also made a violent attack on Morel's aim of providing in French public libraries all the services that the Anglo-Saxon public libraries were offering: open access, lending and reference libraries, information bureau service, and newsrooms, as advocated by Morel in his book *La Librairie Publique*[85] and in his article, *"La Librairie Publique en Angleterre et aux Etats Unis."*[86] In his book, *L'Organisation des Bibliothèques,* Victor Chapot went on to caricature Morel's concept:

> Apart from newspapers, what else can libraries offer? And which public are they going to cater for? Here, I think Mr. Morel is making a fool of us, and amuses himself, undoubtedly, by reducing his paradox ad absurdum. The mainstay will be *Le Bottin*; please add to it the railway timetable, posters etc.[87]

The last comment, to say the least, displayed a misunderstanding of what Morel meant by practical life.

Morel's professional advancement was hampered by a regime where scholastic assessment, including the passing of examinations and tests, and promotion by seniority carried more weight when a promotion to a high post in a public institution was being considered than the unbiased assessment of the personal work of an employee.

But it is difficult to gauge Morel's influence on the development of public libraries because many of the results escape analysis. However, his criticism came at the right time, and Morel could darken the picture when representing the state of public readership in France,[88] which was not very bright. He laid the foundations of a modern librarianship based on the experiences which he had gathered from the United States and England.[89]

Lucien Maury, in an article entitled *"'Lavènement du livre' in Revue Politique et Littéraire"* of 1910, wrote about Morel's experience of free public libraries in England and the United States:

> We need the bibliothèques livres publiques, and it is here that the book by Eugène Morel (*Bibliothèques*) will prove most useful. For it is concerned with a new concept which it is high time for France to adopt. England and America have given us models. There is nothing more astonishing to a bourgeois of a French province than to look at this prodigious development of the free library (sic) of England or America. When we look at it our desire is to emulate this serviceable institution. Therefore, let us stop boasting about our non-existent municipal and popular libraries.
>
> Popular theatre, popular university, popular restaurant, popular library...it is with this word 'popular' that the best intentions become an insult to the work that these undertake. When will we put an end to these charitable gestures?[90]
>
> 'A library,' an American whose name I do not remember has written, 'should not be a reservoir, but a fountain.' So that this fountain of intellectual life be beautiful, welcoming, perpetually flowing, a library should be opened everyday from nine in the morning to ten in the evening: it should offer to passers-by cheerful, brightly lit, and attractive rooms. In England, Eugène Morel has seen hundreds of them: It is a thing which is more beautiful than the church, the Town Hall, more gay than the bar; it is as brightly lit as a theatre. At night, even on a cold night, it invited readers up to ten o'clock. Readers are cozy and warm, and it is clean there. One always feels in good company. One can see that in England, in America: but not in France.[91]

If there were people in France like I.E. Chatelain and Victor Chapot who were against Morel's advocacy of free public libraries, his efforts for the promotion of modern librarianship were accepted not only by the Americans and the British, but by the Italians also.

The partnership of E. Morel and Ernest Coyecque started when the Americans, after the First World War, wanted to establish an American library system in the devastated region. Coyecque's moral support was instrumental in consolidating the French library pioneer's efforts in bringing reform to the apathetic state of public libraries. The joint activities of these two library pioneers were summed up in an obituary written by Marguerite Gruny for Ernest Coyecque, published in the *Bulletin d'Informations de l'Association des Bibliothécaires Français* in 1954.[92] They brought a vitality to the French public library movement until the death of Morel in 1934. They also had a considerable influence on library reorganization after the Second World War.[93] In this obituary, Marguerite Gruny wrote:

> As soon as Ernest Coyecque assumed his duties at the *Bureau des Bibliothèques*, he wanted to look into the public library affairs. At that time, in 1910, Colin had published a work of 322 pages, *La Librairie Publique* by E. Morel, readapted from another work, *Les Bibliothèques*. It bore this epigramme: 'What pedant invented the word bibliothèque, leaving the French word libraries to the English?' It was an exact picture of the Library as the Anglo-Saxons conceived it; the 'free public library,' which, since the Ewart Bill, that is to say, since 1850, has developed in England and the United States. With the help of numerous examples the vast organization of the 'free public library,' with its extended and diverse services, was described: information, reference, and home reading facilities, reading rooms, provision of lectures and book exhibitions, and a junior library. *La Librairie Publique* examined the French possibilities for developing libraries. The conclusion of the book emphasized that our country, which had no reason to lag behind in library service, should take the Anglo-Saxon libraries as a model...
>
> *La Librairie Publique* was the book which Ernest Coyecque was looking for. He immediately agreed with all the views of Eugène Morel, and went to see him at the Bibliothèque Nationale. The writer and the man of action got along very well, and each knew that he was not on his own in his pioneering efforts for the advocacy of public libraries. Their patriotism, as well as their sense of justice, made them feel that France was very backward when compared with other countries where libraries were concerned, and their intelligence gave them both an insight into the future of libraries.
>
> The meeting between E. Coyecque and Eugène Morel strengthened Coyecque's convictions and encouraged him to set up his plan for reorganizing libraries with more breadth and clarity. Coyecque knew that 'the time has come to modernize the Municipal Library, but not to abandon it like a wretched and derelict relative in comparison to the other municipal services, such as the fire brigade service...water reservoirs of the water department...sewerage, and transport and electric tramways services...'
>
> However, in spite of this tenacity, the inspector of libraries realized that his efforts were inadequate and inoperative. But events which were of major importance for the history of libraries in our country were going to support their efforts.
>
> Between 1917 and 1924, at a period which knew neither the Atlantic Pact nor the Comité de Defense Européenne, in a magnificent act of

generosity, the memory of which all those who had known it would keep, the American Committee for Devastated Regions devoted its efforts to the rehabilitation of four cantons of the department of the Aisne. It was a general plan of reconstruction which included houses as well as institutions. Coupled with a modern social service were five 'Public Libraries' open at the same time to children and adults...

Easter Day of 1921 saw the inauguration of the most important of these libraries, that of Soissons. Eugène Morel, who for several years had attracted the sympathy of the Americans by his comprehension of their grandiose achievements, was invited there, as well as Ernest Coyecque. The two Frenchmen could not help marveling at the humble lodging of the troops, its windows adorned with pot plants, which accommodated their new creation. The new library was a living illustration of the book of the one and of the reports, brochures, and articles of the other.[94]

It was at the inauguration of the Soissons Library that Morel's efforts to develop an effective library system were approved and proclaimed by the Americans. An extract from an article in the French newspaper, *L'Argus Soissonais,* March 27, 1921, gives further evidence of Morel's pioneering efforts in comments like these:

...the establishment of public libraries according to the American plan of open shelves with books accessible to one and all will do more good towards producing reforms in the French library system than volumes of reform propaganda, according to Eugène Morel of the *Bibliothèque Nationale* in Paris, who made a speech at the opening ceremony. M. Morel has been advocating for many years the necessity for reform in French public libraries. 'They are serious formal gathering places for spectacled literati, whereas they should be cheerful rooms where the public feels welcome and at home,' he said in his speech this afternoon. 'In the future, when I am asked what I mean by the modern popular libraries I have preached and written about for decades, I shall recommend a visit to this library at Soissons.'[95]

The creation of Soissons Public Library, an American self-help project, after the 1914-1918 war, represented the first step in this movement of rebuilding or setting up libraries in France by the Americans with the help of library pioneers like Morel and Coyecque. Many of the large municipalities also responded to the call of the American Library Association and were ready to collaborate with the Americans in this worthy and far reaching movement.

Morel, in his monograph, *L'Enseignement Post Scolaire: La Bibliothèque Nationale*, written in 1927, also stressed the participation of the Town of

Soissons in setting up a library in the region of France called the Aisne, and showed how the Mayor, the Chief Superintendent of buildings of the *Region Dévastées,* and other important personalities had contributed to the project. In short, Morel wrote:

> Everybody has contributed to the creation of this library; this is the reason why libraries have started to become an integral part of the life of the community.[96]

However, among all those who contributed towards the setting up of this library, the contribution of the two French library pioneers was of paramount importance. This was recorded by the Americans, who recognized their initiative in making the free public library at Soissons a success. The French newspaper, *L'Argus Soissonnais,* wrote the following on Morel's contribution to the project:

> ...M. Morel, who has studied the organization of libraries in America, Scotland, England tells us how happy he is to see the realization in Soissons of a concept for which he has been fighting for quite a long time. He enumerates all the advantages that a well-organized library brings; it is both a place where research can be undertaken and an information centre. There, one learns to enjoy good reading and is made aware of the problems which one's municipality, one's town, one's country, the entire world has to face. For a long time, Americans have had libraries like this which have developed the habit of seeking for themselves the information they need.[97]

Ernest Coyecque also attended the inauguration of the Soissons Library and delivered a speech on the occasion. A part of the speech was reported in the *Argus Soissonnais* of 1921:

> ...M. Coyecque warmly thanks the Committee for its initiative. For many years he has been struggling with Morel to secure the transformation of the libraries of Paris and to adapt them to the needs of the present day. He said 'Look at the English, American libraries.' But America and England are so far away, and the argument was not as successful as one had hoped. Now, I am able to say to those who are incredulous: take the train and go to Soissons and see for yourselves...[98]

After the inauguration of this library, Morel and Coyecque still hoped that there could be a change in the French public library system.

A photograph shows them in front of the door of the lodgings. Their faces showed a restrained, but deep joy. But, ironically, above their head, on the door of the library could be read these words on a notice board: 'Popular library of Soissons' (Bibliothèque Populaire de Soissons). In utilizing this term *'populaire,'* which was so often criticized (especially by Morel), the founding Committee had in mind no doubt to try to overcome the shyness of the population before their newly created property.

> This type of library has become today (1954) a familiar feature of public life, even though French people have never had the opportunity to recognize it as such. In some corners of the world it has already become obsolete, but thirty years ago it astounded and delighted people at the same time. The two Frenchmen could not help voicing their admiration: 'Alas, if Soissons were Paris.'"[99]

Miss Jessie Carson, chief Junior Librarian of the large public library service of New York, remembered their statement. A few days later, she gave E. Coyecque and E. Morel to understand that the American Committee was ready to offer to Paris a library which would be an exact replica of the one at Soissons. The library's initial expenses were to be borne by the Committee, then the City of Paris was to take charge of the service. The Inspector of Libraries applauded with enthusiasm. Both Morel and Coyecque sought the help of a politician to help them with the administrative formalities. André Tradieu agreed to help. On November 2nd, 1922, the library in La Rue Féssart, at Belleville, was solemnly inaugurated.[100]

An extract of an article appearing in *L'Argus Soissonnais* of 1922 covered the inauguration of this library by the American Committee for the benefit of French readers in Paris at Féssart on November 22nd, 1922. This article reveals Morel's advocacy of public libraries and gives the gist of the many speeches delivered on the occasion. Among them were those of Myron Herrick, Ambassador of the United States of America; Louis Pench, chairman of the Municipal Council; M. Julliard, Prefect of the Seine and of André Chevrillon, member of the French Academy and Chairman of the Comité Français de la Bibliothèque Moderne, of which Morel was a staunch member and a former chairman. In his speech, André Chevrillon extolled the expertise and devotion of Morel in having promoted the setting up of the Library at Féssart. It is interesting to quote an excerpt of his speech on this occasion if only because it reveals how Morel, together with E. Coyecque, had brought about this great achievement:

> At least, in the name of the French Committee for the Promotion of the Modern Library, I would like to thank our American ladies who inspired this work and the two French technicians—why should I not mention their name?—and thank them for all the benefits that their technical know-how and dedication have brought to the organization of this work.

These two Frenchmen were M. Morel of the Bibliothèque Nationale and M. Coyecque, Inspector of the eighty-four libraries of Paris and of the Department of the Seine. M. Morel, in his book, *La Librairie Publique* (1910), which is an authority on the question, had pointed out the imperfections and the out-of-datedness of French libraries—here I speak especially of the local regional libraries and of those found in the wards of the town. [Morel] had spoken of reforms and the necessary development of libraries.

What the American Committee had achieved in this field in Soissons would interest these gentlemen very much. They showed their admiration for this project. The American Committee complied with their wish and offered to organize a library in a ward of Paris—a library that could be used as a prototype. The offer was transmitted to the Municipal Council, which eagerly accepted it.[101]

At the inauguration of the library at Féssart, Morel mounted an exhibition on American libraries. An extract from the proceedings of a meeting held at Féssart on November 15th, 1922, gives the following information on Morel's activities regarding his desire to enforce the principles of building French libraries on American models:

> Eugène Morel expressed the wish to organize a small exhibition to show what American libraries look like. He says that he has contacted La Maison du Livre, who will lend their premises, and Mr. Johnston, who has promised E. Morel a nice collection of big posters. 'There is a need,' says he, 'to overcome the ignorance on the world of this phenomenon, the library, which is still very unknown…One could not imagine how little people with whom one comes into contact know about libraries. They know that libraries exist where there are books. Apart from that, they do not know anything about libraries.' [Morel] even says that he has delivered lectures on this subject in working class circles and has not found any resistance.[102]

In 1929, the Municipal Council of Féssart, at its meeting on December 19th of the same year, adopted the project of rebuilding the library of Fessart, which was given to the French in 1922. The reconstruction project was to replace the wooden building with a two story brick building.[103] Regarding the renovation of the Rue Féssart Library and the new institutions, a journalist, Jules Bertaut, in an article in *Le Temps* of July 27th, 1929, entitled *"La Librairie Claire,"* quoted Morel's writings and emphasized that they had had some influence in changing the attitude of the French towards the setting up of libraries:

A few years before the First World War, Mr. Eugène Morel in a book full of new ideas, entitled *Bibliothèques*, had said almost everything that could be said on *La Librairie Claire*. He was the first or one of the first to have recommended the creation of what one could call *La Librairie Claire*.[104]

In 1927, Morel, in his monograph, *L'Enseignement post-scolaire: La Bibliothèque Moderne*, described his *La Librairie Claire* and exposed his slum clearance campaign to get rid of gloomy libraries:

> [*La Librairie Claire*] is not one of these miserable rooms where from a 'wicket-gate' a civil servant hands over to you a black and filthy book. Nor is it one of these libraries which people have labeled '*bibliothèque populaire*,' so as to distinguish it from scholarly libraries to which people who have some spare time in the evenings go in order to read these same black and filthy books.
>
> This is a new institution. It is the free library, the bright home open to one and all. It should have books for everybody—adults, young people, scholars, and students as well. It should provide its services in far off places which it reaches by mobile libraries. It should cater for rural readers, workshops, factories, fields...[105]

Finally, of the many advantages that the creation of the Library at Féssart had brought to the French, Morel wrote in 1925:

> The Library of Belleville, rue Féssart, is the work of this same American Committee who, in the department of the Aisne, had erected in the midst of the ruins the library of Soissons, and the branch libraries in the countryside: Blerancourt, Anisy, Coucy-le-Chateau, Vic-sur-Aisne. The one that stands in Rue Féssart, in the most densely populated quarter of Paris, is a 'reproduction' purposely placed there for those who are preaching the cause of libraries so that they may show that these are not words, but deeds. This may show that where one used to lend a hundred volumes per day, one can lend a thousand; that there are readers who belong to all trades, of all ages, and both sexes who come to the library everyday, that three librarians who have studied their special trade in a special school can hardly suffice to cope with the public demand, and that in the face of such a success, only one question is asked: 'Is it a plucked flower which looks nice in a pot and adorns the place or is it an offshoot which will multiply?'[106]

Two years after the inauguration of La Bibliothèque de la Rue Féssart, in November, 1924, in similar conditions, the Committee for Children's Libraries of New York offered to the City of Paris the library L'Heure Joyeuse. It should be pointed out that Morel used his contacts with the Americans to promote L'Heure Joyeuse. This library was to find a strong supporter in Ernest Coyecque and E. Morel, though Coyecque was to retire from the library scene and leave Morel to struggle like a deserted champion for the development of public libraries in France.[107]

The greater part of Morel's advocacy for public libraries was supported by the Americans, as well as E. Coyecque. Both Coyecque and Morel wanted a reorganization of French municipal libraries as early as 1910.[108]

This was pointed out by E. Coyecque in his article on the municipal libraries of Paris in 1915. Just like Morel, he spoke of reform which was stifled by a spirit of skepticism, indifference, and inertia:

> We are under a regime where reforms are in full swing, and at a time when favoritism and routine are also out of favor, and it is not advisable to show skepticism, indifference, and inaction.[109]

Even 17 years after Morel had started his campaign for free public libraries, he and E. Coyecque faced strong antagonism from French librarians. These called themselves conservators at the Congrès de Bibliothécaires et de Bibliophiles, held on April 2nd, 1923, at the Sorbonne, Paris.[110]

W.C. Berwick-Sayers, who attended the Conference, wrote a report on it in the *Library Association Record* of 1923. He gives the reader the following information on E. Coyecque's and Morel's advocacy of public libraries in France and his own appreciation.

> There [at the Congress of librarians and bibliophiles, in 1923] was more emphasis laid on conservation rather than diffusion of books. M. Louis Varthon, who presided over the preliminary gathering, addressed the meeting and welcomed the delegates from all over the world as conservators of books. The words 'conservators of books' ran through the whole Congress. When E. Coyecque, the Inspector of Public Libraries in Paris and an enthusiast for the methods which prevail in England, and America, pleaded for the modern spirit in libraries and for their service for the people, one venerable librarian arose and retorted gravely: 'We are not destroyers, we are conservators.' One gathered from the discussions which took place that the spirit, however, was making itself felt as an incalculable and disturbing force, even among the older librarians.[111]

Six years after the Congress had taken place, Morel and Coyecque noticed that remarkable progress had been achieved in the development of public libraries in France. It was apparent in the following paragraph of E. Coyecque's introduction to his two volumes of *Le Code Administratif des Bibliothèques d'Etudes* (Paris, 1929) that a new vitality had come into French library activities after the Congress of librarians and bibliophiles of 1923:

> After a long period of indifference, total neglect, and ultra-conservatism in formulas which have become inadequate and out of date, French libraries have in the last few years gone through an era of revival, progress and readaptation to the conditions and needs of modern life and work.[112]

Morel and Coyecque's partnership in developing public libraries was also praised by W.C. Berwick-Sayers in 1923. He was then the Chief Librarian of Corydon Library, England, and had already become a well known personality in the British Library Association. After a visit to the Belleville Library, on his "Easter Pilgrimage to Paris in 1923," he made the following remarks and emphasized the importance of the work of E. Morel and E. Coyecque and the library's future development:

> The issues from the library average 500 daily. This is significant and proves that Paris has a large book-loving population. The total number of books issued from the old 'bibliothèques municipals' as a whole must be very large indeed, and if only these libraries were modernized according to the example which the Americans have generously given them, the advantage to the population would be incalculable. Fortunately, men like M. Eugène Morel and M. E. Coyecque, the Inspector of Public Libraries in Paris, are aware of the needs and possibilities of public libraries, and it may be that a much needed evolution, if not a revolution in methods, will come.[113]

The revolution that W.C. Berwick-Sayers anticipated did, in fact, occur through the activities of Morel and Coyecque. For their partnership was not restricted to the above-mentioned achievements, but was directed towards the completion of more important projects. Both of them were bitter critics of the short opening hours of libraries. E. Coyecque often quoted from E. Morel's writings to emphasize his point. A typical example is the quotation used by E. Coyecque when he states that:

> The great misfortune of French libraries, our colleague Eugène Morel has said somewhere, is that they are always closed.[114]

In 1915, E. Coyecque emphasized the importance of public libraries in words like these, which are mainly repetitions of what Morel had already written in his books, *Les Bibliothèques* and *La Librairie Publique*:

> The complete service of the library is based on the close juxtaposition, the collaboration, and the constant cooperation between pleasure and profit. It contains three sections. Each section should contribute to the success of the other two. If the Municipal Library operates under these conditions, it will transform itself; it will become not only a 'popular,' but a free, public library. For it is equipped with all the necessary means to serve one and

all; it can and will be used by everybody... If this is understood—as one can understand it in England and America and even at Levallois-Perret, the Municipal Library must necessarily take the place which it deserves in the machinery of the town.

In society, it plays its role for the same reason as the other services of the community and those of education do. In the fullest meaning of the word, does not the Municipal Library represent continuous education, that which takes charge of the adolescent before he leaves school to accompany him throughout his life until his death? However, it must be remembered that while most of the other public services improve as social life becomes daily more complex and strenuous, the service of the Municipal Library is misunderstood, neglected, forgotten, and remains aloof from general progress.[115]

Finally, E. Coyecque attempted a definition of the municipal libraries as seen through the eyes of E. Morel, who advocated a democratic use of the public municipal libraries:

The Municipal Library should change from being dedicated to an individual group to being open to everybody. It should be a library used as a tool, it must have as its motto: "The Municipal Library is neither a conservation Library where books are collected, nor is it a museum. But it should be used democratically.'[116]

In 1927, two years before E. Coyecque spoke about revival in favor of the expansion of public libraries[117], Alexandre Vidier, deputy chief librarian at the Bibliothèque Nationale in 1910 and recognized as a great librarian, laid stress on this budding revival in the *Annuaire des Bibliothèques et des Archives* of 1927. He pointed out that the keynote of this revival was coordination and development towards cooperation.[118]

However, the concept of the free public library had not made much headway, and the state avoided the new challenge presented to it by this revival. Morel's movement towards providing a free public library service for all without discrimination of class or rank was by no means understood by everybody. Those who were fighting for reform sought remedies in the light of foreign achievements, especially in the enforcement of a *Public Libraries Act* based on the British and American model, leading to the establishment of free public libraries. There are few instances in French library history where a strong movement for the setting up of free public libraries from the proceeds of local rates and state taxes has been launched. The old style popular libraries which still existed seemed sadly unadapted to the needs of the general public, and the municipal library was tolerated and maintained just because it happened to be there. Very few people were interested in knowing whether it could play a significant role in the social life of the town or city. The municipal council's lack of interest in its library was the natural result of the lack of public interest. It was simply a custom to set up libraries in the municipalities. New municipalities depended on the whims of the mayors whether libraries were set up or not. No legislative acts were envisaged to call on the French municipalities to found, finance, and control a free public library (as in America or England).

However, the library movement initiated by the passing of a *Public Library Act* in France grew from Morel's dynamic and open conception of the "pennyrate" that should support the free public library. His activities regarding this spanned the years 1910[119] to 1927.[120] In France, Morel was the first to propose the passing of a French library law based on the British Ewart Bill.[121] In his book, *La Librairie Publique*, Morel clearly reminds the reader that

> the British Ewart Bill could authorize a municipal council to levy a rate not exceeding one half-penny in the pound for the setting up of a library. and that admission was to be free of all charges. Town Councils were empowered to rent or purchase appropriate land or buildings for the creation of free public libraries with an adequate library service.[122]

Morel was the first to suggest that municipal councils should follow their English counterparts and levy a special library tax. He wanted a Public Libraries Act to be enforced in order to make the state recognize that the library should be a public and national concern. By providing reading matter and a means of self-instruction, the library could be regarded as being in the interest of the community.[123]

In devoting himself to securing library legislation to support his advocacy of free public libraries, Morel was not as fortunate as Edward Edwards who, at the right moment, had found politicians like William Ewart and Joseph Brotherton to help him in influencing the passing of a Public Libraries Act.[124] In his *La Librairie Publique*, Morel explained:

The Free Public Libraries Rates

> This is only a tax which is regularly imposed, but is not subjected to the annual vote of the House of Parliament. It is a tax levied by every municipality to ensure that public libraries are run according to certain standards. This can also ensure that the advantages that come unexpectedly from other sources are efficiently looked after. These resources are gifts, grants of money, lotteries, rates, fines, etc. What would the penny rate (sic) accrue to in France? Of what avail would the penny rate (sic) be in France? According to the Ewart Act, English towns were

authorized to levy a penny rate per book on the rate value (sic) on behalf of the free public library. This authorization has become compulsory, and the penny-rate was suppressed. Every town in England and the United States with a population of above 30,000 inhabitants has the penny rate (sic). We have witnessed that the penny rate has passed from one franc per head of the population to reach three francs in Boston.

We should not have to worry about the resources that we will receive from the State, such as book donations, gifts etc. This exists elsewhere, and we should not rely on it. This is just an insignificant contribution. It is only the municipal rate that can permit the free public library to be kept alive. We do not have to bother about universities, scientific institutions, and so on. If one has to levy taxes to set up municipal libraries, then one is right. But the budget must be increased. For if a library is not serving everybody, then it becomes a special service.

## ABOUT A PUBLIC LIBRARIES ACT IN FRANCE

We will not be in a position to assess the real value of the *penny rate* [Morel's italics] in France, as long as a library levy is not imposed. There is no basis to set it up.

We can only base our calculations on a comparison of the population and the income collected from the communes in France and abroad with the money allotted to books. If one were to count the proceeds per head of population or per figure collected from tax which is levied, no town of France can actually meet the expenses which are needed for the maintenance of public libraries. None… if there is one thing we can teach librarians abroad, it is thrift.

A Public Libraries Act could be much more limited in France than anywhere else. But it must contain a regulation whereby it is compulsory to levy rates and to fix the minimum charge.

(1) Every town below 35,000 population should have the statutory power to allot yearly an amount of money which will be exclusively used for the upkeep of a public library. This amount should neither be less than 0.50Fr. per head of the population, nor less than one hundredth of the municipal income.

(2) Every town below 35,000 inhabitants is authorized to levy rates in the same conditions either for the setting up of an independent free public library whenever the annual income thus obtained exceeds 20,000 francs, or for the maintenance of a branch library in the region when the income is less than 20,000 francs.

(3) By the same act, the State undertakes to increase by one tenth the budget voted for the communes which have a population above 35,000 inhabitants.

(4) Every commune which does not have a free public library can, if 24 electors sign a petition, ask for one and assign a person to be responsible for it, be authorized to allow its citizens to borrow books from the nearest town. But the loan of books will be subject to special regulations. The rate of the cost of sending the books will be fixed and will be defrayed by the borrowing commune.

(5) The free public libraries will acquire legal status. Funds which have not been put to use at the end of the financial year will be put by for their benefit and can be employed later either from the purchase of books or the construction of libraries. On no account should these funds be used for other purposes except building reading rooms or increasing their stock.

(6) During the 3 months following the actual passing of the law, it is necessary that a committee be nominated in each of the towns affected by it. This committee will be in charge of regulating the use of these funds and of providing for the founding of free public libraries.

We emphasize particularly the words 'for the maintenance of a library' as far as ordinary resources are concerned. If there is the problem of establishing a library, this can be overcome by a loan or by special taxation or from special rates. But in many towns, the site will be donated and gifts will more or less ease the cost of establishing it. Finally, even though the free public library is a very modern phenomenon and required almost new buildings, one cannot reject in advance plans for transforming existing buildings, even if they are old libraries.

The library budget must only be used to pay for expenses incurred by the library service. This was often not the case, I will quote an example: some municipalities have paid from the library budget the expenses of political meetings in terms of heating, and lighting bills. One can add anything one wants to a library: an auditorium, a school, a theatre, a museum etc. But these new additions should be supported by special funds.

Thus, towns which do not have any library to transform can set aside the proceeds of rates until they can have enough money to establish a free public library. It seems right that after 5 years every town will be in a position to establish the initial services. While keeping a large part of the funds for future construction, they could allow the general public enjoy the benefit of a small newsroom and a more or less extensive loan service. It is to be noted that in almost all towns, the existing library and the popular library will provide a good starting point. The latter offers almost everywhere miniature branches and book stocks which have only to be centralized.[125]

This was written when Morel saw that nothing had been done regarding the enforcement of a public libraries act on the lines of the British Penny Rate. Thus, from Morel's writings, one can see that the movement for a Public Libraries Act in France started in 1910 and continued for sixteen years to advocate the necessity of supporting the library by public rates.[126]

Morel wrote in his book, *L'Enseignement post-scolaire: la bibliothèque moderne*, in 1927, that there should be:

laws passed and special taxation levied... in order to ensure that every Frenchman has access to the Free Public Library (sic).[127]

In short, the leitmotiv of *Les Bibliothèques*, as well as his *La Librairie Publique*, and of most of his writing, emphasized that:

France also should have her Free Public Libraries.

Another example of his advocacy for free public libraries is found in his article of 1911 in *Library World*, entitled "Municipal Libraries for France." This article not only gave an interesting view of the library act in England and in the United States, but also that of library activity in Great Britain, America and the Continent. It also emphasized that the manner in which E. Morel's advocacy of the establishment of *Free Public Libraries* had progressed in France. He showed in this article the superiority of the Anglo-Saxon public library system over the French one, which consisted of the *populaires* and the *municipales*. Morel wrote:

People who go to London see the British Museum; those who go to America see Washington and Harvard; they return astonished but discouraged at such a waste of money, and do not see that side by side with these large libraries England and America, have, during half a century, created a new institution without equal in France which upsets our ideas and our systems of information and gives an immense impetus to industry and commerce by keeping them up-to-date; an institution so important that it might be said that 'the era of cathedrals' has succeeded the' era of public libraries' of the 'Free Public Library.' These are what we call libraries. Some libraries we have: some less old, others richer; but this is beside the question. A library preserves books; they are used. One makes use of them as often as possible; and always replaces them. It is a vast system of organizing public reading. The Germans, who are attempting something in this direction, call it *leschalle bucherei*... We have the old French word, *librairie*—let us keep it.[128]

To all those who were interested in knowing what a public library in Great Britain and America consisted of, Morel gave the following details:

(1) Of a Newspaper Room. Here one can see the news of the day. In London, at six o'clock, one has the French newspapers. By the side are reviews arranged on special tables, from which they can be taken. Here also are found annuals, bottins, commercial directories of all countries, digests, dictionaries of all languages and trades, steamship and railway time-tables, maps of the locality…Ah! If the Touring Club would only, as regards this, organize a campaign for the libraries of France!

(2) A Lending Library, with books available for the public. One chooses his own book from the shelves. This system, called open shelf, has not, in the thousands of libraries where it is in operation, caused more thefts than the old system of grilles and wickets. But what benefits! Enquire at our fancy goods stores, which make use of it for their fashions.

Here, not only is the level of advanced reading maintained, for one chooses the best books, but the falling off in novels points to the gain in instructive reading. At Sarnia (Ont.), in 1903, the issue in novels fell from 17,227 to 9,937, while that of science rose from 673 to 903, history from 791 to 1,384.

(3) A room called the Reference. It is operated like our libraries, and issued for studying purposes, but does not close at four o'clock. Here one can sit down, write, and rest.

(4) Other rooms. Many have special rooms for ladies. Some of them are real drawing-rooms, with a fire, and arm-chairs that can be placed where the reader likes. At Homestead, there are two billiard rooms (one of which is for the ladies), a gymnasium, and an immense lecture hall. Besides, there are museums and temporary exhibitions. At Glasgow, a library is added to the municipal baths. Thus, the antique thermal baths, which were museums, baths, gymnasiums, libraries, and clubs all together, are revised in grey Scotland.

(5) Children's rooms. Here woman's genius has done wonders in ten years, especially in the United States. Today, the public library, cooperating with the school and college, is upsetting all the systems of teaching, and that is a great point about which French professors do not trouble much.

It is no longer the academic library which supplies us with such and such a book—one at a time—suggested by the professor. The student is placed before a mass of volumes, he has to choose, read, make extracts, sum up, prosecute his studies himself. Here, we commence by learning a lesson off by heart; the teacher explains it, advises a few reading, the extracts are all

> ready, Raffy, Lanier, and only the good ones (Oh, reward of merit!) will be admitted to the library. Down there, it is the reverse, by the pupils themselves. In the class, personal research takes the place of theoretical teaching. And those who despise books and 'book knowledge,' and prefer any kind of frivolous prattle to the written page, will be able to learn from the Public Libraries thus organized that it is the books which give experience, which show initiative and precise information, and develop a practical spirit.
>
> I heard it said: 'It is curious, but they are not for us. It is the Anglo-Saxon spirit...they read, we do not read.' This libel on the intellect of the people amuses the drawing room, but is disproved by deeds. The French do not go into libraries. No, when they are closed.[129]

In the final paragraph, Morel asked for a change in the public library movement which he knew would need to come sooner or later. But social attitudes are extremely difficult to change. He looked into the state of libraries in France in relation to the state of libraries in other countries and asked if the authorities could remove the prejudices and discrimination that impeded the advancement of the concept for Free Public Libraries.[130]

Not only did the Americans applaud Morel's pioneering efforts for the development of public libraries, but his efforts were appreciated by the British as well. He was made an Honorary Fellow of the British Library Assistants' Association by unanimous vote of the Council as early as May 22nd 1912. The certificate issued to Morel on December 16th, 1913 reads as follows:

> At a meeting of the Council of the Library Assistants' Association held on May 22nd, 1912 M. Eugène Morel was, by unanimous vote of the Council, elected Honorary Fellow of the Library Assistants' Association for, "distinguished professional service in promoting cordial relationship between British Library Assistants and the Librarians of France, and for his consistent advocacy of public libraries.'[131]

It was signed by the honorary secretary, W.C. Berwick-Sayers in 1913. Ten years later, Berwick-Sayers, after paying a visit to France, wrote, in an article entitled *"The Paris Pilgrimage"* in the *Library Association Record* of 1923 that:

> the French public library spirit was alive and developing

but was surprised to note that

> financial conditions seemed to have been against libraries in France.[132]

In the same article, W.C. Berwick-Sayers wrote about the many activities that Morel undertook in order to bring to the French a concept of the free public library and to promote it:

> M. Eugène Morel, to whose good offices we owed the visit, had put up a Technical Exhibition at the Pavillon de Maison. It was more novel to the French librarian, and Morel used it to make a valiant attempt to introduce plans, pictures, publications, and appliances illustrating the methods of modern libraries. In this exhibition several countries of Europe participated.[133]

Though Berwick-Sayers laid stress at the end of his article on the fact that the British Library Association rarely entered into definite relations with continental library associations,[134] it is clear from the above examples that Morel's advocacy of public libraries had transcended this isolation.

The development of Morel's activities and influence on the improvement of the free public libraries was to have far reaching impact not only in the immediate 1910s[135], but also during the decade that followed the Second World War. This is made clear by René Lemaitre in his article, *"Des Livres Pour Tous,"* published on the occasion of *Le VIIe Festival International du Livre*, held in Nice from May 3rd-8th, 1975.[136]

In the French speaking world, Morel's pioneering efforts were emulated by other librarians. The national archivist-librarian, Gabriel Esquer in Algeria[137], was influenced by Morel's writings, and wrote on the Ewart Library Act and on the freely accessible public libraries.[138] This influence was reflected in his article on public libraries in Algeria, which appeared in the *Annales Universitaires de L'Algérie* in 1912. This article is reviewed in the French professional journal, *Bulletin de l'Association des Bibliothécaires Français* of 1912.[139] The review reads as follows:

> *Les Bibliothèques Publiques en Algerie:* this article by Mr. Gabriel Esquer, archivist-paleographer of the central government of Algeria, published in the *Annales Universitaires de l'Algérie* lère année, March, 1912, is very interesting. It deals with public libraries in Algeria. It was entirely inspired by the ideas which our colleague, Mr. Eugène Morel, has continued to propound on the necessity of having libraries which are freely accessible with day long service without interruption, open to all classes of the community who come to look for information.
>
> Following the example of Eugène Morel, Mr. Gabriel Esquer traveled to England, the United States of America, and the Scandinavian countries. During his visit to these countries, he gathered enough data to show the Algerian government how to effectively adapt the library system found in these countries to the Algerian public library service, so that the latter

would serve the public better. He stated his objectives, which were similar to those of E. Morel. They were:

1. Libraries should be open all day so that everybody will be able to use them;

2. to put at the disposal of readers newsrooms, new titles, directories, almanacs and other works which may be of practical use to readers, books on Algerian topography and a junior library etc.

In order to make these ideas become a reality, Gabrial Esquer recommended that local rates should be imposed on the citizens. In the meantime, he recommended that contacts should be established between libraries and newspapers for the publication of press releases. These should be related to libraries, for example, a list of new acquisitions could be given.[140]

Even in Italy, there were people who recognized the work achieved by Morel in the development of public libraries in France. Virginia Carini Dainotti, in her book, *La Bibliothèca Publica in Italia tra cronaca e storia*, Volume 2, described the poor state of public libraries in Italy, but she also points out that Morel faced similar problems in France. She wrote:

> It is true that common grief is half delight, but we may be consoled at the thought that this happened also in France, where only in 1908 was there a courageous librarian, Eugène Morel, who launched the crusade against the Popular Library. In one of his writings of that year about libraries, the chapter dedicated to popular libraries starts with the war cry: Down with the popular libraries... before uttering one single word about popular libraries we can state that France will never have any libraries until she ceases to have these 'populaires.' Special libraries, conservation libraries, and other libraries are necessary. There are so many trades, and each trade has its own clientele. But apart from this, there is only one category of French. Only after 40 years did France heed Morel's warning...[141]

The great stumbling block to Morel's advocacy of public libraries was the unfavorable ambience in which he moved. This did not help him to forward his concept of modern librarianship.

In the early years of his career at the Bibliothèque Nationale, he started advocating strongly for the creation of a body that would support his ideologies[142] and combat all antagonistic movements. Morel was the first in France to envisage the setting up of a league of friends for the creation of libraries. As early as 1910, in one of his lectures given at the Ecole des Hautes Etudes Sociales for training of librarians in France, which is entitled

*La Librairie Publique en Angleterre et aux Etats Unis,* he made the following comments which were used as propaganda for his concepts:

> Those who believe that the Free Public Library is an impossible achievement in France do not see the tremendous efforts deployed everywhere in this direction, the thousands of books which are scattered, and that this scattering of efforts renders the result insignificant.
>
> But perhaps people who believe that France, in this respect, can put herself on a par with other nations could set an example and form groups. We thought that the normal way of grouping people together is to form a league. There are already many of us who are prepared to initiate a league in order to found public libraries in France. We are making an appeal to all men of good will who would like to join our league. Here and now you can send in your application for membership. We need, first of all, a league for propaganda. Then we must coordinate all efforts, look for points of agreement, keep a register of addresses of those who would like to donate money, books, or help, and, more particularly, will we not need an organization to receive donations?...
>
> France abounds in donors, but they are mostly concerned with competitions and prizes. Gentlemen, much could have been done to promote literature—just by the influx of readers which would have been attracted—if the money given for only one of these prizes which represent a private income of many thousands of Francs, had served to build a Free Public Library. And please do not doubt that when the town possesses a model construction, it will be its duty to maintain it as it maintains the museums given to it.[143]

Two years after Morel had suggested the setting up of this league, the idea began to make an impact on the country. A league was formed not only in Paris but in other towns. There were many who supported Morel's advocacy for a league, but the most prominent figure among them was Henri Michel, librarian at the Library of Amiens, in 1912. He recognized Morel's propaganda efforts in these words:

> Books like those of Maurice Pellisson [*Les Bibliothèques Populaires à l'étranger et en France* (Paris 1906)] and those of Morel [*Les Bibliothèques* and *La Librairie Publique*] and his courses of lectures ... are forms of action that one should not get tired of emulating if one wants them eventually to bear fruit.[144]

In 1912, Henri Michel followed the path that Morel had traced, and proposed the creation of a number of Sociétés d'Amis des Bibliothèques. He stressed that the influence of these groups would, in the long run, have a tremendous impact on the decisions of public authorities regarding library matters, and they could also urge private bodies and individuals to give freely to libraries. This would be a remarkable application of American methods. The attempt that Henri Michel had made in Amiens did not have, before 1912, all the results expected, but it had led to the creation of similar organizations in many other towns.[145]

Furthermore one of the extracts from Morel's book, *La Librairie Publique*, completes the evidence of how Morel wanted to lay down the arrangements for the establishment of a Ligue for the creation of free public libraries. This was entitled: Ligue pour la creation de libraries publiques. The concept was taken up and discussed successfully in all subsequent professional meetings. The conclusive chapter of Morel's book contains the following plea for his league:

> League for the Creation of Public Libraries
>
> What can we do now...talk, write...but there are thousands of ways we can adopt to launch a publicity scheme. Another thing we can do also! Join a league. During the month of April 1910, some librarians and the director of a journal launched a marvelous appeal for truth and common sense. The result was that teachers and skilled workers got together and discussed the question.
>
> They all agreed that a new concept of libraries had been born and that the word '*bibliothèque*' itself was not suitable to designate the new invention, but that a special term be either bureau for documents on present day life, or, reading centre for urban and rural regions which would manage lending in town and the country or, a place where people can meet, splendid monument! The basilica of the modern city, the lycée especially made for self-instruction, the school for research and initiative which is an auxiliary to school, to the lycée, and takes the place of the old method of teaching. And instead of all that—should the library be closed for the student when the latter is more likely to benefit from it for his personal self-instruction; or should it open its doors wider to him and accompany him throughout his life, in this active life where one never stops learning.
>
> The word '*Librairie Publique*' which is found in this volume [*La Librairie Publique*] was chosen at one of these meetings. And it was proposed that a league be thus formed to fight for the creation of free and modern libraries in France.
>
> Is this league really going to be founded?
>
> A league is essential, and the reason for its creation is as follows: If it happens that an individual who wants to make a will or a gift is willing to set an example by endowing a public library or an ordinary periodicals' room and a reference library, he will not know to whom to apply in order that his wish be executed. Surely he would make his request to Academies

who would found prizes or undertake to print costly and ostentatious publications. Or, he would make it to libraries who would print catalogues, to organizations, to public assistance, to...to the town... But what a considerable number of nice gifts have been lost in this way. Who will tell them that providing facilities for self-instruction is more constructive than offering prizes which can turn a whole nation into intriguers and beggars. With such a *raison d'etre* the league can work.

Now let us talk about propaganda. The first move towards propaganda is to be made among librarians. Provisions of yearbooks, books on modern topics, commercial and industrial directories, maps, guidebooks... periodicals and daily papers... longer operating hours, better facilities for loan and shelf browsing... Many things can be done in libraries ... but all this is active propaganda. We are glad to say that in this field we have recorded good results. Libraries are undergoing considerable change in Paris and in the provinces. If they are changing so much that the words Librairie Publique are becoming obsolete, then they will at least have achieved something...

A league also serves to rally its partisans. Morel's book, *La Librairie Publique*, is an appeal for the formation of a league. The league will survive only when it has a sufficient number of, not only adherents—to have them would be easy but misleading—but also reliable collaborators.[146]

E. Morel's main preoccupation was not only the development of public libraries, but also the promotion of the services that special libraries could offer to the general public and to their particular clientele. As a student of law, Morel had used special libraries, namely the Bibliothèque Nationale and the library of the University of Paris. These experiences had shown him their shortcomings from a user's point of view. He would continue as long as he lived to try to find ways of spreading the development of the special library, libraries of higher studies (academic libraries), research libraries, and the national library.

Before 1908, he went to London to study the administration of the British Museum in person. He did not confine his visit to the British Museum, but discovered with enthusiasm the English free public libraries and special libraries. He was naturally impressed by the variety of services which they were offering at this time to their readers. On his return, he set to work, and, in 1908, he recorded a considerable amount of his British experiences in his two volumes called: *Bibliothèques: Essai sur le développement des bibliothèques publiques et de la librairie dans les deux mondes.*[147]

As for academic libraries, he bitterly criticized their administration and organization in his books. He compared the budgets of German and French university libraries and showed how inferior France's funding was.[148] Morel wanted libraries of higher education to promote science and technology.[149] He described to the French the *Auskunftasbureau* of Berlin, and strongly advocated in his writings the setting up in France of a similar service.[150]

In *Bibliothèques* he described the *Auskunftasbureau* as

> a bureau which is responsible for tracing any book which is found in public libraries and answers any question relating to it if this request is accompanied by a postage stamp. It lets the applicant know where a particular book is found and forwards the request to any country which applied for any book.[151]

In 1908, Morel also pointed out that all the special libraries that have existed for the past 50 years have been administered by paleographers, and history has been the prevailing subject.[152] He wrote:

> There are only special libraries with one specialty only: history.[153]

He insisted that the French government set up effective special libraries which would cater for the scientific and technological needs of the country. In support of this, he quoted these words from the founder of the Ligue de L'Enseignement:

> M. Massé (1815-1894), in his budget report for 1904, states: to persist in keeping general libraries and to continue to maintain them is the only way not to serve science. They are hampering the advancement of science. For it is like attempting an impossible task. It is only when we have specialists who will administer special libraries and make people aware of the fact that there exist bibliographies of scientific libraries that we can render service to the nation.[154]

Finally Morel compared the three National Libraries: Washington (used most of the time for the Library of Congress), the British Museum, and the Bibliothèque Nationale de Paris.[155] He also made a comparative study of university and research libraries of the world.[156]

This was the only complete picture of the organization of these libraries that was ever made in France.[157] He also discussed the construction of these libraries, and stressed the building criteria which were used abroad but not applied in France.[158]

Morel wrote:

> There is an enemy: a great enemy of libraries, the most dangerous after the archivist; it is the architect. We have great artists. They build for eternity.

> But a library is not a work of art, it is a tool. It is not a palace but a machine. It must serve the public, it must be extensively used. The construction of libraries should not be a question of architectural beauty, but of utility.[159]

Morel was also among the first to promote the advancement of information bureaus, documentation centers, and the use of mechanization in libraries. According to his theory, the librarian should be seen as a purveyor of information to the people and not merely as a conservator of books hidden mostly behind huge counters, which served as a difficult barrier between the reader an the librarian. The library should not only cater for the recreational needs of the users, but provide an information service which would counteract the emphasis laid on the conservation of stocks and the importance of documentation. The latter were nevertheless a vital part of any library.

> Gone is the day when the memory of a man could contain all the knowledge useful to his trade... and everything that was necessary for him to carry on with his civic and political activities. One learns how to use books as the worker learns how to use his tools. One needs to know how to extract information from books, but not to learn everything that is found in books... [There are many] beautiful libraries in France which hold so many books that they can never provide the reader with the right book... But the art of extracting information from books must be taught to everybody.[160]

Thus, he stressed that one of the aims of the public library was to act as an information center which would "provide quickly and at any time," according to the requirements of the moment, the information and documentation of life, sciences, and trades. It should be an information bureau which answers queries on all topics and helps the general public in their research.[161]

Morel clearly foresaw the needs of the public library of his time. He laid stress on the organization of library work to provide users with scientific and technological information:

> French libraries have remained for a greater part of their time the monopoly of historians and scholars; they have rejected scientific classification and at the same time, scientific subjects and technology...[162]

Morel was also a fervent supporter of the introduction of automation in libraries. He advised the use of certain mechanically operated processes that would facilitate research work or could multiply catalogue cards. For example, he quoted the *Bibliophote,* which, in 1912, he brought to the attention of librarians and the general public, together with a card duplicating machine.[163] He laid stress on the impact that mechanization could have in libraries in two of his last articles published in *La Revue du Livre* of 1933, under the titles: *"Les Machines au secours de la bibliographie"* and *"Mécaniques et bibliographie."*[164]

In 1933, Morel criticized the obsoleteness of the printed catalogue, which was then extensively used, and which in many cases absorbed without profit all the resources of libraries, including those of Bibliothèque Nationale. He believed that the *Bibliothèque Nationale* should have a more economical cataloguing service. He advised that most of these libraries should revert to the classified catalogues. These had been given up for the author catalogues which were preferred.

In the early 1910s, in a remarkable chapter on Legal Deposit, he began to lay the foundations of his work which would later concentrate on the complete conservation and compilation of bibliographies of French publications.[165] He expounded the idea that the Dewey Decimal Classification should be used by the National Library with a view to compiling a national bibliography. He even advocated the photographic reproduction of texts on films, a process which was called *Film Silf*.[166]

Morel became a pioneer of information bureaus in France. In highlighting the backwardness of France compared to America and England in this field, he used figures, statistics, and documentary evidence extensively, as he had done in his comparative studies of public libraries in these countries. He reviewed the services of information bureaux in these countries and assessed the value of libraries which could help serious readers in their research. The study of Morel's life reveals the conditions in which the development of libraries in France was to be achieved; it is also a contribution to the cultural history of France.

# Morel and Legal Deposit in France

In addition to his many other library activities, Morel played a considerable part in the development and reform of legal deposit in France. This aspect of his work is not as well known as his advocacy for free public libraries, but it had a far-reaching influence on the whole structure of the French legal deposit law as it stands today.

The system of legal deposit in France was introduced in the time of absolute monarchy as a royal privilege when François I established the Royal Library at Blois, which was controlled by the great scholar Guillaume Bude from 1522 to 1540. During this period, François I founded the legal deposit system by the *Ordinance of Montpellier 1537*, which allowed for the deposit of one copy of each French book and the offer for purchase by the library of every book printed abroad but on sale in France. Initially this system proved extremely unpopular and was not functioning well even by the Revolution.[1] Many collections were added, but the next period of great prosperity for the Bibliothèque Royale (the original name of the Bibliothèque Nationale) was under Louis XIV and his minister, Colbert, during the period of 1643 to 1683.[2]

As the Bibliothèque Nationale alone had enjoyed copyright facilities since 1537 in the domain of printed books in Paris this tended to centralize the legal deposit there, thus preventing the eventuality of having depository libraries in other parts of France, for example in the provinces. In 1935 J.H.P. Pafford explained how the Bibliothèque Nationale had benefited from this centralization when compared to other libraries:

> "France is such a highly centralized country that the Bibliothèque Nationale is an example of the national library par excellence. Not only is there in France no other library which can compare with it in size and importance, but since it received the right of the legal deposit as early as 1537 (then of course as the Royal Library) and has held it, with some lapses, ever since, its collection of national literature is probably more nearly complete than that of any other national library."[3]

In 1903, Jean Gautier, sub-librarian at the Faculty of Law of the University of Paris, published a book entitled *Nos Bibliothèques Publiques*. This gave a description of the legal situation of French public libraries and contained all the decrees, orders and circulars relating to Public Libraries published in the twenty years preceding 1903. In this he wrote:

The growth of public library stock depends on many sources, first on the gifts and also on the legal deposit which the printers are compelled to effect. The legal deposit (the founding of which dates back to François I) is presently governed by the law on the printing press of July 29, 1881 (Articles 3 and 4). Two copies of every printed work should be deposited at the Ministry of the Interior for the region of Paris. In the departments they should be deposited at the prefectures and sub-prefectures. These are assigned to the national collections; one copy is always set aside for the Bibliothèque Nationale, which increases in its own right to about 25,000 volumes yearly.[4]

Jean Gautier also gives ample information in a footnote about other writers who were interested in the early reform of legal deposit and how legal deposit was dealt with in 1881 and 1883. Thus, footnote no. 2 on pages 119 and 120 reads as follows:

> For further information on legal deposit, the main aim of which should be the enrichment of our public libraries, see PICOT: 'Le depot Légal': Comptes rendus de l'Academie des Sciences morales et politiques 1883 Tome 119, p. 632. The text of a law to redress the big inconveniences which the present legislation of legal deposit presents has been submitted to the Chambre des Députés by M. Masieres but has not been discussed. (Journal Officiel Document Parlementaire. Chambre 1883, p. 589, annexe no. 1824.)[5]

The author gives information on the poor acquisition policy of the Bibliothèque Nationale in 1903, which could not cope with preserving scientific literature because the organization of legal deposit was not adequate:

> Its budget, even though very high, hardly allows it to keep abreast of what is being published in science and literature; the acquisitions are made up above all of foreign books, for a copy of all French books should be handed over to the Bibliothèque Nationale through the legal deposit.[6]

In 1910, La Société Française de Bibliographie published a book entitled *Histoire du Dépot Légal*, written by one of Morel's colleagues, Henri Lemaitre, archivist-paleographer, and sub-librarian at the Bibliothèque Nationale.[7]

A. Vidier, in reviewing Lemaitre's book in the *Bulletin de L'Association des Bibliothécaires Français* of 1912, under the section *Publications nouvelles concernant les Bibliothèques Françaises. Rapports présentés aux Assemblées Générales des 23 avril 1911 et 13 avril, 1912*, reported that according to Lemaitre it was necessary that a reform of legal deposit be contemplated:

The growth of the collections is closely linked with the application of the law on legal deposit. This law is not functioning properly, and there has been sufficient systematic criticism leveled at it. It is by finding out how legal deposit originated, was transformed and is presently organized, that we are preparing, to a certain extent, the reform of the law. It is to our colleague, M. Lemaitre of the Bibliothèque Nationale that we owe the first part of the history of legal deposit.[8]

In a very long introduction which runs to fifty pages, Lemaitre gives a history of legal deposit from *L'Ordonnance de Montpellier* of 1537 to the law of 1881. The work is a collection of all documents: ordinances, laws, circulars, letters, memoirs and plans concerning legal deposit in France. In concluding his preface, Lemaitre enumerates the number of organizations which had echoed the complaints of a certain Mr. Picot, who wanted a reform of legal deposit. These organizations were *Congrès International des Imprimeurs de France; Congrès International des Bibliothécaires; Société d'Histoire Moderne; Association des Bibliothécaires Français;* and finally, *La Société Française de Bibliographie*. Lemaitre also voices his own opinion on an eventual reform of legal deposit:

> If in spite of the goodwill of the administration, in spite of the officials to lodge complaints, the deposit does not yield the results that are expected of it, it is because the legislation needs to be revised. We are not running short of plans to reform.[9]

After Lemaitre had visited the Copyright Offices of the Library of Congress in Washington, he described in 1912 the functioning of this service in the *Revue des Bibliothèques*.[10] A summary of this article casts light on the services of the Copyright Offices of the Library of Congress, and draws a comparison between legal deposit in France and America:

> While in France, because of its origins, legal deposit is effected at the Ministry of the Interior where the volumes go, one copy to the Bibliothèque Nationale and one to the Ministry of Public Instruction to be distributed among libraries of secondary importance, in Washington there exists a centralized system and it is organized with minute precision which ensures both the guarantee of the author's rights and that the volumes deposited are quickly utilized at the Library of Congress.
>
> The benefit of the copyright is reserved for citizens and inhabitants of the United States and for nationals of countries who treat American citizens on the same footing as their own. In order to benefit from it, one must:
>
> (1) print on every copy put at the disposal of the general public the notice of copyright;
>
> (2) ask for the application of the law for the work in question;

(3) deposit two copies;

(4) pay a tax of 5 francs. The deposited volumes are immediately numbered; the certificate of the deposit is sent to the proprietor and the cards for the work are made within five days. The cards are arranged in three ways: in numerical order, in alphabetical order by the names of the proprietors, and in alphabetical order of author's names. The Library of Congress makes a selection among the deposited volumes. Books that it does not wish to keep are put at the disposal of libraries of the district of Columbia, the agents of which come on the spot to indicate the volumes that they would like to take and fix wrappers on them bearing the name of the institution then turn them upside down. Volumes that are left are either returned to the authors or sold. The Copyright Office employs no less than seventy-eight persons. It is administered by a 'registrar' (sic) drawing 20,000 francs and subjected to a surety bond of 100,000 francs. At present, he is the competent M. Thorvald Solberg.[11]

In 1912, Morel, in an article entitled *"La Livre Français et la Production Mondiale,"* published in *Mercure de France,* wrote on the same lines as Jules Lemaitre that only a re-organization of legal deposit could reinforce the Copyright Act in France:

> Should not the reorganization of legal deposit be a French copyright (sic) for the benefit of the state, men of letters, libraries, publishers? But up to now no agreement has been reached among them.[12]

As early as 1908 Morel was interested in the reform of legal deposit. His chapter on Dépôt Légal in his book *Bibliothèques,* vol. 2 reveals his far reaching knowledge of the functioning of legal deposit and his strong desire to reform the law in France. An analysis of this chapter[13] will bring to light his pioneering efforts in this field. Morel stressed the inadequacy and deficiencies of legal deposit and showed that everybody seemed to agree that it should undergo a reform, though it had taken almost a quarter of a century to discuss it. Thus Morel emphasized that legal deposit must be studied and reformed with a threefold aim so that the reform should be contemplated at three levels and from three points of views:

(a) From the point of view of libraries. The legal deposit must ensure that everything that is published goes not only to the *Bibliothèque Nationale* but to a regional library which should be a special library;

(b) From the point of view of the literary, artistic and scientific property and of copyright. He pointed out the important commercial role that it should play; that it must work in straight collaboration with what was being done abroad and must be aware of what advantages the American copyright brings to the United States.

(c) From the point of view of the establishment of a national bibliography: the organization of legal deposit must exempt libraries from producing their own catalogue cards and provide important regional or special centers with complete bibliographies.[14]

Morel's aim, justification for a reform of legal deposit at this early stage of his career, was explained in these few words:

> the legal deposit has not been set up to furnish our libraries with free copies of what is being published but to maintain political control. However, today it should aim at these two things:
>
> (a) to be a medium for protecting literary and artistic copyright; and
>
> (b) to be a small tax levied in favor of libraries. Therefore it should be reformed.[16]

Before giving further information on the advantages that legal deposit could bring to the National Library and many other types of libraries, Morel gave a brief list of names of persons who had campaigned for the reform of legal deposit in France: Pico (1883), Vachal (1884), Philippon (1889), Bonnerot (1907). Morel stressed that legal deposit could promote advances in technology,[117] and that if libraries were to benefit from it, the plans for a new law should favor all libraries which must agree on one point: it should be the publisher, not the printer, who would be compelled to deposit.[18] The establishment of a copyright should be based on the Copyright of the Library of Congress, "which gives us not a model but a project and solid basis for discussion."[19] Morel advised that the Bibliothèque Nationale should administer a similar service to the Copyright Office and "Bureau de Bibliographie," which were two important sections of the Library of Congress:

> Before concluding, Morel wrote:
>
> "(a) There should be a legal deposit for three libraries in France: one for the *Nationale*, the second copy for a regional library, and the third for a special library.[20]
>
> (b) Legal Deposit awards the privileges of artistic and literary property copyright.
>
> (c) Legal deposit is not a special question, a petty business for librarians; it is a big commercial and national affair."[21]

By way of conclusion, Morel expressed the wish that the government would take seriously his appeal for a reform of legal deposit:

> We do not achieve anything at all by finding fault at plans of reform of legal deposit which we know about already. All of them would be much better than the present state of things. And we wish that the Chamber votes for one of them. But we think that it would be a pity not to benefit from the interest of the Chambers to obtain more than the minimum regulations and not to initiate more extensive and prolific reforms.
>
> To these plans which have been lying dormant for a quarter of a century without achieving anything but a sterile approval we add these suggestions, which might bring to libraries a trifle more than the gift of a few complimentary copies of books.[22]

Morel also wanted, side by side with the legal deposit service, the establishment of a *Bibliographie de la France* which, he thought, would not be complete unless it gave an indexing to periodical literature and furnished to various catalogues of libraries a centralized cataloguing service.[23] He wrote:

> By providing libraries with ready-made cards, you are at the same time insisting upon up-to-date and useful catalogues. It is economical and it enables the librarian to do his work: to give service to the public.
>
> To create bibliographical centers is to organize science in France, to give a better service in the provinces, to establish on a regular basis the lending and dispatch of scientific materials and to decentralize research.
>
> These are important reforms, or rather innovations, which according to us should keep pace with the reform of legal deposit.[24]

According to Morel, the setting up of national bibliographical centers depended entirely on the reform of legal deposit. In *Bibliothèques* he wrote:

> *La Bibliographie* is not only a special science; it is also a new industry, the rapid progress of which allows us to forecast its future development. The Institut Bibliographique has its headquarters in Paris, which sells ready-made cards. These are more complete and cheaper than any of those which are handwritten, typed, or printed.
>
> Belgium has made of its Institut an official institution. When will France follow this example? In America, the cards of Boston and Washington are used, and Washington has given us the indication of a useful centralization: Legal Deposit, Library, Catalogue, and Bibliography. These last two bureaus are quite distinct: Catalogue represents the manufacture and commerce of cards for all libraries; Bibliography equals information service to the general public, publication of lists of books on

current events, and possible collaboration in an international scientific bibliography.[25]

However, the State, which through legal deposit receives all books, already has a centralized service and is better equipped than private individuals to establish bibliographical centers. And in a country where all education depends on the state, where it cannot be expected that the general services appertaining to science be set up by the generosity of individuals, it is normal to look to the State, who has all these things—all the libraries, all the specialists. If individuals manage set-up, in spite of opposition from authority, an undertaking of a scientific nature, it is to be expected that it will fail, because anything which belongs to the 'State' is not made use of. Things which have been done informally will be done again officially... only Medicine has had some success because it has outside the state a potential clientele of about 25,000 doctors.

It is in fact from a reform of legal deposit that one can expect the setting up of bibliographical centers. We need general bibliographical centers for French books, and special ones (pure science, commerce, etc.) are required for international bibliography.

These special centers, whether part of a library or an Institute or not, will be dependent on legal deposit. Their duty would be to ensure the delivery and dispatch of French publications, to distribute them, to make cards for them, to abstract periodicals and books, and to sell or distribute in great numbers these cards to libraries.

Now, the legal deposit even reformed, will never have but from two to five books to distribute. If twenty libraries cannot have all the books, twenty at least can have the list of all the books.[26]

Ready-made cards provide not only the orthodox catalogue but a host of them...

The question of 'form' and the discussion of a system are here irrelevant. Money does not enter into it. The *Bibliothèque Nationale*, which prints the reviews of new books twice, once in the bulletin and the second time in its catalogue, could be authorized to print them only once and to sell ready-made cards. It will benefit much by completing its catalogue. This should be done immediately, while waiting for something better: the reform of legal deposit.[27]

In 1907, The French Library Association's organ, *Le Bulletin de l'Association des Bibliothécaires Français*, reported that it was the first time that the various questions relating to the personnel and the organization of public libraries were seriously discussed and examined in a report on the budget of the Minister of Public Instruction. The author of the report, Mr.

Steeg, Member of Parliament, had tackled all the problems of libraries—promotion of personnel, training problems, specialization of libraries, creation of a *Caisse des Bibliothèques Publiques* and a *Conseil Supérieur*—and has accompanied his report with reasonable comments.

Apart from these comments, Mr. Steeg reported on the poor status and low salaries of librarians in various categories of library, from the National Library to the less important popular libraries, and proposed reforms, among which are the following:

> Other questions, adds M. Steeg are cropping up and must be studied, like the specialization of libraries and the reform of legal deposit. Only a meeting of competent men and delegates of librarians can study all these questions."[28]

In 1910, the French Library Association found two "competent" members who became involved in the reform of legal deposit. These were Maurice Vitrac and Eugène Morel.

At the General Assembly of the French Library Association held on April 3rd, 1910 at the Hotel des Sociétés Savantes under the chairmanship of Charles Mortet, two sessions were held, one in the morning at 9:30am and the other at 3:00pm.

At the morning session, a reform proposal of legal deposit was submitted by Maurice Vitrac to the members of the French Library Association:

> The Agenda calls for the examination of the Projet de Reforme du Dépot Légal submitted by Mr. Maurice Vitrac at the General Assembly. The conclusions of the project of Mr. Vitrac are adopted after a discussion in which Messrs. Giraud-Maugin, Fontana, Morel, Mortet, Cagnieul and Gautier took part. The Committee is commissioned to carry out the plan.[29]

The bulletin of the French Library Association of 1910 gave the essential excerpt of the speech delivered by M. Vitrac to the Assemblée Générale of April 3rd, 1910. This reads as follows:

> It is not my intention to 'lecture' on legal deposit... What I plan to study here is only Article 3 of the Law of July 29th, 1881, which at present regulates legal deposit. I will examine with you the deficiencies of the law and we will see in what spirit and to what extent it is applied and if it can be applied.
>
> This communication is intended to be practical. When this critical account will be over, I will then have the honor to present to you a modified text of Article 3 of the law of 1881. Then you will have the option to discuss it unambiguously. You will see if this new text, which, to my mind is clear

and simple, solves the difficulties in a practical manner and you will decide, finally, whether it is convenient that the Association takes the initiative to request the legislative authorities to adopt it.[30]

Article 13 of the law of July 29th, 1881 stipulates the following:

As soon as any printed matter is published, the printer, under penalty of 16 to 300 francs, should make a deposit of two copies intended for the national collections. This deposit should be effected to the Ministry of the Interior in Paris, to the prefecture for the chief towns of the 'departments,' to the sub-prefecture for the chief wards of administrative districts and for other towns at the town hall. Ballot-papers, commercial circular letters, jobbing-works or places of job-work are exempted from this arrangement.[31]

Maurice Vitrac took line by line the clauses of Article 3 of the above law and analyzed them one by one. After which he wrote:

As you can see, Article 3 of the Law of 1881 deserves many criticisms. Its drafting is obscure and incomplete. Because of these deficiencies, its application is not followed. Too great a number of publications are not deposited: Many are deposited but are incomplete. It appears that the necessity of modifying the law of 1881 has made itself felt and has bothered many people. The projects of reform of legal deposit are numerous. Conceived by people who did not at the time have the opportunity of studying practically the machinery of legal deposit, these are projects which unfortunately come from ideologists with ambitious intentions to whom the enormous difficulties did not matter.[32]

Legal deposit does not work well, it is true, but it functions. We are used to its present form. So, let us deal with it, but with moderation. Let us not forget that legal deposit is concerned with public and private interests worthy of respect. The enrichment of national collections, the respect of the publishers and authors' property and the goodwill of printers can and should be reconciled.[33]

It is along these lines that we propose to you to ask the Chambers to adopt the following modifications to article 3 of the law of 1881.

Law of July 29, 1881

Article 3: Paragraph 1: Within the maximum delay of eight days, every publication coming from the printer's press will be deposited in one copy by him, intended for the national collections. This copy will be in all respects an exact copy of the current copies printed by him. If he fails to effect this deposit a month after he has been asked to do so by the competent services, the printer will be liable to a fine of 10 to 100 francs. In no case can the 'prescription' be acquired.

This deposit is to be effected at the Ministry of the Interior in Paris and at the prefecture for the 'departments.' Free post is granted to printers other than those of Paris and main towns of the 'departments' for the dispatch of the copy of legal deposit. Under pain of being declared null and void a deposit certificate should be enclosed with every deposit. This should mention: firstly, the title of the deposited printed matter; secondly, the name of the author; thirdly, the name and address of the person in whose favor the printing has been made; fourthly, the number of printed copies.

A deposit is demanded for ballot-papers and works called 'jobbing works' or 'pieces of job-work.'

Paragraph 2: Within the maximum period of three months, every publication put on sale by a publisher should be deposited by him. One copy is intended for the national collections. This will not give enough time to the rightful claimants to be able, after the expiry of this delay, to initiate proceedings against counterfeiters of this publication.

The deposited copy should be in all respects an exact copy of the copies put on sale. The deposit will be effected at the Bibliothèque Nationale; the publishers other than those of Paris will for this deposit benefit of postal franchise. Against every deposit received a receipt signed by the librarian will be delivered.[34]

In 1912, the Bulletin of the French Library Association confirmed the involvement of E. Morel and M. Vitrac, both librarians at the Bibliothèque Nationale, in a project for the reform of library deposit. This journal gives the following information and shows how Morel and Vitrac sought the help of the Société des Gens de Lettres to put forward their plan of reform:

For a reform of legal deposit.

The project of modification of the law of July 29, 1881, worked out by our colleagues MM. Morel and Vitrac, had been adopted by *La Société des Gens de Lettres* upon the official report of Mr. André Couvreur at the Special General Meeting of June 30 last. This project consists, if you still remember, of a double deposit to be effected, one by the printer to the Ministry of the Interior, the other by the publisher at the Bibliothèque Nationale, with a statement of the number of printed copies.[35]

In 1912

the Section des Bibliothèques Modernes at the Ecole des Hautes Etudes Sociales announced the following lecture by Morel in the 1912-1923 course: 'The French Book in France—statistics by Eugène Morel.'[36]

This lecture, together with many articles on the printing output of France, clearly indicates Morel's early interest in what was being published in France and the connection this material had with legal deposit.

In 1912, Morel confirmed in an article, *"Le Livre Français et la Production Mondiale,"* in the journal *Mercure de France,* that

> It's now fifteen years since I have been trying to take into account with some accuracy, of the printing output of France. I have spent many weeks rummaging in registers and counting volumes on the shelves of the Bibliothèque Nationale.[37]

This article, which was an essay on the printed output of France, was a sequence to the many essays which had previously dealt with this matter. In 1910, Morel wrote in an article entitled *"La Production de l'Imprimerie Française"* en 1909 in the above journal[38] that he had published in the *Mercure de France,* and for the publisher of the journal some essays of statistics on the output of the printing press in France.[39] His main objective was to draw public attention to the need of a reform of legal deposit in France.

Indeed, the above article, with the others published in *Le Mercure de France,* i.e. *"Production et le Dépôt Légal en 1908"* (no. du 1er mars 1909) and *"La Production de l'Imprimerie Française en 1909"* (no. 307, 1er avril 1918) and chapters of his book, *Bibliothèques: essai sur le developpement des bibliothèques publiques et de la librairie dans les deux mondes.* (Vol. 1, p. 286; vol. 2, Livre III. *"Devant l'invasion des livres: Le Grand Cimetere des Livres. Le Dépot Légal,"* etc.), covered the main problems that legal deposit was causing at the French national library. A clear picture of what was being deposited up to 1909 is given in the above articles of all categories of materials deposited at the National Library. The book, *Les Bibliothèques,* represents on page 286 a good example of the graph Morel talked about in his article, *"La Production de l'Imprimerie Française en 1909,"* appearing in *Mercure de France* of 1910, in which Morel wrote that he had tried to set up a graph between 1884 and 1906 which showed the ups and downs of legal deposit.[40]

However, in 1913 more people became interested in the reform of legal deposit. A *Société des Amis de la Bibliothèque Nationale et des Grandes Bibliothèques de France* was founded at 5, Quai Malaquais in Paris. The principal aim of this organization was "to enrich the Bibliothèque Nationale of Paris, which collects not only books but manuscripts, autographs, prints and rare books."[41]

In the same year, A. Vidier, member of the French Library Association, reviewed in the Association's journal some new publications concerning

French libraries which appeared in 1912 in a report to the General Assembly of the Association of 30th March, 1913, and noted:

> LEGAL DEPOSIT AND RUBEN DE COUDERO
>
> The question of the reform of legal deposit is always very much in the news and has remained one of our main preoccupations. Since 1883, it has been examined by publishers, bibliographers and librarians. Today, it is a jurist, M. Ruben de Coudero, judge at the Supreme Court of Appeal, who, in the wake of many others, is devoting himself to criticizing the law which ensures so imperfectly the growth of our national collections.
>
> Mr. Ruben de Coudero finds a solution to the present state of things in the deposit of one copy by the printer and one by the publisher of the author; he recommends that the deposit should be effected at the Direction des Beaux Arts in Paris, departmental archives and the town halls in the provinces.
>
> We should profit from the judicious comments on the question by M. Ruben de Coudero. But we should not conform to his findings, for they do not seem to set right the damages caused by legal deposit.
>
> The reform of legal deposit is included in the programme of work of an extraparliamentary commission whose terms of reference are to study the reorganization of the Bibliothèque Nationale. Therefore, it is superfluous to start a new debate on the question. In this connection, we do not doubt that the members of this commission tackle the question from the correct angle, from which it is fitting to consider the various interests concerned, namely those of authors and publishers, governing bodies, and those of the public collections and research workers.[42]

Charles Mortet, in his presidential address to the General Assembly of the French Library Association, held on April 20th, 1914, revealed that the French Parliament had begun to take an interest in the reform of legal deposit:

> I could also show to you that the reform for which we have been asking for the past 30 years to modify the articles of the law of 1881, which regulates so imperfectly the Legal Deposit, is probably on the eve of the Chamber of the budget of the Public Instruction, and the discussion which followed this report foreshadow the incorporation in the law of finance of 1915 of clauses which will, at last, work out this reform.[43]

In fact, the budget of the Ministry of Public Instruction at the Chamber of Deputies, at its meeting of March 2nd, 1914, gave rise to an exchange of views and observations which were of major importance and interest to members of the French Library Association. An extract of this discussion concerning the Bibliothèque Nationale and legal deposit of chapter 81 of the *Journal Officiel* (pp. 1201 & 1203-1205)[44] describes the parliamentary debate in which a parliamentarian, Mr. Gustave Rouanet, deplored the inadequate functioning of legal deposit:

> Mr. Chairman: Chapter 81. Bibliothèque Nationale—Personnel 501.475F.
>
> I now call on Mr. Rouanet to take the floor.
>
> M. Gustave Rouanet: I call the attention of the Minister of Public Instruction to the situation at the Bibliothèque Nationale in general and to the personnel, more particularly the caretakers. There is much to be said on the Bibliothèque Nationale, the running of which leaves much to be desired. For some time, it was leading the way along institutions of its kind, but for the moment, it is lagging behind all the great public libraries of Europe.
>
> The very bad running is especially due to the lack of personnel, to the bad state in which it is, and also, I must say, to the way in which the law on legal deposit is carried out at the Ministry of the Interior.
>
> Printers are in the habit of sending to the Bibliothèque Nationale the odds and ends, the waste of their printing. Some years ago, I called the attention of the Ministry of Public Instruction to the possibility that exists, it seems to me, to force printers to give to the Bibliothèque Nationale copies of work printed on a special paper which could be provided, if necessary, by the administration in order to prevent these copies from deteriorating rapidly.[45]
>
> The Minister of Public Instruction: Mr. Rouanet I quite agree with the rapporteur that an effort is in fact necessary...
>
> As far as the second request of Mr. Rouanet is concerned, I more than fully agree with him, if this is possible. He has spoken of legal deposit which is effected in conditions which he has qualified very severely; he could not have given more eloquent expressions to his criticisms. Presently, printers should deposit at the Bibliothèque Nationale two copies of all works printed by them. Either they do not effect this deposit or they deposit worn out books... I intend asking the Minister of the Interior, who is also an authority on the subject, to give his consent to table a bill which will deal in a more positive way with legal deposit.
>
> This question has been completely and competently dealt with by the rapporteur, and he is certain of the fact that we should have our attention focused on the importance and necessity of this deposit on which the future of French culture partly depends...

Mr. Chairman: The floor is now to the rapporteur (Mr. Veber.)

The Rapporteur: I thank the Hon. Minister for what he has said, because it is a fact that what is accorded to the personnel (of the Bibliothèque Nationale) this year as salary is a first step...

The Minister of Public Instruction: Exactly.

The Rapporteur: ... As far as legal deposit is concerned, I thank the Minister for signifying his adhesion in principle to some remarks which I had the honor to include in my report... He has promised us to table a bill in order to better enforce legal deposit. But we all know what is in store for all bills which are not included in the appropriation bill..."

I believe that the Minister of Public Instruction could agree with the Minister of the Interior while awaiting the appropriate bill to be discussed, not to table a complete bill on legal deposit but at least to attend to the most urgent matters.

We could, in one or two articles to be inserted in the appropriation bill, meet the most urgent needs on which I would not like to dilate again, as these had been excellently reported to us successively by Mr. Rouanet and by the Minister.

Mr. Gustave Rouanet: I add that without his having to table a bill, the Minister of Public Instruction could ask various departments to deposit all their publications. The Legal Deposit applies to the printers but does not apply to the State Press or administrative services with the result that a host of official documents and even publications specially printed under the auspices of the state are not to be found in the Bibliothèque Nationale, because legal deposit is not always effected or the administrative services have not deposited the required copies.

Mr. Chairman: Mr. Bluysen.

Mr. Paul Bluysen: While I am all for the reform which has been requested, please allow me, Mr. Minister, to ask you a question relating to a word which you have just used.

You have said that the responsibility of legal deposit in your mind and in the spirit of the bill which you will table, will rest almost exclusively with the printers. Don't you think that it is necessary to examine whether this responsibility should not be at least shared by the publishers, for this is what happens as far as legal deposit is concerned, for the deposit of a volume.

When a copy is deposited, one printer can have printed one part, another one the other part. Therefore, the printer will be responsible literally for the part of the book which he has produced. But if, on the contrary, you shift the responsibility to the publisher and require that the deposit be effected by him, he will become responsible for the whole work. Thus you will make the legal deposit become more effective...

The Minister of Public Instruction: I agree with Mr. Rouanet and I remind you that as far as the principle of the deposit is concerned, no law is necessary.

I agree with Mr. Bluysen that provision should be made for the responsibility of the publisher, and if the publisher does not exist, that of the printer. In fact, this is found in the form of a text at page 537 of the report of Mr. Veber, and this text seems perfectly acceptable.

As far as the insertion of a text in the appropriation bill is concerned, I do not see an inconvenience. I simply want to take some precautions since I am not taking this responsibility alone, but it does not depend upon me that this reform be made at the appropriation bill.

Chapter 81 put to the vote is adopted.[46]

While some of the plans put forward before the year 1918 proved useful in attracting public attention to the need of a reform of legal deposit, this piece of information in 1918 by Charles Mortet, Chief Librarian of the Bibliothèque Sainte Geneviève and in charge of the courses at the Ecole des Chartes, shows that no great step had been taken towards a thorough reorganization of legal deposit. He gave in an article, entitled *"Un nouveau pas vere la reformed u Dépot Légal,"* published in the French Library Association's Journal of 1918, a thorough idea of what was expected for a new step towards a reform of legal deposit.[47] While in Switzerland in 1918 it was made known that an agreement had been reached, between the Swiss National Library, the *Schweiser Buchhandlerverein*, and *La Société des Librairies et Editeurs de la Suisse Romande*, that the National Library should receive a free copy of their publications for legal deposit as from January 1st, 1918, there was evidence in France that unfortunately there was much to be done before a law could be enacted for a reorganization of the legal deposit law of 1881.[48]

It is probable that it was the slackness with which things had been carried regarding a new reform of legal deposit that goaded Morel, elected as chairman of the French Library Association on May 21st, 1918, to bring this law up to date. It will be seen chronologically from Morel's tenure of office as chairman and from 1918 onwards how great changes and improvements took place in the reform of legal deposit. In all the decisions and discussions made regarding the reform of legal deposit, Morel showed perspicacity coupled with foresightedness of the needs of the National

Library and the general public, as well as a knowledge of legal matters. For one must not forget that Morel had been a lawyer before he became a librarian. In 1918, Charles Mortet, in the above article, reviewed the work of Morel on legal deposit, which was entitled *"Le Dépot Légale etude et projet de Loi."* It will be interesting to reproduce in full length this review of Morel's book by a contemporary because its vital importance in the reorganization of the law is emphasized therein:[49]

*A new step towards the reform of Legal Deposit*

The two articles which our colleague M. Eugène Morel has published recently in La Revue Nouvelle (15 October – 1st November 1917), and which he had published simultaneously in a brochure entitled: *"Le Dépot Légal, etude et projet de loi"* (Paris: Bossard 1918. 80, 46p), deserve special attention, because this well-documented study deepens and enlightens better than any other which had previously treated the delicate questions which its reform raises. This should have been treated with urgency for quite a long time. This study proposes solutions which seem more practical than those of previous plans of reform.

First, the concept that predominates the paper of Mr. Morel is that if legal deposit, from its origins, had been concerned with the idea of submitting to the control of public authorities everything that is printed in France and was intended to build up with deposited copies, the principal stock of one or several State libraries, this two-fold consideration does not suffice today to make us accept the reforms by which the imperfections and deficiencies of the 1881 law are to be remedied. The main *raison d'être* of legal deposit which justified best and in all respects the means by which one endeavors to render it more strict and effective, is the necessity to collect, classify and preserve officially in a public institution everything that is being printed in France in order that the copyright on books and other categories of printed materials could be ascertained, acknowledged and guaranteed.

Thus, conceived legal deposit does not only interest administrators, librarians and the intellectual public who use the large libraries of Paris. It interests also, in the first place, all those—authors and publishers—who cooperate in book publication; the concentration in the one and same institution of every publication that comes from the French printers and the official registration which gives to every deposited publication an exact date, provides to the author and publisher the surest means to prove that they can establish their rights of authorship in case these are contested or usurped. To those whom the law compels to effect a deposit, this obligation appears no more than a vexation tax, arbitrarily levied on literary works and publishing businesses for the benefit of those who do not buy books, but, as M. Morel shows well, as a "safeguard of French thought" in its most substantial and legitimate interests. From that time, the objections that authors and publishers raised too often to the reforms which had been initiated by librarians and public authorities for the practical functioning of legal deposit must disappear. Instead of complying unwillingly with, or evading a formality which seems to have been made only to enrich at their expense the public libraries, the authors and publishers, more enlightened, will lose no time in adhering to it in order to reap immediately the benefits and at the same time with the greatest exactitude with which it is probable that the deposit will henceforth be effected, will be found ensured on one hand, the regular growth without which the national libraries cannot offer the services for which they have been instituted.

On this concept are based the essential broad lines of the new plan of reforms which M. Morel has worked out, drawing his inspiration from

> the wishes expressed recently by the Association des Gens de Lettres and by Le Congrès du Livre held in Paris in the month of March 1917. By striving to give in precise details a practical form to the general concepts expressed by their wishes. In agreement with these associations and members of this Congress, he considers that if one wants the legal deposit to have the desired effects that one would like it to have, it is indispensable that on one hand, the deposit of two copies, effected at present by the 'printer' be maintained and be subjected to stricter control. On the other hand, in view of the fact that more frequently the copy as deposited by the printer is incomplete or imperfect, the deposit of the 'publisher' (or by the author when he is his own publisher) of a copy in good selling condition should be added to it. More particularly and more rightly he lays stress on the necessity to maintain and strengthen the printer's deposit which some people wanted, in order to simplify things, to be replaced by the publisher's deposit of two copies. Relying on the long experience which he has acquired from his services at the Bibliothèque Nationale, and on the statistics which he has been able to compile during the past years, he shows with a great force of argument that it is only on this condition that legal deposit can keep its true character and justify the changes that it imposes. In fact, only the deposit effected by the printer ensures the complete collection of printed materials, and M. Morel proves, with figures, that against a total of 3,000 to 4,000 volumes having a recognized publisher, there are every year at least 7,000 items (books of which the author is the only depositor, official and administrative publications, yearbooks, catalogues, societies, deeds, brochures and sections extracted or not from periodicals—which no publisher puts on sale and which would become rapidly undiscoverable if the printer did not effect the deposit

immediately after the printing). Also, only this immediate deposit registered at the Ministry of the Interior gives a definite date to the rights of literary property. It is the only means not to render illusory the role of supervision which the state cannot give up for social and moral, as well as political, reasons. Finally, the declaration of the printer of the number of books printed is the necessary control of the declaration which is asked of the publisher and which should be between him and the author, the normal basis for the contract of impression of a work.

If it is true one objects to the boring task, the less of time which the immediate deposit subjects printers to, and which many among them, are more inclined at present to evade. M. Morel answers very justly that their penalty could be sensibly alleviated if the law authorized delivery of deposit by free mail to be addressed to the Ministry of the Interior and to a special office depending on this ministry. On the other hand, in order to avoid that the obligation of the immediate deposit be not easily evaded, he asks that, following the wish expressed for quite a long time, if a printer infringes the regulations, the prescription, which after the law of 1881, took place at the end of three months, could not henceforth be called upon only during a period of five years no legal proceedings have been instituted against him. But with more reason, he thinks that the punitive sanction that is necessary to give to the obligation imposed by the law, cannot consist but of a fine and should go further as to deprive the author of a publication not deposited of the right of literary property. The provision of article 6 of the law of July 1793: stipulating that failing a receipt to ascertain that a deposit has been effected 'the author will be unable to initiate legal proceedings against infringers of copyright': has not expressly been abrogated by the law of 1881 on the press and the jurisprudence of the Supreme Court of Appeals holds this law applicable to this case. Consequently, it is extravagant that if through the mistake of the printer or the publisher, the deposit of a work has not been effected within the prescribed date limit, and if subsequently on the eve of the trial, the omission cannot be made up because an accidental circumstance has caused all the copies of an edition to disappear from the market, the author loses in this very case not only the surest means to prove his authorship, but what is more, the power to sue in court, and consequently his right is reduced to nothing. It is no less extravagant that in this case, the printer or the publisher who has failed to effect a deposit, is considered as pecuniarily responsible for all the harm done to the author by the complete loss of his rights. The draconian provisions of the law of 1793 must then be formally abrogated, and it is essential that this should be laid down as a principle that the deposit regularly effected has, legally, as a unique consequence, the 'official registration of a fact' (at what date, such and such a thing was printed and such and such a number of copies are preserved in such public institutions), but also that if the deposit has not been effected, the right of literary property, independent of this administrative formality, continues to exist in its completeness and can be established by other means of proof."

Secondly, the essential basis of the new plan that M. Morel proposes and the whole text of this project will be found at the end of this article. Now it is necessary to examine the second facet of the problem. Let us suppose that the reform of legal deposit were accepted and voted as it is proposed, in what manner would the three copies coming from the deposit effected by the printer on one hand and the publisher on the other hand be distributed, preserved and utilized?

This important question is answered by two short articles[19, 20] in M. Morel's project. Naturally, one of these allots to "the Bibliothèque Nationale and its outbuildings a copy of every item deposited, while the other one makes the Ministry of Public Instruction responsible for designating by region the institution destined to receive the second copy of everything that is being printed or published there." This last arrangement is a trifle vague and requires to be discussed. As far as to where the third copy should go, the one that the publisher deposits, no article makes an allusion to it: this is a regrettable lacuna. On the other hand, in the explanations that precede or follow the text of the project, M. Morel does not take sides with anybody on the question of knowing whether it is the Bibliothèque Nationale which will receive directly the two copies coming from the printer's deposit, responsible for preserving one and distributing the other or whether there would not be the need to create for this service to which the project gives a great extension and a new importance, a special bureau of Legal Deposit forming part of the Bibliothèque Nationale, as in the United States, where the "Copyright Office" is juxtaposed to the Library of Congress of Washington.

This is, to my mind, how these various questions could be answered.

> The function which M. Morel wants to see predominate in the institution is the one that will ascertain and guarantee officially the rights of intellectual property in collecting in the same public institution, not only the best part, but the total printing output of France, in whatever type of impression they appear, that is to say, apart from the books and the engraved prints, the photographic, typing and cinematographic prints. The consequence would be to increase considerably the weekly contribution of the deposit effected by the printer a contribution which is, at present, already considerable, because according to the figures that M. Morel gives for the period 1911 to 1913, the average was for books, brochures, maps, and prints about 14,000 items, excluding posters, the

number of which varied between 2,300 and 11,600, and for periodicals, three quarters of which arrive incomplete, the total deposit should annually amount to about 636,000 items. The result is that there is a massive piling up of printed matter, the daily registration and the submission of which to institutions responsible for preserving them will require large promises and larger personnel. To meet the needs of the new development of this institution, the present organization through which the two copies deposited reach the Ministry of the Interior, directly when the deposit is effected in Paris by the administrative channel. When this is done in the province they are transported from there every week, one at the *Bibliothèque Nationale,* the other at the Ministry of Public Instruction which in fact is responsible for the distribution among various public libraries—this organization, I say, will evidently be inadequate. It has the big inconvenience of multiplying the conveyance of things from one place to another, this is for deposited items the cause for deterioration, and at times for disappearance.

If one were to remove the responsibility of the direct reception and the distribution of deposited copies from the Ministry of the Interior to devolve it exclusively on the *Bibliothèque Nationale,* one would have three inconveniences, i.e. to suppress the control which the central authority should exercise on the printing output of France, to confer upon the *Bibliothèque Nationale* an administrative supervision for which it is not armed sufficiently with necessary powers, and to impose on it the temporary storage of a second copy which it should preserve and will clutter up the exiguous premises.

The natural conclusion is that the printer's deposit, as M. Morel conceives it, should be effected in a special institution under the jurisdiction of the Ministry of the Interior, but distinct from the other offices of this ministry, and which, fitted out in view of the new organization, would be responsible for receiving, recording and distributing according to precise regulations two copies of every printed materials coming from the French printing press. One can take as a model by adapting it to our legislation and administration, the Copyright Office of Washington, the working of which, fixed by the law of March 9th, 1909, has been carefully described by our colleague, M. H. Lemaitre, is an interesting account published by *La Revue des Bibliothèques* (année 1912, pp. 1 to 19.)

In the United States, according to the law in force, the deposit is not compulsory, but optional only (which does not prevent this from being, in fact, universally practiced by authors and publishers because of the effective protection that the deposit ensures to their rights.) Also, the author or the publisher must, after all, show his intention to guarantee his rights of property in printing on the half-title or opposite to the title the declaration of the *Copyright*, and by sending to the *Office*, with the two copies demanded, a request for the registration of his rights. Furthermore a tax of one dollar (5 francs) is levied by the *Office* every time that a copyright is effected. In this country, where the deposit by the printer is compulsory, consequently exclusive of all request and taxation, the preliminary formality would consist solely in the declaration which is laid down by the law of 1881 and which the new project provides. The 'Central Bureau,' set up to receive the legal deposit, would deliver, as does the *Copyright Office*, an acknowledgement of receipt of deposit reproducing the declaration, inscribing immediately on a counterfoil register the title of the printed material by giving it an accession number and by mentioning the date of deposit! It would reproduce this number, on one hand, on the two received copies, and on the other hand, on the catalogue card written according to the usual rules (author's name, title, bibliographical address, date of publication, format, number of pages etc...)

It would print in agreement with the *Cercle de la Librairie*, and if it is possible, in conjunction with it a weekly bulletin, which will reproduce the series of titles of printed materials received in the previous week—a bulletin which will make up a really complete *Bibliographie de la France*. These titles which are printed, cut up and stuck on cards would serve, on one hand, to set up in the office two indexes which could be consulted without any charge by anyone interested; one of these indexes would be arranged by author's names or anonymous titles, the other by names of owners. On the other hand, they would be used like cataloguing cards by libraries to which would be directed the copies coming from legal deposit.

Finally, this Central Bureau would be responsible for the distribution of the two copies deposited by the printer. One of these would go direct to the *Bibliothèque Nationale* and would be delivered to it as soon as possible, with the printed cards corresponding to the items deposited. If the regulations of the law as proposed were strictly complied with, the printed matter which would come thus into this institution, will record as we have seen, a considerable increase, but probably with no great benefit to readers who use the reference libraries, for a great part of printed materials which would increase the present contribution would be of interest only to authors or publishers who deposited them and who would like to safeguard their right of property. These printed materials would be utilized only in exceptional cases for scientific, literary, artistic or technical research. In order to provide against the overcrowding which would result from the multiplication of this category of printed matter, there must be some arrangements made, the greatest effectiveness of which could be achieved if the series of works which are less used like provincial newspapers, posters, almanacs, could be transported into special premises which will be under the jurisdiction of the *Bibliothèque Nationale*...

The second copy deposited by the printer would be, following the wish often expressed and which the plan of M. Morel adopts, sent *en province* in one of the libraries of the region where the work was printed. For this, two reasons are given: Firstly, as a remark was made about this, 'it is advisable that if one wants to preserve French book production, the two copies should not be centralized in the same town where a great disaster would jeopardize both of them'; secondly, it is useful to contribute towards the literary and scientific decentralization in favor of regional libraries. Thus, one can designate a dozen towns, preferably University towns where there exists already an intellectual activity which is more or less developed— namely Lille, Caen Rennes, Poitiere, Bordeaux, Toulousse, Marseille, Grenoble, Lyon, Dijon, Nancy, Clermont—in order to receive and preserve in the same conditions as the *Bibliothèque Nationale*, the second copy of the printer's deposit. The Central Bureau, which would have received this second copy as well as the first, would distribute them while taking into consideration their sources and would send it post free to the libraries called to profit by it.

Now it remains to determine how the copy which the publisher has to deposit (or the author when he is his own publisher) would be used. The reason which has goaded to include in the majority of the projects of the reform of legal deposit this new obligation imposed on the publisher is well-known. In most cases, the printer who is only compelled to deposit what he prints himself hands over to the representatives of the Ministry of the Interior incomplete copies, for instance, when the cover and the title of a book are printed separately or when the plates, which should go with the text, have a special printer. More often than not, through negligence, he deposits two rejects, badly printed, soiled or torn. Finally, those copies that he deposits in good condition, can, because of accidents or misappropriation in postal dispatch or in the conveyance from one office to another, never reach their destination. Presently one is compelled to make up for these drawbacks, to appeal to the goodwill of publishers, which entails long discussions or correspondence and never gives the result that one expects. This is why it has become indispensable to include in the contemplated bill the *perfect obligation* for publishers to deposit at the *Bibliothèque Nationale* a complete copy in *non de luxe* edition of all printed material which they are putting on sale. This copy, destined to replace, *in case of flaw*, the one which the *Bibliothèque Nationale*, will have received from the printer's deposit, should naturally be addressed directly and post free to this institution which will deliver an acknowledgement of receipt for it and where the substitution of one copy for another, when there will be the need to do it, will be immediately effected.

No sooner will this work be over than the *Bibliothèque Nationale* will find itself in possession not only of one copy intended for its collections, but

# LEGAL DEPOSIT

also, because of the great part of its entries, of a second copy which will come at one time from the printer's deposits which would be replaced by publisher's copies at another time from the publisher's deposits which would not have been utilized because the printer's copies were in an acceptable state. What will become of the second copy? The answer to this question is clear: it must be allotted to the *Bibliothèques Publiques de Paris* (Arsenal, Masarine, Sainte-Geneviève) which even presently, benefit from the distribution made by the Ministry of Public Instruction, from one of the two deposited copies. The representatives of these libraries would then go at regular intervals to take delivery not at the Ministry of Public Instruction but at the *Bibliothèque Nationale* to whom an acknowledgement of receipt will be given.

I believe that this could be the main outline of the new organization of legal deposit as put forward by the plan of M. Morel. There is no doubt that objections will be raised that such an organization will require an extensive personnel and will involve very high expenses. I do not contradict this and I am not unaware that the personnel of the *Copyright Office* (where anyway things have been done grandiosely within the American spirit) comprises besides the *register* (sic) who directs it, an *assistant register* (sic), six heads of section, about sixty clerks, a dozen office employees and typists. But I must call to your attention that here in France at this very moment, the poor functioning of legal deposit compels us to run simultaneously three services: one at the Ministry of the Interior, the other at the Ministry of Public Instruction, and the third at the *Bibliothèque Nationale*. In grouping together in the same office the officials and agents of the first two services one can have already an important personnel to whom it will suffice perhaps to add some auxiliaries. Though all things have been considered, the actual cost would be double: this increase of expenses will be justified by the advantages that the new organization will bring to the various points of view which I earnestly want to point out to your attention in this study.[50]

Finally, Charles Mortet quoted the work of Morel on the bill on legal deposit:

> Here are the passages of a report by M. Eugène Morel, entitled *'Dépot Légal,'* containing the statement of the characteristics of a draft bill and text itself of this bill. This report has appeared in one brochure in 80, published by La Librairie Brossard.
>
> *CHARACTERISTICS OF DRAFT BILL*
>
> 'We have thought it our duty to group under the form of a draft bill the entire work on the measures and innovations which seem to deserve to

make the basis of discussion for the new legislation on legal deposit. This plan distinguishes itself by the following characteristics:

(a) Specification of the items submitted to the deposit which an antiquated law, one century old, could not provide for;

(b) the deposit of the printers first and that of the publisher to follow the first one should be that of two copies; that of the second of one copy only if the copies of the first are complete, but three in case they are not;

(c) obligation to deposit three copies, namely for publishers who have their materials printed abroad;

(d) allotment of one copy to a provincial library;

(e) granting of books published abroad to be submitted for legal deposit;

(f) special article, concerning *de luxe* works and prints published in very limited edition and reducing the deposit to one copy only;

(g) special article, concerning photography and cinematography;

(h) double declaration of the number of printed books submitted to the same sanctions as the deposit;

(i) extension of the prescription;

(j) admission of those interested to attend to application of the law;

(k) concentration of the declarations and documents provided by legal deposit;

(l) legal obligation to classify the deposited materials by titles. Organization of imparting of information to those interested.

(m) the making of rules for the loan of unpublished books and others in libraries;

(n) formal enunciation of the role of deposit; declamatory and non-assigning of propriety.

Many consider that one can go further into the case in question and draw a more complete project, giving far deeper into the details of the application, providing for a new institution attached to the *Bibliothèque Nationale,* an *Office du Dépôt Légal.*

We have avoided, even when writing before the war, all proposals which will imply that the organization is still inexistent, or demands transfers of difficult assignments to obtain from competent ministries.

Two important points were essential: achieve, obtain something, be it the extension of the delay of claim, the accuracy with which items are

# LEGAL DEPOSIT

deposited, the sending of items without postal charges, the deposit by the publisher of the complete work etc.—everything on which we have agreed and which is not achieved, perhaps because of the enormous needs of the projects submitted. Secondly, we have always rejected the opinion put forward many times that the printer's deposit cannot be suppressed, replaced, and reduced. We consider that it would be disastrous for libraries, the national bibliography, and writers.

These have been consulted twice on the question, and their wish corresponds to that of librarians:

'In the interest of writers, as well as that of libraries, *La Société des Gens de Lettres* expresses the wish that the responsibility of legal deposit be left to the printer and that in any case, the formality of the deposit should not question the rights of literary propriety. It recalls that it has put forward previously a formal wish that one copy be deposited accompanied by a declaration of the number of copies printed by the printer and another one with the same declaration by the publisher under legal sanction.'

## TEXT OF THE BILL

### Title I – Printer's Deposit

Article 1: Within eight days which follow the printing of the last page a deposit should be effected by the printer of two copies of all printed materials consistent with the usual copies delivered by him;

Article 2: All the products of graphic arts without any other exception than those enumerated in Article 3 are considered as printed matter and compelled to be deposited;

Article 3: Jobbing works, such as visiting cards, ballot-papers, office stationery and, more particularly, patterns and trademarks, commercial labels, titles of publications not yet printed, are excluded from deposit;

Article 4: *De luxe* editions and artistic prints printed to less than 100 copies and numbered can be deposited by the printer in one copy only if they are in perfect condition;

Para.2: This deposit will be confused with the publisher's deposit provided for in Title II, for the prints and artistic reproductions when the author himself sells the products of his art, and will be effected directly to the *Bibliothèque Nationale;*

Article 5: Para.1: All sorts of photographs, as well as photographic prints, are subject to the printers deposit when they are not meant for sale: in this case, they must bear the author's mark and the year in which the deposit has been effected;

Para.2: The Minister of Public Instruction will regulate the form of deposit in special or new cases. Proofs on paper are received in lieu of proofs on perishable material (glass, cellulose, etc.), cinematographic proofs can be reduced on a proof of about 30 images;

Article 6: The printer's deposit will be effected post free direct to the Ministry of the Interior for the *department* of the Seine to the prefecture for the other *departments* at a place fixed by the governor or the President for the colonies or protectorates;

Article 7: Para. 1: The deposit will be accompanied by a declaration extracted from the counterfoil register, dated and signed, mentioning the title of the work, the names and the subjects for prints and photographies, the number of printed copies, and the name of the person for whom the printing has been done, a mention of the quality of the deposited material if it concerns a bookseller-publisher;

Para. 2: The depository service will issue a receipt of acknowledgement which will reproduce the declaration. These receipts, extracted from a counterfoil register, will bear the numbering set up this year on the 1st of January, and reproduced marked with the stamp of the legal deposit of the department on every document deposited;

Para. 3: Can be grouped in the same declaration publications of lesser importance and of the same nature as posters, circulars etc.;

Article 8: Every new printing of books is subject to deposit. However, if the work has been deposited for less than five years, the new printed number of books does not bear any modification other than the number of mark of edition and the date, no new copy will be able to be added to the declaration which will have to reproduce the number of the previous deposit;

Article 9: Engravers and photographers making by hand, by units, as orders are made, proofs of a plate or negative preserved, should mention that the printed number is limitless and made by hand, they will be subject to new deposits only if alterations are brought to their prototype or on request of the *Bibliothèque Nationale* if the proofs furnished by them are seriously damaged.

*Title II – Publisher's Deposit*

Article 10: Para. 1: Every person who puts on sale as publisher or principal depository a printed work or product of graphic arts bearing the name of the firm, must, within the month it is being put on sale, send a complete *non de luxe* copy to the *Bibliothèque Nationale;*

Para. 2: There should be a deposit of 3 copies if the whole or a part is printed abroad;

# LEGAL DEPOSIT

Article 11: Foreign publishers having a branch in France, booksellers or commissioners advertising in a special way or taking out a subscription at their French firm for a work published abroad should effect a deposit of three copies for works in French and one only for those in a foreign language, music, prints, maps, and photographs;

Article 12: Foreign publishers who will direct to the *Bibliothèque Nationale* a copy of their publication will be considered depositors, and they will be delivered a dated acknowledgement of receipt for all useful purposes;

Article 13: The publisher's deposit should be accompanied by a declaration extracted from a counterfoil register if the publisher is a tradesman in France. This declaration should mention the authors' names and printers, the date the work is put on sale, the price of the work, the number of the printed work, and the number of copies which have entered France. The prescriptions of Article 8 concerning the successive impressions apply to the publisher's deposit.

*Title III: Sanctions and Effects of the Deposit*

Article 14: Failure to deposit an item within the prescribed delay, deposit of incomplete work, omissions, or errors in the declaration are liable to fines between 16 and 300 francs;

Article 15: The application of the fines does not exempt one from effecting a deposit and the printer or publisher who will not be able to present the item will be liable to a statement of claim from the State;

Article 16: The bookseller or retailer acquiring a good number of works of which the deposit has not been effected is responsible for the deposit;

Article 17: The prescription is for five years with regard to legal deposit. However, the State can for thirty years claim or cause to seize among publishers or booksellers who possess them in great number, a copy of items to be submitted for deposit which have not been deposited;

Article 18: Authors, joint authors, illustrators, publishers, beneficiaries or agents and other persons interested in deposit of printed matter are allowed to take action against the strict application of the laws on legal deposit, one month after having directed to the Ministry of the Interior a claim which must be certified by the governing body of the *Bibliothèque Nationale;*

Article 19: A copy of any deposited item should be preserved at the *Bibliothèque Nationale* or in its outbuildings. The printer's and publisher's declarations will be submitted to it and will also be preserved by it;

Article 20: The Ministry of Public Instruction will designate by region the institution destined to receive the second copy of the printed matter or the publications which will be made in this region;

Article 21: A decree concerning the public use of documents will lay down the rules and regulations for allowing the general public and those interested to have access to works coming from legal deposit, more particularly of those documents not yet put on sale, or deposited before they are put on sale, and for the declaration of printers or publishers and for authorizing them to copy, photograph, or to make extracts or certificates of deposited items;

Article 22: Any prosecution, any request for subscription or offer of materials to a public service regarding an item submitted to legal deposit should state the number of the deposit of this item or justify that a claim has been made according to the conditions laid down in Article 18;

Article 23: The legal deposit records the acquired rights but does not confer in itself any right of propriety. It cannot take the place of the real publication, it cannot be contrary to the person who justifies himself as the author of literary work nor replaces the formalities prescribed for the guarantee of patent rights or by the law of July 14, 1909 on the deposit of designs and patterns. It is independent of the administrative and judiciary deposits prescribed by the law of the press of July 29, 1881.

Article 24: The provisions prior to the present law and more particularly to Article 6 of the law of July 19-24, 1793, Article 3 and 4 on the law of the press of July 29, 1881 are abrogated.

*NOTES*

Article 1: Delays are necessary to avoid that the printer awaits for a claim to deposit. The deposit can always be effected more particularly before an action for infringement of copyright is instituted; but the fine should be incurred for five years for late deposit. However, it is useless to overcrowd the deposit with scattered parts of publications and as far as volumes are concerned, time must be given to the printer to sew the book;

Article 2: It is indispensable that the new law specifies better than the old one what is to be deposited. Terms like 'commercial circulars' and 'pieces of job-works' are vague. It is important that the trade catalogues be deposited. As far as pieces of job-work (biblioquets) are concerned, the meaning of the work itself is not well-known among printers themselves. The legal formula must provide for the future operating process of reproduction not only for the processes derived from photography but for those from typewriting the advancement of which baffles the notion of printing.

Article 3: We have used the word 'excluded' *(exclus)* instead of 'exempted' *(dispenses)* from the deposit in some cases. There is a tendency, in fact, to transform the legal deposit of printed matter and prints into a service of deposit of patterns, and for the guarantee of the patent rights (deposit of brand, labels, titles of publications which are not brought out etc.).

Article 4: The previous law makes compulsory the deposit of three copies for maps and prints. The result is that nothing is being deposited. Artists at times offer a copy of their works, but they never deposit three copies. No sanctions will succeed in levying a tax which in case of a limited edition becomes loathsome.

Many times the amendment of the value of the object, the loss of rights of artistic property, has been proposed. It is one of the best ways of protecting art, and it seems, that the desire to preserve works of art should not go so far as to discourage artists from producing them and give rise to artistic emigration in order to evade such a tax. Penalties which will be less severe will encourage artists to deposit more in the Print Room of the *Bibliothèque Nationale.*

Article 5: This article is very debatable. This is because there is no special legislation regarding photographs and the legislation can be contradictory. As far as legal deposit is concerned, one cannot think of compelling everyone who does photography to deposit his work. It will be compulsory for all those who sell proofs to the public or want to claim rights of reproduction. French legislation tends to give to the photographer on his negative the right for a period which is equal to that given to the artist on his work. But the artist, the writer signs his work, can be located. At his death—the starting point of the time allowed for the deposit which will culminate into the expiry of his patent—will be known. Even the printer is bound by the law to give his name. The photographer, author of a negative, is but a daily paid worker. The owner of a negative is neither a publisher nor is he bound to put down his name nor to deposit and declare his print. At times he comes to claim the right on the reproduction of a work of art which the artist himself has authorized, and it is impossible to find out the name of the author of the photography and if the copyright of it has lapsed or not. No doubt a law on legal deposit has nothing to do with the question of copyright as its aim is to record only the items. But it would settle once and for all a question which deserves a special law rather than compare anonymous photographs with personal works of art. Publishers and literary men, authors of artistic and scientific publications necessarily have to illustrate their works and need to be protected from demands which culminate at times into real interdictions when the work is destroyed or the authorization to photograph the item is refused by the governing body under various pretexts; the result of this has been to reserve the reproduction of a document to those whose duty it is to make this accessible to the general public.

Article 6: The text is borrowed from the plan of Messrs. Pol Neveux and Vidier.

Article 7: Documents which cannot be identified reach the legal deposit. Then the subject has to be enunciated. The name of the publisher or the client is necessary not only for the claim of the complete work if there is the need, but for the complementary particulars on the subject which the printer is often unable to provide. The yearly numbering is rightly claimed by Messrs. Pol Neveux and Vidier. Uniformity of method is the condition for the strict application of the law.

Article 9: It is essential that the number of copies printed is regularly declared. It is one of the raison d'etre of legal deposit. But what about legal deposit itself? Hundreds of identical copies of the same work clutter the shelves of the *Bibliothèque Nationale*. One grows weary of claiming a useless work and it is through these loopholes that the law breaks down. In the case of successive printed numbers of copies the declaration required by Messrs. Neveux and Vidier can dispense with useless deposit and will ensure a strict application of the law.

Article 10: The definition of the publisher proposed here includes the author who puts his address on the work and the bookseller who occasionally receives the deposit of a private individual. One knows very well that it is these works from private individual that escape legal deposit. No bibliography allows one to locate them. The collection of the works of posts is particularly incomplete at the *Bibliothèque Nationale*.

Para. 2: This article will redress an anomaly. French publishers who have their works published abroad are in fact exempted from deposit.

Article 11: The increasing competition of foreign publishers settling in France renders this innovation important. A way should be found to ensure that all the books in the French language should be in the *Nationale*. Books in French are published not only in Belgium, in Switzerland and Canada but in Scotland as well.

Article 12: Will the effort to attract foreign deposits be followed effectively? One could think this hope chimerical if this was not a question of regularizing the tendency of foreign publishers rather than of making a platonic appeal. The publicity made for deposited works, the assurance that all formalities are fulfilled in case of infringement of copyright, interest foreigners due to the fact that several publishers of music and books of art have started to deposit. Consequently, the *Bibliothèque Nationale* hesitates to classify these books as French deposits. It seems certain that a receipt duly

# LEGAL DEPOSIT

signed and the option to deposit only one copy will attract to the *Nationale* interesting foreign collections.

Articles 18-19-20: These articles establish the *Bibliothèque Nationale* as the depository responsible for the total French book production. Even if an office or a central bureau of legal deposit should be created outside it, this bureau should be constantly in touch with it.

Whether the *Bibliothèque Nationale* should be in charge or not of this administrative function, it must be admitted that the shelving of books in a library is but a minor part of the role of legal deposit. This includes the delivery of certificates, classification and making accessible, with such and such reservation, the declaration of the number of printed matter, statistics, information on trade and politics, the distribution of double copies etc. There is here a network to be created of which little mention has been made in the plans of the reform of the deposit.

In admitting the principle that the *Nationale* always keeps the best copy, it is just that the province benefits of the others. It is useful to contribute to the progress of provincial depositories in promoting the regional libraries. It is advisable if one wants to conserve French book production, not to centralize the two copies in the same town where a great disaster would put both copies in danger.

As far as periodicals and writings without any publisher's deposit are concerned, by allotting one of these two copies to the province this will deprive the Arsenal.

Funds of some thousands of francs would be more useful to this big library than the deposit which weighs it down. But one must also realize that newspapers, brochures, and local writings are more useful in their place of origin than in Paris, where the *Nationale* possesses them already, then papers (prospectuses, programmes, circulars) ,which one would know what to do with in Paris. In their country of origin, these would form religiously classified collections.

Article 21: Article 21 sets up and organizes the regular control of legal deposit. This does not exist presently. This article is also important for literary men, newspapers' publishers, and magazines etc. Presently, only a process server can make an affidavit at the *Bibliothèque Nationale* that a deposit has been effected. There is no rule for making accessible at the Ministry of the Interior the declarations of the number of printed materials. A research worker who wants to know if a title which he wants to take is free sees his request routed from the Ministry of the Interior to the *Nationale,* which can give him neither any guarantee nor usually any information.

The claims of the *Nationale* themselves come up against the presentation of a regular bulletin; the book which has been notified as missing having the usual title different from the one which the bibliographical cards have inscribed.

The present chaos means that the legal deposit, besides the low value that it brings to deposited items, is without practical use.

Article 22: The tax imposed on publishers should not prejudice their interests. We do not know whether there has been a report of damaging fact, but the mistrust would be justified. Many are the works sent to the *Bibliothèque Nationale* long before they are put on sale, this delay extends to more than a year when a great publishing house gave up business. Many also are the statements of the facts of family lawsuit, private circulars, theatrical drama reporting 'printed matter as manuscript,' with which one can make oneself acquainted and which one can copy.

The copy and the photograph lend themselves to abuses. These publishers of music, liberal with their pianoforte scores, refuse to deposit their full scores, fearing lest they would be transcribed. One cannot consider making librarians responsible for abuses which they cannot often know about, but one can aim them against those which they see. At all events, the law must specify that the deposit of a document in a library, made in the name of the law, does not *ipso facto* constitute the right for the public to have immediate access to it, even less to copy it, to model upon it or make it public.

Article 23: We have considered that the law has never been clear regarding the rights that depositors assumed, and this in their own interest. Many inventors, authors or proprietors of patterns confound various deposits. Finally, a work imitated by surprise and deposited before the original must give to the depositor but a circumstantial evidence of right of priority.

The publisher who has published but is late with his deposit pays an overdue fine, but as a matter of fact cannot lose any of his rights. The only harm that the absence of deposit can do to him is to have the onus of giving proof of ownership if this is contested.[51]

At a meeting of the French Library Association held on February 26, 1918, under the chairmanship of Paul Marais, Morel was invited to communicate his views on the question of legal deposit to the General Assembly of the Association, which was going to be held on Sunday, May 12, 1918.[52] He promised that he would do so but no mention is made of this in the Association's *Journal*, which gives an account of the proceedings of the meeting of May 12th.[53]

In the same year, the French Library Association was invited to visit the American Library in Paris on November 28[54], with particular attention to La Bibliothèque de l'American Library Association, situated at 10 Rue de l'Elysée in Paris. The French Association accepted the invitation. At the reception, Morel delivered a speech and thanked Burton E. Stevenson of the Chillicote Public Library (Ohio), vice-president of the American Library Association, but added these few words regarding legal deposit and requested from the American Library Association a mutual exchange of publications, especially those as acquired by the American National Library by its legal deposit rights:

> This organization of the exchange of publications of copyright (in this country it is Le dépôt légal) of national bibliographies are also branches where cooperation between allied countries could be practiced…
>
> No doubt we are looking too far ahead, but if the ideal thought of does not put us off our everyday effective work, this ideal is good, and we can always, on condition that we start with something, foresee a closed union, an effective collaboration and the unification of what is possible to be unified.[55]

In his presidential address in 1919 to the Association des Bibliothécaires Français, Morel stressed that it was not enough to impose legal deposit as an obligation, but recommended that means should be found to locate problems which could make even the best legislative intentions inoperative. Thus he recorded his feelings and revealed his reactions to the magnitude of the task that had confronted him and all the various committees which had helped him:

> Please allow me to tell you that although we have not yet got a result at least we have made good progress. The reform of legal deposit undertaken by the Association has made big strides. The *Congrés du Livre* in which the Association distinguished itself, had expressed a series of wishes useful to libraries, which have not been lost sight of, and amongst which appeared the project of the reform of legal deposit. This project has been submitted to the *Syndicat de la Propriété Intellectuelle,* and your President has been defending it as best he could at several meetings of the *Syndicat.* I cannot say that our final project will be met with unanimous acceptance. But librarians are not the only persons interested: they are far from being the most interested. It is a peace treaty that is being proposed to you, a treaty of peace with those whom we have considered as foes, and I can say that it gives hope to our interests. It is not the work of our Association alone, but also that of the *Syndicat des Editeurs* printers who have given us the best technical know-how; *Société des Gens de Lettres,* authors and playwrights,

photographers and other corporate bodies which form part of the *Syndicat de la Propriété Intellectuelle*. Drafted in the form of a bill by the legal advisors of the Syndicat, it has received unanimous approval, and I can promise that it will soon be tabled in the Chamber of Deputies.

It essentially brings us recognition of the double deposits of the printer and publisher, of the control and delay of normal prescription, of declarations in double, and of the essential machinery for the purchase of technical books, of compulsory date of deposit, which is the wish of the *Congrés du Livre*.[56]

In 1922, Morel, in an article entitled *"Le dépôt legal ou le droit d'imprimer pour soi tout seul,"* in *Mercure de France*, criticizes in one way or another all those who had thwarted the rapid application of the new legal deposit law to reorganize the law of 1881, and, as in his presidential address, dilated on the efforts made by many others who wanted to have the text of the project of a law on legal deposit to be approved by the French parliament:

> The text of the bill on legal deposit of printed material which is now submitted to the Chamber of Deputies has been the result of the 'bargains' which have been studied at length between interested associations: authors, publishers, printers, librarians, etc... A wide publicity campaign has been conducted of the preliminary studies made by *Le Congrès du Livre* (1917) and *Le Syndicat de la Propriété Intellectuelle;* all publishers particularly have been aware of the text prepared and have had the time to make comments on a project, the entirety of which was published and discussed at the *Congès du Livre* of 1917. The interventions which are taking place now cannot but be those of private individuals who, by not giving their approval... object to the concessions which the general interest for the French printing output requires of everybody.[57]

He also criticized two parliamentarians, Vuibert and Roches, who, by analyzing in minute detail every article of the new proposed law, caused the voting of this law to be delayed. This showed how Morel analyzed an article written by Vuibert and Roches, who in the journal *La Librairie*, Vuibert took in detail every article of this project of law, tried to find printing errors, and succeeded particularly in proving his strong desire to defer the voting of this law indefinitely.[58]

This polemic between Morel and Vuibert revealed new aspects of a comparison between the legal deposit law of 1881 and the newly proposed legal deposit law. Morel talked copiously about those who had studied very closely the project of the new legal deposit law. He said that those who had a sound knowledge and technique of library legislation should be approached before the new law was promulgated. He explained how

Vuibert and Roches had retarded the enforcement of the application of the law:

> In giving to the publisher or to anybody the right to delay the printer's deposit and interpret the meaning of the word *publier*, we cut out all control and relegate the deposit tone of goodwill with the difference on the *status quo* that that which is a tolerance would become a right."[59]

> "It is not, in fact, an improvement of the text that Messrs. Vuibert and Roches are aiming at, it is the abolition of the principle of legal deposit itself.[60]

Finally, Morel gave advice for the effective implementation of the new law on legal deposit, and in view of this he recommended the reorganization of the Bibliothèque Nationale:

> In order that the new law is carried out better than the old one, it will be necessary to consolidate somehow the present services, and there will be the need to see if this can be done at the expense of other services.

> But, if, in admitting, that there is the need to increase the establishment of the host of officials of the Republic with a clerk and a typist, if these recover some of the nice books which certain publishers refuse to deposit, or five or six of these pictures which in the time of Daumier came by the hundreds into the Print Room, one can state that France will not grow poorer.[61]

In 1924, Morel's efforts in campaigning for the reform of legal deposit had already been rewarded, and the *Bulletin de la Maison du Livre Français* of April 1924 made a special mention of his endeavors in bringing a reform of legal deposit. In this journal Georges Girard, a collaborator, wrote:

> Apart from the other qualities mentioned earlier, let us add that as librarian, M. Eugène Morel is a specialist of legal deposit, the reform of which everybody wishes today.[62]

But the collaborator revealed that it was unfortunate that it was in Belgium and not in France that Morel's recommendations on the improvement of the legal situation of libraries was given full approval by the Central government. He wrote:

> But the greatest success he had achieved as a librarian skilled in the technique of the library was not in France but in Belgium. For the *Loi Destrée* de 1921, which organizes public reading in Belgium, was directly inspired by his work. History has its odd side: during the war (1914-1918) his book, *Bibliothèques*, fell into the hands of a Belgian woman imprisoned by the Germans; she read it, meditated upon it and made it known to Mr.

Destrée, who used it to work out the law that we do not have in France, and thanks to which every Belgian free-town is today provided with a suitable library. This is an achievement of which Mr. Morel can be justifiably proud.[63]

In 1921, Morel became known as the initiator and active collaborator of the movement to which the Belgian Libraries owe the Destrée Law on Libraries.

In 1923, he attended the Congrès International de Bibliothécaires et de Bibliophiles. This was organized by the French Library Association with the participation of La Société des Amis de la Bibliothèque Nationale et de Grandes Bibliothèques de France, and held in Paris at the Sorbonne from April 3-9, 1923.

At the opening of the Congress on April 3rd, under the chairmanship of M. Louis Barthou, member of the French Academy, president of the Comission Supérieure des Bibliothécaires, speeches were delivered by the following: H. Martin, President du Congrès, Chief Librarian of the Arsenal Library; Eugène Morel, Librarian at Bibliothèque Nationale; F. Maserelle, General Secretary of the Congress, Paris, delegate of the Belgian Government; Tourneur, delegate of the Association of Belgian Archivists and Librarians; Aro Naito, delegate of Japan; Gravit, delegate of Lettonia; Virkenmayer and Koezorowski, delegates of Polonia; Jorgan, delegate from Romania; Emler from Czechoslovakia.

At 4:00 pm, the exhibition *"L'Exposition Technique de Bibliothèques,"* mounted by Eugène Morel, was inaugurated at La Maison du Livre with the help of M. Gillon, Chairman of the Council of that Establishment. The exhibition attracted more than one thousand visitors, and from a bibliographical point of view interested many librarians.[64]

At this Conference of Librarians and Bibliophiles the Destrée Law was discussed at length and it was agreed that every community in each participant country should be ordered to provide funds for the setting up of public libraries. An example to Europe was set by Belgium, which passed the first compulsory library law mentioned in the resolutions adopted by the Committee of the Second Session of April 19th.

The Congress, in its plenary session of that day, adopted the following resolutions:

Second session:

3(a) That the French government proposes to Parliament the voting of a law modeled after the law of 1919 of Tchekoslovakia and the Belgian Law of 1921, known as *Loi Destrée* on libraries.

(b) That the Municipal Council of Paris proceeds immediately with a modern and technical reorganization of municipal libraries. This should be done by modeling the law on that of the Belgian Law of 1921, known as *Loi Destrée*, and the libraries on that of the American model library of Belleville. (Members voting: Tulten, Coyecque, Morel, Tobolka)[65]

In this same session Dupuy, Morel, and Marty adopted the following resolution:

> that libraries be organized to deliver photographic reproductions from negatives, the conservation of which will prevent the subsequent loan and useless dispatch of the originals.[66] (Members voting: Dupuy, Morel and Marty)

Max Leclerc, one of the chief administrators of La Librairie Armand Colin, published an article on the "Reform of Legal Deposit" in *Bulletin de la Maison du Livre Français of 1924*. This provided its readers with ample information on this last work of Morel, which can be included among his most successful activities. This shows that Morel was genuinely interested in the question of the reform of legal deposit and how he successfully contributed to the passing of the law which reorganized legal deposit.

This article, which was of great interest to publishers and printers, would undoubtedly cast a new light on the Legal Deposit Law of 1925 and the important role that Morel played in the promulgation of this law.

It will be interesting to quote it in extenso:

> In 1921, a bill was tabled in Parliament to envisage a reform of the law of legal deposit. This draft bill was adopted and represented by the *Commission de l'Enseignement*. However, it has not yet been discussed.
>
> A decree which was issued upon the proposal of the Ministry of Public Instruction and Fine Arts, dated February 20, 1924 (*Official Journal* of February 25th), lays down that henceforth the service of legal deposit depending on the Ministry of the Interior and that which depends on the Ministry of Public Instruction, which constitute an autonomous office, will acquire legal status. This office will bear the name of *Régie du Dépôt Légal.*
>
> The establishing of the copyright department aims at making practical progress through the ordinary channels of rules and regulations, pending the time when the new legislation will be promulgated. The report which precedes the decree indicates one of the most successful results of the initiative taken by the Ministry of Public Instruction and Fine Arts:
>
> 'It is possible even now to give recognition to and to make rules for, the organization of publicity for legal deposit which in fact exists already, even though the law of 1881 did not make provision for a case of the kind, and

which now publishers and authors consider as one of the most essential grounds for contractual agreement.'

In fact, article 6 of the decree stipulates:

'The acts of declarations of deposit of all printed materials and reproductions intended for public use which are effected in compliances with Articles 3 and 4 of the July 29, 1881 Law, can be consulted by the depositors themselves, the authors, and respective beneficiaries.' These will have the right to obtain the delivery of certified copies corresponding to these declarations.

An advisory committee composed of a limited number of members will maintain control... This will include representatives from the *Representative of the Syndicat des Editeurs*, the *Cercle de la Librairie*, the *Société des Gens de Lettres*, *des Associations de Presse* and *La Confédération des Travailleurs Intellectuels*.

The report recalls to mind that the bill presently submitted has sanctionable agreement concluded between the representatives of the *Gens de Lettres*, composers, artists, printing and publishing houses to ensure, thanks to the innovation of the double declaration imposed on printers and publishers, the regularity and faithfulness of the execution of contracts concluded between intellectual producers and publishers.

Thus, a reform which concerns all intellectual producers[67] has been carried out, and this from a double point of view. Firstly, its principal objective is to ensure at last the regular growth of our national collections to which research workers come and look for documents indispensable to their work. For a long time, this growth was jeopardized because of the fact that this law was not enforced. Our national collections were becoming more and more incomplete.

The establishment of the double deposit to be made, one by the printer to the Minister of the Interior, the other—and this is where there has been one of the principal innovations of the law—by the publisher to the Bibliothèque Nationale ('the one serving to control the other'—thus the bill stressed it)—this establishing of the double deposit which does not add anything, in fact, to the existing charge of the duty in kind, because the deposit of two copies had been laid down by the law, will have as a matter of fact to allow the author to easily ascertain upon a mere request made by him to the Bibliothèque Nationale, the number of copies published at every printing or reprinting of his work.[68]

This reform originates from a wish expressed by the *Congrés Nationale du Livre* of 1917. The Executive Committee of the *Congrés du Livre,* under the chairmanship of M. Pierre Decourcelle, has been working for long in conjunction with MM. Taillefer, lawyer at the Court of Appeal, general secretary of the *Syndicat pour la Protection de la Propriété Littéraire;* Eugène Morel, librarian at the Bibliothèque Nationale, and Max Leclerc, publisher, to prepare the draft of the law, which, after it had been successively approved by *La Société des Gens de Lettres, Le Syndicat des Editeurs, Le Syndicat pour la Protection de la Propriété Intellectuelle,* was presented to the Government, adopted unaltered, and tabled in June 1921.

It was reported to the House in December 1921 by M. Marcel Plaisant. It raised some routine objections and was amended since then by an Interministerial Commission convened at the Ministry of Public Instruction, under the chairmanship of M. Coville, director of *l'Enseignement Supérieur.*

It was during the examination of the question by this Commission, consisting of the heads of various departments of the *Bibliothèque Nationale,* the director of National Archives, Inspectors of libraries, a delegate of the Ministry of Finance as well as M. Eugène Morel and M. Max Leclerc in association with M. Grunebaum-Ballin, that the idea of setting up a legal deposit department was brought forward by the latter—felicitous idea, in particular as it ensures, following the very terms of the report which introduces the decree, the permanent participation of competent persons concerned with the effective running of this public service.

A little industrial organization will no doubt make an impact upon a service which has suffered for many years from the absence of such an organization. In fact, the Bibliothèque Nationale only received 20,000 items every year, while more than 40,000 should have been sent to it. The head of this service himself reports this.

The Print-Room of the Bibliothèque Nationale suffers more than the Printed Department from the deterioration of legal deposit: there it is a real disaster. The prints are no longer deposited, and the work of our most illustrious artists runs the risk of being lost forever for posterity.

Up to the end of the 19th century and since the reign of Louis XV nearly all the French prints got into the National Collection through legal deposit. In 1920, there were only four items among those deposited which an amateur would have liked to keep for his personal collection. For the past twenty years, the Print-Room has received one print of Forain, one of Beanard, and five of Steinlen, none of Maudin.

It is high time that measures are taken, but for the past long period since the beginning of the twentieth century—that is to say, more than twenty years, the wrong is irreparable. If the work of Daumier was not already in the Print-Room, it would take hundreds of thousands of francs in auction sales to acquire it.

Let us now revert to the origins of legal deposit, which dates back to the Ordinance of François I of 1537, confirmed by an edict of 1617 and definitely set up by the law of 1793 on literary property.

The law of July 19-24, 1793, which is still in force, stipulates thus under its article 6:

'Every citizen who will be responsible for the creation of a work either of literature or of engraving in whatever style it be, will be compelled to deposit two copies at the *Bibliothèque Nationale* or the Print-Room of the Republic, where he will be delivered a receipt signed by the librarian, without which he will not be in a position to institute legal proceedings against infringers of copyright.'

The law of the press of July 29, 1881 has in its articles 3 and 4 made rules for this. From now on, the deposit will be effected by the printer to the Ministry of the Interior for Paris; at the prefecture for the chief towns of the *departments*; at the sub-prefecture for the *arrondissements* and for other towns at the town hall. The act of the deposit will mention the title and the number of copies of the printed material.

It is unfortunate that the sanctions are inadequate and the time limit too short. Many copies are lost in transit and do not reach the Bibliothèque Nationale. The Ministry of the Interior is badly equipped to serve as a repository and an agent for the transfer of the enormous output of the printing press.

These are the reasons why these lamentable results have been recorded as shown above. However, when the new law will be voted, the Bibliothèque Nationale will receive, direct from the publisher, a copy that will no longer be able to get lost in administrative transference.

This deposit will be accompanied by the declaration of the publisher, who will have to mention the following:

(1) the names of the author, printer or maker, and the publishers;

(2) the date when the printed material is put on sale;

(3) the price of the work;

(4) for books, the format in centimeters;

(6) the number of pages and inset plate;

(7) the date of the completion of printing.

(Article 9) and article 19 stipulates:

'*The declaration provided for in article 7 (declaration of the printer made to the Ministry of the Interior): it contains also the number of printed copies; and in article 8*

# LEGAL DEPOSIT

> *(declaration of the publisher) can be freely consulted by the depositors themselves, the authors... They have the right to obtain the release of certified true copies of these declarations.'*
>
> Until the bill is passed, article 6 of the decree offers to authors and publishers the same guarantee. Thus, a reform which will not fail to have the most felicitous effects is carried out not only from the point of view of the good administration of our national riches in respect of literature and the arts but also from the point of view of the regularization of the agreements between authors and publishers.
>
> All the persons concerned are associated with the smooth running of the copyright department, which, under the sponsorship of the State, will undertake to restore this magnificent service of public interest."[69]

On May 27, 1925, the main recommendations, as laid down by Max Leclerc in the above article and those of Morel in his *"Projet de Loi sur le Dépôt Légal"* and *"Le Dépôt Légal, etude et projet de loi"* were tabled and the new law of the legal deposit was passed.

In 1934, E. de Grolier and G. de Grolier, editors of *La Revue du Livre* wrote in their journal that E. Morel deserved credit as one of the first who was responsible for the passing of the law.

> He was establishing in a remarkable chapter on legal deposit the foundation of his future activities for the conservation and the compilation of the complete bibliography of French book production. He asked for reform with a threefold aim:
>
> 1st for libraries—three libraries should enjoy legal deposit, namely the *Nationale*, a regional library and a special library;
>
> 2nd for the literary, artistic, and commercial copyright;
>
> 3rd for the establishment of a national bibliography, to set up a centralized catalogue service by providing various libraries with card catalogues.
>
> Eugène Morel had summarized and developed these ideas on legal deposit and the national bibliography in *Le Dépôt Légal* published in the middle of the war, then in *La Loi sur le Dépôt Légal* published in 1925 on the morrow of the passing of the law, achieved after fifteen years of perseverance. If there had not been Eugène Morel, this law would not have been passed, and it can be said that it is to Morel that the French owe this chapter of the French book *(charte du livre français)* the basis for a complete national bibliography. He has been able to achieve the most important thing: the principle of the double deposit—that of the printer and the publisher—and the extension of the date limit from three months to three years. This

will enable the authorities to take action against defaulters. He succeeded in obtaining the means which relieved the *Nationale* of useless and cumbersome material: the replacement of legal deposit by the declaration of the number of printed copies. He had not been able to achieve other reforms which he had initiated: the deposit of several copies, creation of a unique legal deposit department which would centralize the services of the *Nationale* and the Ministry of the Interior. On the other hand, a reform which had he not been able to bring in the bill he had been able to achieve thanks to his efforts of a few months, before his death: the enforcement of the deposit of periodicals.[70]

His writings after the passing of the law of 1925 reveal the kind of initiator he wanted to be. Preoccupations like those shown below, mainly with unprofitable and impossible targets, reveal something of the manner in which Morel's mind worked. Thus he wrote in 1933 in *La Revue du Livre*, directed by the Groliers, that he would like to give all his attention to the compilation of the National Bibliography and the legal deposit of periodicals:

> Mr. and Mrs. De Grolier, in a useful report to the 1933 *Conférence de l'Institut de Documentation* at Bruxelles, showed that more or less the various business concerns, namely Segaud, Valdas, Lorenz, based themselves on the *Bibliographie de la France*; this is itself incomplete and not published punctually, nor does it have a systematic index (the other part, *Livre du mois de l'année* reclassified only notices).
>
> In its official part, *La Bibliographie de la France* based itself on legal deposit. This should be double from the printer and the publisher. The publisher's deposit brings in 13,000 to 14,000 titles per year; the printer's deposit a trifle more... the day when the Ministry of the Interior decides, the legal deposit which has trebled since the law of 1925 will be practically complete. At the moment it brings in between twenty to thirty thousand titles, 10,000 of which go to the *Bibliographie de la France*.[71]
>
> But one must know that *Le Bottin* has appeared in 1933 even though it does not appear in *La Bibliographie*. Such and such a novel which is known to have run into 200 editions has, in fact, run into 20 and appears only once. Finally, the separate reprints from medical journals which in 1924 contributed two to three hundred titles now bring in more than 3,000 with the law of 1925, and these are not included, justifying thus the 'decline of research' as established by international statistics.
>
> Who does not see that next to the *Bibliographie de la France*...there is a place for a general bibliography, which will be better protected from commercial needs, complete and so to say immediate. It is by centralizing legal deposit, that the *Bibliothèque Nationale* would be the only competent

> institution to establish it as it alone has the means to compile it. What the *Bibliothèque Nationale* needs, to make it work easily, is a small organization.
>
> And what about the abstracting of periodicals? The law of legal deposit for periodicals which underhand manoeuvres of librarians had deferred will be in force in some months' time. The *Bibliothèque Nationale* will have enough staff to open the largest periodicals room possible and will be in a position to lend many thousands as soon as they appear."[72]

Thus, the reorganization of the legal deposit law is regulated by the law of May 19, 1925. This requires the deposit of books, brochures, prints, engravings, photographs, cinematographic and musical works, and commercial catalogues. Invitation cards and similar materials called "bilboquets" are excluded. Two copies must be submitted (special rules apply to *de luxe* editions and prints before sales and circulation).

The *Régie du Dépôt Légal* was organized by the decree of November 1925, and stipulated that copies should be sent to an agent in Paris and to agents or delegates in the provinces. In Paris, the copies were deposited at the Ministry of the Interior for Paris which held an office outside of Paris.[73]

In 1926, the Réunion des Bibliothèques de Paris grouped the national institutions into one body. These were the Bibliothèque Nationale, the Nasarine, Sainte Geneviève, and l'Arsenal.[74] This merging had been able to unify the regulations and methods of administration so as to better control the purchase of books and to promote legal deposit by the setting up of a Comité Consultatif du Dépôt Légal.[75]

In the same year, Morel became involved in the American Library Association's fiftieth anniversary conference. He had to attend this conference because M. Roland Marcel, the chief librarian of the French Library Association, gave up the trip to the United States of America. Morel represented the Association des Bibliothécaires Français and wrote to Miss Bogle in a letter dated September 7, 1926, that he would arrive in New York on Wednesday, September 29. He also informed his correspondent that L'Alliance France has asked him to organize several lectures, including one of his personal memories of the period 1880-1900 (Goncourt, Le Grenier, Théatre Libre, A. Daudet, Jules Verne etc.). He also wanted to stop in Washington to visit the Bureau of Copyright, as he wanted to see enforced in France the newly reformed legal deposit law of May 1925.[76]

Back from the United States of America, Morel started working on a voluminous article on copyright. In August 1927, the *Mercure de France* published his *"Le Domaine Public Payant,"* which Morel produced as an ambitious contribution to this journal for which he had been writing since the early 1900s. In this article, Morel did not only explain the difficulty of enforcing the law regarding copyright but also stressed the many disadvantages that playwrights and other writers were faced with.[77]

He also wrote about his activities and his involvement with the reform of legal deposit as well as about the opposition he met with when he had to campaign for the law to be reformed.

> I have fought for twelve years for the reform of legal deposit which has at last been voted but benefits up to now the only institution which has opposed it most—the Bibliothèque Nationale—which reaps all its advantages. I had to fight great opposition, but the core of the matter had hardly been discussed or even examined by some persons. All the obstacles came from considerations of facts which did not concern the law but the details of its application—personnel, mode of delivery, control etc.[78]

He presented *"Le Domaine Public Payant"* to the reader as:

> The whole of the works which one can make use of without special authorization, but for a fee. This fee can be fixed or can be proportional, but it must be equal for everybody. The English compulsory licence is but a variant. The *Domaine* which can be extended to a more or less big number of works may vary in type of work and duration... When does it start? When does it end? To what does it apply? Does it include rare or foreign works? Does it cover all forms of art? Whom does it benefit? Is it a privilege for the author and his descendants? Does it make the state responsible for moral right?[79]

> A century ago, the Domaine Public Payant was nearly set up in France. The extra-parliamentary Commission responsible for studying the law on literary property held 18 meetings from December 21, 1825 to May 6, 1826, a third of which were devoted to the *Domaine Public Payant.*"[80]

> The Legal Deposit, with a statement of the number of copies printed for books, existed but was no longer enforced. It is being revived again since the law of 1925.[81]

Finally, Morel, in talking about the Domaine Public Payant, wanted to emphasize that if France wanted to improve her libraries and put into force the newly reformed legal deposit, she had to do what Belgium had been doing since 1921:

> Subscriptions, official books with which libraries without readers, at times without librarians, and which are hardly ever open, are cluttered... If we need a bill, a method, let us use as a model the existing *Lois Destrée*, which in Belgium has laid the foundation of an intellectual Renaissance. It provides aid to only those towns which make an effort...[82]

He was very concerned with defining the proper aims and scope of legal deposit and its relationship with the Domaine Public Payant. He took the view that, in general, legal deposit was the best means of ensuring the recording and conservation of national material. But he recognized the advisability in certain cases, of adopting methods of acquiring national publications. These included arrangements with publishers' associations, writers organizations such as La Société des Gens de Lettres, and other methods.[83]

Jean Cordey, librarian in charge of the *service étranger* at the Bibliothèque Nationale, at the Congrès International des Bibliothécaires et des Amis du Livre, held in Prague from June 29th to July 3rd, 1926, had this to say about the legal deposit law of 1925:

> The large national libraries have grown and continue to grow mostly through legal deposit in two copies...By virtue of the law of May 27, 1925, which has reorganized this deposit, one of the two copies is deposited by the printer, the other by the publisher; these are centralized at the *Bibliothèque Nationale*, which keeps one and distributes the other, dependning on the subject it deals with, among the *Bibliothèque de l'Arsenal, La Bibliothèque Ste. Geneviève,* and certain other institutions...[84]

Cordey's remarks summarized Morel's concept of the reform of legal deposit. Morel had achieved in using it for the preparation of national and specialist bibliographies.

Most of Morel's concept of reform became a reality. A brief summary of these will embrace the following points:

(1) The desirability of drawing up a model law to specify Morel's basic concepts of legal deposit, its reorganization and procedure;
(2) the possibility of having a single authority responsible for compulsory deposit—centralization of service at the *Bibliothèque Nationale:*
(3) to determine on as wide a basis as possible the material to be deposited;
(4) to set up autonomous national agencies to be responsible for organizing and supervising legal deposit, imposing penalties for non-compliance and distributing the publications received;
(5) to standardize as far as possible the number of copies to be deposited, reducing it to the minimum necessary;
(6) to recommend practical measures for operating and regulating the legal deposit services, so as to ensure maximum efficiency, which Morel emphasized was of the utmost importance.

There is no doubt that present day librarians in France still feel the influence of Morel and his work. In his writings on the profession, in his criticism of French librarianship and French library history itself, he set examples which even now still have a living force.

On the whole, his work has many aspects of great consequence. His theories of public librarianship, his work of reform, his training of librarians show a high degree of expertise. Among his achievements were the Bibliothèque de Levallois Perret; the municipal libraries of Paris during their reorganization period; the first children's libraries in France; and the reform of the legal deposit law.

Apart from his writings on librarianship, he tried his hand at literary criticism and made himself a name as a novelist, playwright, and poet. It is unfortunate that his name does not appear in the French Dictionary of National Biography as a pioneer of public libraries, or in a history of French literature.

Fine tribute to his literary and library work was paid to him two months after his death in *La Revue du Livre* of April 1924, by Ernest Coyecque[85] and the Groliers[86] respectively.

One month later, Seymour de Ricci, who wrote *Le Problèms des Bibliothèques Françaises: petit manuel pratique de Bibliothécomie*[87] in 1933, paid the following tribute to Morel in *Beaux Arts*, 1934:

> The premature death of Eugène Morel at the age of sixty-four has grievously moved all his friends of the *Bibliothèque Nationale*. A talented literary man, gifted with a versatile and inventive mind, he had a long standing interest in the ingenious endeavors made in Belgium and in France to produce multiple copies of books, as well as prints, through the process of microphotographic file.
>
> Reorganizer and indefatigable 'animateur' of legal deposit, he managed to get regularly in the *Bibliothèque Nationale* a great number of *de luxe* publications, which printers and publishing houses forgot too often to deposit. All readers of books on the arts and all historians of contemporary illustration owe him in his own right, a real gratitude.[88]

One year later, Alphonse Seche, a correspondent of the *Revue D'Art Dramatique*, wrote in *Dans la melée littéraire*, 1935, the following obituary which dealt mostly with Morel's literary talents:

> Eugène Morel remained my friend. Born in 1869, he died in February 1934 at sixty-five. Physically, he was a strong man. He was a highly cultured man and had a great intellectual curiosity. Literarily, he did not occupy the place that he deserved. The young generation did not know

him. It would have benefited considerably if it had known him. Many writers of my generation knew the same fate. Before the "charcheurs littéraires" who came after the war, they had found new formulas. It was the case of Eugène Morel.

He had a stroke of luck one day. Questioned on French Literature, Tolstoi, one day, described Morel as one of the most original novelists of the time. Immediately, the author of *Les Morfondus, La Rouille du Sabre*, became famous. But Paris consumes an incredible number of celebrities. What ingenuity, enthusiasm, and constancy one must show in order to keep a fame which has been won with so great difficulty.

For the past fifteen years, how many young writers have we not seen being born. Who can tell you their name! In literature, as in all the arts, it is enough to have a little talent to make a good start. But the winner is judged at the finishing line. He who is popular at his start, may disappear into complete oblivion twenty or thirty years later.

Eugène Morel was blamed for seeming reluctant to follow his literary destiny. For years he did not publish anything. He was successful in the theater and in the bookshop, but he did not make the most of it. Would a 'young writer of less than thirty' write *La Parfaite Maraichère*, one would proclaim him a prodigy. It is only fair that this small novel should be made known to the public one day. However unknown it is to the public, it is an authentic masterpiece. It is followed and completed with small poems in prose of an exquisite fantasy and unforeseen and charming imagination.[89]

# NOTES

## Chapter One: The Early Years

1. Polnay, Peter de. Aspects of Paris. London: W.H. Allen, 1968 p. 96.
2. Benedetti, J. Le Marais au 19e siècle. (In Prefecture de la Seine. Le Quartier du Marais. Paris: Imp. Municipale, 1960, p.17.)
3. Ibid., p. 18.
4. Polnay, op.cit., p.16.
5. Benedetti, op.cit., p.19.
6. Ibid,, p. 20.
7. Daudet, Alphonse. Desirée quoted In Benedetti. Op.cit., p. 18.
8. Daudet, Alphonse. Les Contes du Lundi. (1873) quoted In Benedetti. Ibid.
9. Balzac, quoted In Rudorff, R. Belle Epoque: Paris in the Nineties. London: H. Hamilton, 1972. p. 36.
10. Rudorff, op.cit., p.36.
11. Benedetti, op.cit., p.19.
12. Information from Mlle, Marguerite Gruny, Morel's niece.
13. Ibid.
14. Information concerning E. Morel's ancestry and parentage from Mlle. M. Gruny.
15. Rudorff, op.cit., p. 36.
16. Ibid.
17. Letter from E. Morel to A. Salason, 15.2.1876.
18. Seguin, J.P. Regards sur le passé. Les Enfants et les Livres, (numéro special de l'Education Nationale) novembre 1952, p. 7.
19. Grand Larousse Encyclopedique, vol. 6, p. 879.
20. Letter from E. Morel to Frederic Morel, (?) July 1882.
21. Letter from F. Morel to E. Morel, (?) July 1884.
22. Grand Larousse Encyclopedique, vol. 6, p. 879.
23. Oxford Companion to Art. p. 146.
24. Oxford Companion to French Literature, p. 335.
25. Ibid., p. 678.
26. Girard, Georges. Notes bio-bibliographiques: Eugène Morel. *Bulletin de la Maison du Livre Français*, 5e année, no. 64, 1er avril 1924, p. 884.
27. Ibid.
28. Oxford Companion to French Literature, p. 198.
29. Larousse Literature Français, vol. 2, p. 184.
30. Rudorff, op. cit. Preface, p. 13.

| | |
|---|---|
| 31 | Morel, E. Jules Verne, *La Nouvelle Revue*, vol. 33, 1905, p. 440. |
| 32 | Ibid., p. 443. |
| 33 | Letters from F. Morel to E. Morel, 12.1.1884, (?) July 1884. |
| 34 | Dictionary of National Biography, 1922-30. p. 120. |
| 35 | Ibid. |
| 36 | Letter from E. Morel to A. Salanson, 15.2.1876, Letters from A. Salanson to F. Morel, 24.3.1882; (?) July 1882. |
| 37 | Morel, E. Jules Verne, op.cit., p. 443-44. |
| 38 | Girard, op.cit., p. 884. |
| 39 | Curriculum vitae: Bibliothèque Nationale, probably dated 1926, relating to E. Morel's activities in libraries. |

Chapter Two: The Making of a Librarian: 1892-1900

| | |
|---|---|
| 1 | Information from Mlle. M. Gruny and Morel's family. |
| 2 | Information from La Bibliothèque Nationale through Mlle. M. Gruny |
| 3 | Rudorff, R. Belle Epoque: Paris in the Nineties. London: H. Hamilton, 1972. p. 229. |
| 4 | Ibid., p.235. |
| 5 | Morel, E. Léon Cladel. *Revue Blanche*, vol. 3, 1892, pp. 73-84. |
| 6 | Morel, E. Pour nos glories. *Revue Blanche*, vol. 6, 1894, pp. 431-38. |
| 7 | Panizzi Papers. Letter from Forshall to Panizzi., 24.1.1839, quoted in Munford, W.A. Edward Edwards, p. 31. |
| 8 | Munford, W.A. Edward Edwards. London: Library Association, 1963, pp.47-48. |
| 9 | La situation des bibliothécaires, 1ère année, no.4, juillet-sout 1907, p. 82. |
| 10 | Ibid., pp. 82-83. |
| 11 | Information given by La Bibliothèque Nationale and Morel's children. |
| 12 | La situation des bibliothécaires. Op.cit. ibid. |
| 13 | Marcel, H. La Bibliothèque Nationale. Paris: Laurens, 1907. p. 26. |
| 14 | La situation des bibliothécaires. Op.cit.ibid. |
| 15 | Ibid. |
| 16 | Faye's preliminary report quoted in La situation des Bibliothécaires. Op.cit., p.83. |
| 17 | Information from Mlle. M. Gruny and Morel's family. |
| 18 | Information from La Biblithèque Nationale through Mlle. M. Gruny. |
| 19 | Koch, T.W. Bibliothèque Nationale: history, organization and administration. *Library Journal*, vol. 39, 1914, p. 429. |
| 20 | Ledos, E.G. M. Leopold Delisle et la Bibliothèque nationale. *Revue des Bibliothèques*, vol. 34, no. 12, 1924, p. 116. |

# NOTES

21  Pellisson, M. Les Bibliothèques populaires à l'étranger et en France. Paris: Imp. Nationale, 1906. p. 215.
22  Delisle, L. Souvenirs de jeunesse. (translated) *The Library* (new series), vol. 9, 1908, p. 210.
23  Ibid.
24  Le Prince – published in 18th century (about preservation of manuscripts.) Paris, 1782.
25  Delisle, op.cit. ibid.
26  Langlois, Ch.V. La reforme des bibliothèques en France. *Bibliothèque de l'Ecole des Chartes,* novembre-decembre 1905, p. 751.
27  Ibid.
28  Ibid., p. 752.
29  Piper, A.C. Training for librarians in France. *Library World,* vol.12, 1910, p. 421.
30  Glenn, F.H. Technical training in librarianship in England and abroad. *Library Association Record,* vol. 12, 1910, p. 120.
31  Ibid., p. 122.
32  Piper, op.cit., p.421.
33  Ibid., pp. 421-422.
34  Morel, E. *La Librairie Publique.* Paris: A. Colin, 1910. p. 316.
35  Gruny, M. Eugène Morel et les bibliothèques pour enfants. *Bulletin d'Analyses de Livres Pour Enfants,* no. 17, septembre-décembre 1969, p. 24.
36  Morel, op.cit., p. 316.
37  Ibid.
38  Gruny, op.cit., p. 24.
39  Ibid., p. 21.
40  Girard, Georges. Eugène Morel: notes bio-bibliographiques. *Bulletin de la Maison du Livre Francçais,* 5th année, no. 64, 1er avril 1924, p. 884.
41  Letter from F Morel to E. Morel, 24.3.1884: Letter from E. Morel to F. Morel, (?) July 1884.
42  Morel, op.cit., p. 29.
43  Ibid.
44  These were the Bibliothèque Arsenal, the Nasarine and the Sainte Geneviève.
45  Langlois, Ch.V. (Reforme des Bibliothèques en France); 1st letter to *Le Temps,* 27 décembre 1905.
46  Morel, op.cit., p.29.
47  Ibid.
48  Morel's letters to F. Morel in 1884.
49  Grolier, G. & Grolier E. L'oeuvre d'Eugène Morel. *Revue du Livre,* 2nd année, no. 8, avril 1934, p. 144.
50  Morel, E. La Librairie Publique, op.cit., p.29.

51  Ibid.
52  Ibid.
53  Ibid., p. 316.
54  Gautier, Jean. Nos bibliothèques publiques. 2nd rev. ed. Paris: Librairie Chevalier & Rivière, 1903. pp. 175-177.
55  Clavie, Marcel. La reorganization de la lecture publique en France. Paris: La Pensée Francaise, 1924, p. 39.
56  Morel, op.cit., p. 14.
57  Thoraval, J. Les grandes étapes de la civilization francaise. Paris: Bordas, 1969. p. 484.
58  Oxford Companion to the Theatre. 3rd ed. 1967. p. 31.
59  Morel, op.cit., p. 15.
60  Morel, E. Mounet-Sully. *Mercure de France,* vol. 114, 1916, p. 647.
61  Ibid.
62  Ibid. p., 635.
63  Ibid. p., 636.
64  Rolland, R. Oxford Companion to French Literature.
65  Morel, E. Advertissement (In Association des Bibliothécaires Français. Bibliothèques, Livres et Librairies. Paris: M. Rivière, 1912. Préface, v.
66  Crosland, M. Colette ou la difficulté d'aimer. Paris: A. Michel, 1973, p. 71.
67  Girard, op.cit., p. 884.
68  Ibid.
69  Antoine, A. (In Oxford Companion to the Theatre. 3rd ed., p. 31, 1967.)
70  Girard, op.cit., ibid.
71  Guignol. (In Oxford Companion to the Theatre, p. 420.)
72  Morel's own handwritten list of novels and plays.
73  Girard, op.cit., ibid.
74  Ibid.
75  Coppee, F. (In Dictionary of Modern European Literature. London: Oxford University Press, 1947, pp. 172-173.)
76  Koch, op.cit., pp. 339-350, 419-430.
77  Macfarlane, J. The national libraries of Great Britain and France, and their catalogues. *The Library* (First Series), vol. 10, 1898, p. 37.
78  Ibid.
79  Masson, A. & Salvan, P. Les bibliothèques. Paris: Presses Universitaires de France, 1963, p. 21.
80  Ibid., p. 49.
81  Macfarlane, op.cit., ibid.
82  Masson, A. op.cit., ibid.
83  Ledos, op. cit., p. 145.

# NOTES

84  Masson, A. op.cit., ibid.
85  Ledos, op.cit., ibid.
86  Ibid.
87  Rudorff, op.cit., p. 237.
88  Ibid., p. 235.
89  Ibid., p. 237.
90  Girard, op.cit., ibid.
91  Ibid.
92  Ibid.
93  Funk and Wagnalls. New Standard Encyclopaedia of useful knowledge. London, 1931. Vol. 23. Transvaal, p. 506.
94  Morel's handwritten list of magazines and journals to which he contributed.
95  Girard, op.cit., ibid.
96  Morel's handwritten list of novels.
97  Morel, E. La Prisonnière. Paris: Flammarion, 1900. 295p.
98  Morel, E. La Prisonnière. *La Nouvelle Revue*, vol. 4 &6, 1900.
99  La situation des bibliothèques, op.cit., ibid.
100 Ibid.
101 Morel, E. Les bibliothèques: essai sur le développement des blibliothèques publiques et de la librairie dans les deux mondes. Paris: Mercure de France, 1908. vol. 1, p. 17.
102 Ibid.
103 Ariête: Direction de la Bibliothèque Nationale: 1.3.1900.
104 Ibid.
105 Ibid.
106 Morel, E. Le Congrès de l'Art Théatral. *Revue d'Art Dramatique*, Septembre 1900, p. 770.
107 Rudorff, op.cit., p.229.
108 Morel's handwritten list of contributions to magazines.
109 Morel, E. Projet de théaters populaires. Paris: Ollendorff, 1900. 78p.
110 Morel, E. Le Congrès de l'Art Théatral, op.cit., p. 777.
111 Ibid.
112 Girard, op.cit., ibid.
113 Ibid.
114 Morel, E. Mounet-Sully, op.cit., p. 645.
115 Henriot, G. France. (In Bostwick, A.E. Popular libraries of the world. Chicago: American Library Association, 1933. p. 100.)
116 Morel, E. Les bibliothèques..., op.cit., p. 162.
117 Edwards, Edward. Freetown libraries. London: Trubner, 1869, p. 221.
118 Morel, E. La Librairie Publique, op.cit., pp. 177-178.
119 Henriot, op.cit., p. 101.

| | |
|---|---|
| 120 | Munford, W.A. Edward Edwards. (1812-86). Portrait of a Librarian. London: Library Association, 1963. p. 77. |
| 121 | Great Britain. *Parliament.* Select Committee on Public Libraries. Report from the Select Committee on Public Libraries. July 23, 1849. 1st ed. New impression. London: Cass, 1968. (Facsimile reprint of 1st ed. London, ordered by the House of Commons to be printed, 1849). Appendix III. |
| 122 | Grolier, op.cit., p. 144. |
| 123 | Bouvy, M. A review of J. Hassenforders book: Developpement compare des bibliothèques publiques en France, en Grande Bretagne et Etats Unis…1850-1914. Paris: Cercle de la Librairie, 1967. *Bulletin de Documentation Bibliographique: Analyses no. 2180.* (In *Bulletin des Bibliothèques de France, 14th année, no. 9-10, septembre-octobre,* 1969, p. 768.) |
| 124 | Gaussen, F. Des bibliothèques sans lecteurs. *Le Monde,* August 1, 1967. July 29, July 30 and August 1, 1967. |
| 125 | Bouvy, op.cit., ibid. |
| 126 | Ibid., p. 767. |
| 127 | Pellisson, op.cit., p. 154. |
| 128 | Bouvy, op.cit., pp. 767-768. |
| 129 | Edwards, E. Public Libraries in London and Paris. *British Quarterly Review,* August 1847, p. 114. |
| 130 | Morel, E. La Librairie Publique, op.cit., p. 13. |
| 131 | Ibid., p. 4. |
| 132 | Ibid., p. 13. |
| 133 | Ibid. |
| 134 | Ibid., p. 14. |
| 135 | Hassenforder, J. Histoire d'une tentative pour la promotion des bibliothèques populaires : La Société Franklin. *Education et Bibliothèques,* no. 6, mars 1963, p. 34. |
| 136 | Ibid., p. 27. |
| 137 | Bouvy, op.cit., p. 768. |
| 138 | Ibid., p. 767. |
| 139 | Chevalley, H. Education populaire des adultes en Angleterre, Notices sur les principales institutions. Paris: Hachette, 1896. pp. xxiv & xxv. |
| 140 | Keogh, A. English and American Libraries: a comparison, *Public Libraries,* July 1901, p. 388. |
| 141 | Edwards, E. quoted in Minto, J. A history of the public library movement in Great Britain and Ireland. London: Allen & Unwin, 1932. p. 50. |
| 142 | Langlois, Ch. V. Programme du bulletin. *Bulletin des Bibliothèques Populaires,* janvier-fevrier, 1906, p. 13. |
| 143 | Morel, E. La Librairie Publique, op.cit., p. 189. |

NOTES                                                                201

144    Pellisson, op.cit., p. 173.
145    Morel, E. Les Bibliothèques, vol. 1. op.cit., p. 17.
146    Morel, ibid., p. 162.
147    Ibid., p. 19.
148    Grolier, op.cit., p. 144.


Chapter Three: Moving Spirits in the French Library Movement

1      Macfarlane, J. The confiscated libraries in the French Revolution. *The Library,* vol. 8, 1896, p. 102.
2      Henriot, Gabriel. France. (In Bestwick, Arthur E. Popular Libraries of the world. Chicago: American Library Association, 1933, p. 100.)
3      Gautier, Jean. Nos bibliothèques: leur situation légale, 2$^{nd}$ rev. ed. Paris: Librairie Chevalier & Rivière, 1903. p. 20.
4      Henriot, op.cit., ibid.
5      Pellisson, Maurice. Les bibliothèques populaires à l'etranger et en France. Paris: Imprimerie Nationale, 1906, p. 146.
6      Ibid., p. 149.
7      Henriot, op.cit., p. 100.
8      Pellisson, op.cit., p. 149.
9      Philipon de la Madeleine. *Nouvelle Biographie Générale.* Paris: Firmin Didot, 1865. vol. 39, p. 850.
10     Gautier, op.cit., p. 29.
11     Naudé, Gabriel quoted in Smith. G. Gabriel Naudé: a librarian of the seventeenth century. *Library Association Record,* vol. 1, July 1899, pp. 425-426.
12     Ibid., p. 426.
13     Smith, G. G. Gabriel Naudé: a librarian of the seventeenth century. *Library Association Record,* vol. 1, July 1899, p. 426.
14     Philipon de la Madeleine, op.cit., pp. 850-851.
15     Pellisson, op.cit., p. 146.
16     Marcel, Thomas. Les bibliothèques. *Tendances,* no. 24, aeut 1963, p. 8
17     Ibid.
18     Guizot, P.F.G. (In Great Britain. *Parliament.* Select Committee on Public Libraries. Report from the Select Committee on Public Libraries, 23 July 1849. 1$^{st}$ ed. (new impression). London: Cass, 1968, pp. 36-44.
19     Ibid.
20     Pellisson, op.cit., p. 170.
21     Saint-Albin, Emm. de. Les bibliothèques municipals de la ville de Paris. Paris: Benger Levrault, 1896. p. 100.

| | |
|---|---|
| 22 | Pellisson, op.cit., p. 171. |
| 23 | Ibid., p. 198. |
| 24 | Ibid., p. 199. |
| 25 | Le Robert. Dictionnaire Universel des Noms Propres. Paris: S.N.L., 1974. p. 218. |
| 26 | Salvandy, Narcisse Achille de. Minister of Public Instruction. Circular of April 14, 1838. |
| 27 | Nouvelle Biographic Universelle. Paris: Firmin Didot, 1882. vol. 41, p. 719. |
| 28 | Gautier, op.cit., p. 38; pp. 125-126. |
| 29 | Ibid. |
| 30 | Delessert, François Marie. Chambre des Députés. Session de 1836. Comments of F. M. Delessert... on the budget of *L'Instruction Publique* (sitting of May 31st, 1836) Paris: Firmin Didot, n.d. p. 1. |
| 31 | Larousse du XXe Siécle. Paris: Librairie Larousse, 1928. vol. 1, p. 397. |
| 32 | Carnot, H. Le Ministère de l'Instruction Publique et des cultes depuis le 24 fevrier jusqu'au 5 juillet 1848. Paris: 1848. |
| 33 | Ibid. |
| 34 | Pellison, op.cit., p. 158. |
| 35 | Carnot, op.cit. |
| 36 | Duruy, Victor. Grand Larousse Encyclopédique. Paris: Librairie Larousse, 1961. vol. 4, p. 286. |
| 37 | Larousse du XXe Siècle. op.cit., vol. 6, 1933, p. 123. |
| 38 | Ibid. |
| 39 | Macé, Jean. Les origins de la Ligue de l'Enseignement. Paris: 1891. p. 59. |
| 40 | Macé, Jean. Grand Larousse Encyclopédique, op.cit., p. 934. |
| 41 | Larousse du XXe Siècle. op.cit., p. 455. |
| 42 | Berenger, Henry. L'éducation du people en France et en Angleterre. *Revue de Paris,* 15 septembre 1897, p. 268. |
| 43 | Ferry, Jules. Discours et opinions, publiés par Paul Robiquet. Tome IV. Paris: Colin, 1896. |
| 44 | Pellisson, op.cit., p. 178. |
| 45 | Ibid., p. 165. |
| 46 | Ibid., pp. 193-196. |
| 47 | Nortet, Charles. Public libraries of France, national, communal and university. *Library Association Record,* September 1925, pp. 150-151. |
| 48 | Ibid. |
| 49 | *Library World,* vol. 1, no. 7, January 1899, p. 121. |
| 50 | Arreté du ler juin 1862. Ministère de l'Instruction Publique. |
| 51 | Henriot, op.cit., p. 101. |
| 52 | Ibid. |

# NOTES

| | |
|---|---|
| 53 | Hassenforder, Jean. Histoire d'une tentative pour la promotion des bibliothèques populaires: La Société Franklin. *Education et Bibliothèques,* mars 1963, no. 6, p. 25. |
| 54 | Ibid., pp. 21-36. |
| 55 | Macé, Jean. Morale en action. Paris: Hetzel, 1865. pp. 18, 19, 71, 72. |
| 56 | Annuaire Encyclopédique. Paris: 1866. |
| 57 | Hassenforder, op.cit., p. 33. |
| 58 | J.H.P. Libraries in France. *Public Libraries,* 1904. p. 403. |
| 59 | Bowerman, George F. Municipal popular libraries of Paris. *Public Libraries,* vol. 12, 1907, p. 396. |
| 60 | Morel, E. La Librairie Publique en Angleterre et aux Etats Unis. (In Bibliothèques, Livres et Librairies. Paris: Marcel Rivière, 1912, p. 201.) |
| 61 | Ibid., p. 209. |
| 62 | Pellisson, op.cit., p. 197. |
| 63 | Ibid., pp. 198-199. |
| 64 | Ibid. |
| 65 | Ibid., pp. 199-201. |
| 66 | Ibid., p. 198-199. |
| 67 | Ibid., p. 199. |
| 68 | Morel, op.cit., pp. 197-220. |
| 69 | Brown, J.D. Guide to Librarianship. London: Librace, 1909. p. 89. |
| 70 | Official statistics published in 1902. Interpretations of Morel & Pellisson. (In Hassenforder, Jean. Développement compare des bibliothèques publiques en France, en Grande Bretagne et aux Etats Unis dans la seconde moitié du XIXe siècle; 1850-1914. Paris: Cercle de la Librairie, 1966. p.79.) |
| 71 | Hassenforder, Jean. Développement compare des bibliothèques publiques en France, en Grande Bretagne et aux Etats Unis dans la seconde moitié du XIXe siècle; 1850-1914. Paris: Cercle de la Librairie, 1966. p.69.) |
| 72 | Gaussen, Frederic. Des bibliothèques sans lecteurs. *Le Monde,* 29 July, 30 July and August 1, 1967. |
| 73 | Saint-Albin, op. cit., ibid. |
| 74 | Langlois, Ch. V. Programme du bulletin. *Bulletin des Bibliothèques Populaires,* janvier-fevrier, 1906. p. 13. |
| 75 | Ibid. |
| 76 | Chevalley, M.A. *Manuel Général de l'Instruction Primaire,* 29 octobre, 1898. |
| 77 | Pellisson, op.cit., (footnote), pp. 216-217. |
| 78 | Ibid., footnote, p. 217. |
| 79 | Association des Bibliothécaires Français. 1906-1956: Manifestations du cinquantenaire. (20 et 21 novembre 1956), compte rendu, texts des |

80    communications suivi de l'annuaire des Membres de l'Association. Paris: 1957. p. 18.

80    Michel, Henri. Les bibliothèques municipals (In *Associaton des Bibliothécaires Français*. Bibliothèques, Livres et Libraires. Paris: Riviere, 1912. p. 138.)

81    Girand-Mangin. Les Bibliothèques municipals devant l'opinion. *Bulletin de l'Association des Bibliothécaires Français.* Janvier-avril 1912, p. 17.

Chapter Four: Morel and Library Education

1    Pinto, Elena. L'éducation professionnelle des bibliothécaires. *Revue des Bibliothèques,* 1er trimester 1933-1934, p. 51.

2    Ibid.

3    Ibid.

4    Rider, Fremont. Melvil Dewey. Chicago: American Library Association, 1944, 152p. (American).

5    Masson, A. Les Bibliothèques. Paris: P.V.P., 1963. (Que sais-je? No. 944) pp. 48-49.

6    *Bulletin de l'Association des Bibliothécaires Français,* vol. 6, 1912, p. 30.

7    Ibid.

8    Morel's curriculum vitae at the Bibliothèque Nationale. See Appendix C.

9    Bulletin...Français, op.cit., p. 38.

10    Morel, E. Municipal libraries for France, vol. 14, 1911, pp. 109-111.

11    Muhlenfeld, O. The library schools of the Continent. *Library Assistant,* vol. 13, 1913, p. 158.

12    Chronique. Conferences sur les Bibliothèques Modernes. *Bulletin de l'Association des Bibliothécaires Français,* vol. 4, 1910, p. 37.

13    Ibid., pp. 37-38.

14    Girard, G. Notes bio-bibliographiques: Eugène Morel. *Bulletin de la Maison du Livre,* 5e année, no. 64, 1er avril 1924, p. 886.

15    Morel, E. Avertissement. (In Association des Bibliothécaires Français. Bibliothèques, Livres et Librairies.) Paris: Marcel Rivière, 1912, Preface V.

16    French public libraries. *Library World,* vol. 13, 1911, pp. 306-308.

17    Ibid.

18    Grolier, G & Grolier E. de. L'Oeuvre d'Eugène Morel. *Revue du Livre,* 2e année, no. 6, avril 1934, p. 144.

19    Association des Bibliothécaires Français. Bibliothèques, Livres et Librairies, Paris: Marcel Rivière, 1912. 278p.

20    Grolier, op. cit., pp. 144-145.

NOTES

21 Morel. Avertissement, op.cit., pp. i-vi.
22 Ibid.
23 Ibid.
24 Coyecque, Ernest. Un grand bibliothécaire français: Eugène Morel. (1869-1934). *Revue du Livre*. 2e année, no. 6, avril 1934, p. 143.
25 Caillet, Maurice. Inspection des bibliothèques de la ville de Paris et du Département de la Seine. *Bulletin des Bibliothèques de France*. 16e année. No. 3, mars 1971, p. 156.
26 Grolier, pp. 144-145.
27 Ibid., p. 146.
28 Coyecque, op.cit., ibid.
29 Pinto, op. cit., ibid.
30 Curriculum vitae partial relative aux activités d'Eugène Morel touchant les bibliothèques. See Appendix C.
31 Ibid.
32 Association des Bibliothécaires Français, op.cit., iv, 183p.
33 Publications nouvelles concernant les bibliothèques Françaises en 1912. Rapport présenté à l'Assemblée générale de l'Association des Bibliothécaires Français du 30 mars 1913 (*In Bulletin de l'Association des Bibliothécaires Français*, janvier-février 1913, p. 46.)
34 Association des Bibliothécaires Français, op.cit., Preface.
35 Vidier, A. Rapport présenté par A. Vidier à l'Assemblée Générale de l'Association des Bibliothécaires Français du 30 mars 1913. *Bulletin de l'Association des Bibliothécaires Français*, janvier-février, 1913, pp. 45-46.
36 Chronique: Ecole des Hautes Etudes Sociales (1911-1912). Les Bibliothèques Modernes (2e année, vol. 5, 1911), p. 36.
37 French Librarians Association Library Course. *The Library Journal*, December 1912, p. 684.
38 *Bulletin de l'Association des Bibliothécaires Français*, vol. 8, juillet-décembre 1914, p. 90.
39 In fact at a meeting of the French Library Association on May 21, 1915, Morel examined the question of restarting his lectures, on the *Bibliothèques Modernes* which were suspended during the period 1914-1915 because of the first World War (In Séances du Comité: Service au 21 mai 1915. *Bulletin de l'Association des Bibliothécaires Français*, vol. 9, 1915, p. 63.)
40 *Bulletin de l'Association des Bibliothécaires Français*. Vol. 9. 1915, p. 36.
41 Ibid.
42 Muhlenfeld, op.cit., ibid.
43 Ibid.
44 The Easter Excursion. *Library Assistant*, vol. 16, no. 296, May 1923, p. 265.

| | |
|---|---|
| 45 | Ibid. |
| 46 | Ramsden, Michael. Hisstory of A.A.L., 1895-1945. London: A.A.L., 1973. p. 77. |
| 47 | Ibid., pp. 77-78/ |
| 48 | Library cooperation with other countries. *Bulletin of American Library Association*, vol. 16, 1922, p. 194. |
| 49 | Ramsden, op.cit., ibid. |
| 50 | Library Assistants´Association. Minute Book, 1910-1914. p. 148. |
| 51 | Certificate issued by the British Library Assistants' Association on December 16, 1913. See Appendix B. |
| 52 | Bogle, Sarah C.N. Library development in France. *Library Occurent*, vol. 7, 1924, p. 14. |
| 53 | Leavitt, Maria V. Some French libraries as seen by a goodwill delegate. *Library Journal*, vol. 48, 1923. p. 866. |
| 54 | Ibid. |
| 55 | Bogle, op.cit., ibid. |
| 56 | Ibid., pp. 13-14. |
| 57 | Ibid., p. 14. |
| 58 | Gruny, M. Un pionnier des bibliothèques: Ernest Coyecque. *Bulletin d'Information de l'Association des Bibliothécaires Français*, no. 13, mars 1954, p. 11. |
| 59 | Bogle, op.cit., ibid. |
| 60 | Morel, E. Le Bibliophote. (*In Bulletin de l'Association des Bibliothécaires Français*, vol. 5, 1911, pp. 66-68.) |
| 61 | Henriot, Gabriel. *L'Association des Bibliothécaires Français.* Un bilan de vingt ans (1906-1926). *Revue des Bibliothèques* vol. 34, no. 9, 1926, p. 109. |
| 62 | Leavitt, op.cit., ibid. |
| 63 | Bogle, op.cit., ibid. |
| 64 | Coyecque, Ernest. L'Oeuvre Française d'une bibliothécaire Américaine: Miss Jessie Carson. *Revue des Bibliothèques*, vol. 34, 1924, pp. 257-270. |
| 65 | Information from Miss M. Gruny, Morel's niece. |
| 66 | Ibid. |
| 67 | Bogle, op.cit., p. 13. |
| 68 | Carson, Jessie. Report on the Sub-Committee on Children's Work. – being a report to the American Committee for Devastated France, covering the year April, 1921 to April 1922. *Bulletin of the American Library Association*, vol. 16, 1922, p. 200. Information also given by Miss M. Gruny. |
| 69 | L'Oeuvre, November 11, 1924. |
| 70 | Information culled from personal correspondence with Miss M. Gruny who became the librarian of the Junior Library, *L'Heure JoyeuseI* in |

NOTES

Paris. This library was offered to the City of Paris in 1924 by the New York Committee for Children's Libraries.
71 Carson, op.cit., p. 203.
72 Ibid.
73 Ibid., pp. 200-204.
74 Moore, A.C. Annual Report to the American Committee for Devastated France. *Bulletin of the American Library Association.* Vol. 16, 1922, p. 204.
75 Ibid.
76 Carson, op.cit., p. 203.
77 Coyecque, op.cit., p. 264.
78 Ibid.
79 Ibid., pp. 264-265.
80 Morel, E. La"Librairie Publique" en Angleterre et aux Etats Unis. (In Association des Bibliothècaires Français. Bibliothèques, Livres et Librairies. Op.cit., pp. 197-220).
81 Henriot, Gabriel. France. (In Bostwick, Arthur E. Popular Libraries of the World. Chicago: American Library Association, 1933. p. 108).
82 Ibid. (= The Alumni Association of Paris Library School which was the *Association des Aneiens Eléves de l'Ecole de Bibliothécaire de Paris,* 10 Rue de l'Elysée, Paris, was a group of modern librarians, graduates of the school.)
83 Ibid., pp. 108-109.
84 Coyecque, E. Un grand bibliothécaire français: Eugène Morel. Op.cit., p. 142.
85 Gruny, op.cit., p. 11.
86 Ibid.
87 Pons, Jacques. Odette Dourver (1904-1970). Nécrologie. *Bulletin d'Informations. Association des Bibliothécaires Français.* 4e trimestre, no. 73, 1971, p. 217.
88 Gruny, op.cit., ibid.
89 Morel, E. L'enseignement post-scolaire: La Bibliothèque Moderne. Paris: Durand, 1927. p. 7.
90 Ibid.
91 Ibid.
92 Coyecque, E. Les Bibliothèques Municipales de Paris. *Revue des Bibliothèques,* 1928, p. 21.
93 Ibid.
94 Raux, Henri F. Un initiateur de la Lecture Publique en France: Eugène Morel. 1869-1934. (In Festschrift Eugen Strollveither. Erlangen: Universitats bibliothek, 1950. p. 201)

Chapter Five: E. Morel and Children's Libraries

1. New Encyclopedia Britannica. Macropedia. Vol.7. Chicago: Helen Hemingway Benton, 1974. p. 869d.
2. Bérenger, Henry. L'éducation du people en France et en Angleterre. *Revue de Pari,* 15 septembre 1897, p. 267.
3. Huchet, Claire. La Bibliothèque Enfantine: L'Heure Joyeuse. *Revue des Bibliothèques,* vol. 34, no. 21, 1927, p. 270.
4. Subercase, B. Les bibliothèques populaires, scolaires pédagogiques. Paris: Dupont, 1892. (All legislative and administrative documents and official texts concerning school libraries can be consulted in Subercase's work.)
5. Huchet, op.cit., ibid.
6. Pellisson, N. Les bibliothèques populaires à l'étranger et en France. Paris: Imp. Nationale, 1906. p. 195.
7. Langlois, Ch. V. Les Bibliothèqus des Ecoles Primaires. *Revue Bleue,* 3 aout 1907, pp. 131-132.
8. Pellisson, op.cit., pp. 195-196.
9. Ibid., p. 195.
10. Ibid.
11. Heintze, Ingeborg. French public libraries through Swedish eyes. *Library World,* vol. 64, no. 814, April 1968, p. 246.
12. Gaussen, Frédéric. Des bibliothèques sans lecteurs. *Le Monde,* no. 7011, samedi 29 juillet 1967, p. 1.
13. Association des Bibliothécaires Français. Manifestatiens du cinquantenaire (20 et 21 novembre 1956): 1906-1956: compte rendu, textes des communications, suivi de l'annuaire des members de l'Association. Paris, 1956. p. 85.
14. Morel's curriculum vitae relative aux activités d'Eugène Morel concernant les bibliothèques, 1926 kept at the Bibliothèque Nationale. See Appendix C.
15. Association des Bibliothécaires Français. Manifestations...op.cit., p. 40.
16. Gruny, Marguerite. Eugène Morel et les bibliothèques pour enfants, *Bulletin d'Analyses de Livres Pour Enfants,* no. 17, septembre-octobre 1969, p. 22.
17. Ibid, p. 21.
18. Coyecque, Ernest. Un grand bibliothécaire français: Eugène Morel. *Revue du Livre,* 2e année, no. 6, avril 1934. p. 140.
19. Morel, E. Bibliothèques. Vol. 2. Paris: Mercure de France, 1908, pp. 11, 26; 60-61.

# NOTES

20      Gruny, Marguerite. Les bibliothèques pour enfants en France, *Enfrance*, no. 3, mai-juin 1956, p. 177.
21      Fairchild, Salome Cutler. What American libraries are doing for children and young people. *Library Association Record*, no. 11, 15 novembre 1903, pp. 541-551.
22      Keogh, Andrew. English and American libraries – a comparison. *Public Libraries*, no. 7, July 1901, p. 390.
23      Gruny, M. Morel et les bibliothèques pour enfants, op.cit., p. 22.
24      Morel, E. La Librairie Publique. Paris: A. Colin, 1910. p. 125.
25      Ibid., p. 126.
26      Ibid., pp. 126-127.
27      Ibid., p. 130.
28      Ibid., p. 131.
29      Ibid.
30      Ibid., p. 130.
31      Ibid., pp. 131-132.
32      Ibid., p. 132.
33      Ibid., p. 133.
34      Ibid., pp. 133-134.
35      Ibid., p. 134.
36      Ibid., p. 128.
37      Ibid., pp. 134-145.
38      Ibid., p. 139.
39      Ibid., p. 137.
40      Ibid., pp. 129-130.
41      Ibid., p. 139.
42      Morel's curriculum vitae, op.cit.
43      Chapot, V. L'orgainzation des bibliothèques. *Revue du Synthése Historique*, vol. 20, no. 58, 1910, p. 4.
44      Moore, A.C. Children's libraries in France. *Library Journal*, 15 October 1920, pp. 831-832.
45      Gruny, M. Un pionnier des bibliothèques: Ernest Coyecque: 15 aout 1864 – 15 janvier 1954. *Bulletin d'Informations. Association des Bibliothécaires Français*, no. 13, mars 1954, p. 10.
46      Berwick-Sayers, W.C. The Paris Pilgrimage III. The Public Libraries in the Devastated Areas. *Library Association Record*, vol. 1, 1923, p. 105.
47      Ibid.
48      Ibid.
49      Moore, op.cit., p. 832.
50      Bogle, Sarah. C.N. Library Development in France. *Library Occurrent*, vol. 7, 1924, pp. 13-15.
51      Gruny, M. Les bibliothèques pour enfants en France, op.cit., p. 177.

| | |
|---|---|
| 52 | Lemaitre, Jules. La Bibliothèque Enfantine de la Rue Boutebrie: *L'Heure Joyeuse. Revue des Bibliothèques,* vol. 32, no. 3, 1925, p. 35. |
| 53 | Ibid., p. 32. |
| 54 | Morel, E. Discours (In Lemaitre, op.cit., p. 37.) |
| 55 | Ibid. |
| 56 | Ibid. |
| 57 | Coyetaux, Violette. Le centenaire des bibliothèques parisiennes. *Bulletin des Bibliothèques de France,* Ile année, no. 2, fevrier 1966, pp. 66-67. |
| 58 | Morel, E. La Librairie Publique, op.cit., pp. 125-140. (after the bombing of the First World War) |
| 59 | Hollebeque, M. Education thru' books according to the American methods. *Public Libraries,* 1919, p. 204. |
| 60 | Personal information from Miss M. Gruny to author. |
| 61 | Gruny, M. Eugène Morel et les bibliothèques pour enfants, op.cit., p. 24. |
| 62 | Ibid. |
| 63 | Moore, A.C. op.cit., p. 832. |
| 64 | Berwick Sayers, W.C. : The modern children's library. *The Librarian and Book World,* vol. 21, no. 3, 1931-32, pp. 76-78. The children's library. London: Routledge, 1913. |
| 65 | Personal information from Miss M. Gruny to author. |
| 66 | Croydon Public Libraries. Annual Report no. 83, 1925, p. 22. |
| 67 | Ibid. |
| 68 | Personal information from Miss Gruny to author. |
| 69 | Ibid. |
| 70 | Lemaitre, op.cit., p. 54. See Appendix D. |
| 71 | Ibid., p. 35. |

Chapter Six: Advocacy of Public Libraries

| | |
|---|---|
| 1 | Raux, Henri F. Un initiateur de la lecture publiqe en France: Eugène Morel (1869-1934). (In Festchrift Eugen Strolreither. Er.langen: Unversitats bibliothek, 1950, p. 198.) |
| 2 | Gruny, Marguerite. Eugène Morel et les bibliothèques pour enfants. *Bulletin d'Analyses de Livres pour Enfants.* No. 17, septembre-octobre, 1969, p. 22. |
| 3 | Raux, op.cit., p. 201. |
| 4 | Gruny, Marguerite. Un pionnier des bibliothèques, Ernest Coyecque ue (1864-1954). *Bulletin d'Information de l'Association des Bibliothécaires Français,* no. 13, mars 1954, p. 9. |

# NOTES

5     Séances du Comité. Séance du 14 novembre 1918 tenue sous la présidence d'Eugène Morel. *Bulletin de l'Association des Bibliothécaires Français,* vol. 12, septembre-novembre 1918, p. 76.
6     Morel, E. Municipal libraries in France. *The Library World,* vol. 14, 1911, p. 111.
7     French public libraries. *The Library World,* vol. 13, 1911, p. 306.
8     Coyecque, E. Un grand bibliothécaire français: Eugène More (1869-1934). *Revue du Livre,* no. 6, avril 1934, p. 143.
9     Raux, op.cit, p.197.
10     Morel, E. La Librairie Publique. Paris: Colin, 1910, pp. 177-178.
11     Coyecque, E. Les bibliothèques municipales de Paris: au jourd'huidemain. *Bulletin de l'Association des Bibliothécaires Français,* vol. 9, 1915, p. 17.
12     Ibid, p. 49.
13     Morel, E. La"Librairie Publique" en Angleterre et aux Etats Unis. (In Association des Bibliothécaires Français. Bibliothèques, Livres et Librairies. Paris: Marcel Rivière, 1912. p. 219.)
14     Ibid., p. 197.
15     Ibid., p. 209.
16     Ibid., p. 217.
17     Ibid., p. 220.
18     Ibid., pp. 217-218.
19     Morel, E. Bibliothèques, vol. 1. Paris: Mercure de France, 1908, p. 218.
20     Morel, E. "La Librairie Publique"… op.cit., p. 218.
21     Morel, E. Bibliothèques, vol. 1 & 2. Paris: Mercure de France. La Librairie Publique, Paris: Colin, 1910.
22     Morel, E. Free Public Library ( In Morel, Bibliothèques, vol. 2, op.cit., chapter I, pp. 1-19)
23     Morel. La Librairie Publique, op.cit.
24     Grolier, G. de. L'oeuvre d'Eugène Morel. *Revue du Livre.* no. 6, avril 1934, p. 144.
25     Morel. La Libraire Publique, op.cit., title page.
26     Ibid., p. 2.
27     Raux, op.cit., p. 200.
28     Morel, E. Bibliothèques, vol. 1, op.cit., pp. 97-110.
29     Ibid.
30     Bouvy, Michel. Review of Jean Hassenforder's "Development compare des bibliothèques publiques en France, Grande Bretagne et aux Etats Unis dans la seconde moité du XIXe siècle (1850-1914), Paris: Cercle de la Librairie, 1967. *Bulletin de Documentation Bibliographie,* 14e année, no. 9-10, septembre-octobre, 1969, review no. 2180. (In *Bulletin des*

|    | *Bibliothèques du France,* 14e année, no. 9-10, septembre-octobre 1969, pp. 766-767. |
|----|---|
| 31 | Ibid. |
| 32 | Ibid. |
| 33 | Ibid., p. 767. |
| 34 | Ibid., pp. 767-768. |
| 35 | Ibid., pp. 769-770. |
| 36 | Morel, La Librairie Publique, op.cit., p. 29. |
| 37 | Raux, op.cit., p. 199. |
| 38 | Ibid., p. 198. |
| 39 | Morel, E. Bibliothèques, vol. 1, pp. 97-110. |
| 40 | Ibid. |
| 41 | Morel, La Librairie Publique, op.cit., p. 4. |
| 42 | Maury, Lucien. L'avènement du livre. *Revue Politique et Littéraire (Revue Bleue),* 1910, p. 248. |
| 43 | Ibid., pp. 247-251. |
| 44 | Chatelain, Emile. Morel, (Eugène) Bibliothèque. Essai sur le développement des bibliothèques et de la librairie dans les deux mondes. Paris: Mercure de France, 1908. 2 vols. *Revue des Bibliothèques,* vol. 19, 1909, pp. 188-195. |
| 45 | Morel, E. Bibliothèques, vol. 2, op.cit., pp. 1-19. |
| 46 | Morel, E. Bibliothèques, vol. 1, op.cit., p. 218. |
| 47 | Ibid., pp. 138-139. |
| *  | The state library Directorate which is the French Library Board is called *La Direction des Bibliothèques et de la Lecture Publique*; considered an official directorate of the Ministère de l'Education Nationale and cornerstone of the French Library Movement, it has the major task of organizing and administering *La Lecture Publique,* which, in Morel's words, means reading facilities in the widest possible sense of the phrase. *La Direction des Bibliothèques* was created by a decree of August 19, 1945 of the Provisional Government under General Charles, de Gaulle. (Information taken from *Ministère de l'Education Nationale.* Direction des Bibliothèques et de la Lecture Publique. Les Bibliothèques de France au service du public. Paris: 1969.) |
| 48 | Gaussen, Frédéric. Des bibliothèques sans lecteurs. *Le Monde,* 30-31 juillet, 1967. |
| 49 | Lude, Jules. Les bibliothèques publiques. Clermont Ferrand: G. Mont Louis, 1902. p. 22. |
| 50 | Ibid., pp. 20-22. |
| 51 | Ibid. |
| 52 | Morel, op.cit., p. 190. |

# NOTES

53     Febvre, Lucien. Combat pour l'histoire, 2nd ed. Paris: A. Colin, 1965, avant-propos, VIII.
54     New Standard Encyclopaedia. Chicago: Standard Education Society, 1964, vol. 5, p.F. 307.
55     Vidier, Etienne. L'église et les oeuvres socials en 1910. Paris: Ch. Poussielgue, 1901. pp. 34-35.
56     Morel, E. La Librairie Publique, op.cit., p. 189.
57     New Standard Encyclopaedia, ibid.
58     Hassenforder, Jean. Comparative studies and the development of libraries. *Unesco Bulletin for libraries,* vol. 22, no. 1, January-February 1968, pp. 17-18.
59     Edwards, Edward. A statistical view of the principal libraries of Europe and America. 3rd ed. London: (Printed by Hansard), 1849. 48p.
60     Mortet, Charles. Les bibliothèques publiques en France. (In Congrès International des Bibliothécaires et des Amis du Livre tenu à Prague du 28 juin au 31 julliet 1926. Tome II. Communications et Memoires. Prague: Imprimerie d'Etat, 1928. p. 486.)
61     Grolier, op.cit., p. 144.
62     Morel, e. Ecole des Hautes Etudes Sociales. Section des Bibliothèques Modernes. *Bulletin de l'Association des Bibliothécaires Français,* vol. 4, 1910, p. 120.
63     Ibid.
64     Ibid.
65     Ibid., p. 121.
66     Ibid., p. 120.
67     Raux, op.cit., p. 201.
68     Morel, E. Catalogue de la Bibliothèque de Levallois Perret publié sous la directionm d'Eugène Morel. Levallois-Perret, à la Mairie, l'Emancipatrice, (1925). p. 9.
70     Morel's curriculum vitae partiel établi probablement en 1926. See Appendix C.
71     Morel, E. Catalogue de la Bibliothèque de Levallois-Perret. 1925, op.cit.
72     Ibid., p. 4.
73     Ibid.
74     Morel's curriculum vitae, ibid.
75     Gruny, op.cit., pp. 6-12.
76     Morel, E. La Librairie Publique, op.cit., p. 3.
77     Morel, E. Bibliothèques, vol. 1. op.cit., p. 19.
78     Munford, W.A. Penny Rate. London: Library Association, 1951. p. 24.
79     Morel, op.cit., p. 171.
80     Ibid., p. 187.

| | |
|---|---|
| 81 | Raux, op.cit., p. 202. |
| 82 | Chapot, Victor. L'organization des bibliothèques. *Revue de Synthèse Historique,* vol. 19, no. 2, octobre, 1909, pp. 129-149.. |
| 83 | Ibid., p. 138. |
| 84 | Ibid., p. 139. |
| 85 | Morel, E. La Librairie Publique, op.cit., pp. 8-11. |
| 86 | Morel, E. La"Librairie Publique en Angleterre et aux Etats Unis, op.cit., pp. 205-213. |
| 87 | Chapot, op.cit., p. 140. |
| 88 | Morel, E. La Librairie Publique, op.cit., pp. 1-4. |
| 89 | Morel, E. La"Librairie Publique" en Angleterre… op.cit., pp. 205-206; pp. 179-220. |
| 90 | Maury, op.cit., p. 250. |
| 91 | Ibid., pp. 250-251. |
| 92 | Gruny, op.cit., ibid. |
| 93 | Dainotti, Virginia Carini. La bibliotèca publica en Italia tra cronoca a storia. Vol. 2. Firenza: Leo S. Olschai, (editors), 1969, p. 486. |
| 94 | Gruny, op.cit., ibid. |
| 95 | L'Argus Soisonnais, 27 mars, 1921. |
| 96 | Morel, E. L'enseignement post-scolaire: La Bibliothèque Moderne. Paris: Durant, 1927. pp. 13-14. |
| 97 | L'Argus Soissonais, op.cit. |
| 98 | Ibid. |
| 99 | Gruny, op.cit., p. 11. |
| 100 | Ibid. |
| 101 | L'Argus Soissonnais, 2 novembre, 1922. |
| 102 | Estrait d'un compte-rendu d'une séance: à Féssart du 15 novembre 1922. Séance du Comité de la Bibliothèque Moderne, 15 novembre 1922. |
| 103 | Conseil Municipal de Féssart. Déliberation du 19 décembre 1929. |
| 104 | Bertaut, Jules."*La Librairie Claire," Le Temps*, 27 juillet 1929. |
| 105 | Morel, E. L'enseignement post-scolaire… op.cit., p. 2. |
| 106 | Morel, E. Catalogue de Levallois-Perret, 1925, op.cit., pp. 6-7. |
| 107 | Gruny, op.cit., p. 12. |
| 108 | Coyecque, E. op.cit., p. 17. |
| 109 | Ibid., p. 13. |
| 110 | Berwick-Sayers,W.C. Le Congrès de Bibliothécaires et des Bibliophiles. *Library Association Record.* Vol. 1, 1923, p. 102. |
| 111 | Ibid. |
| 112 | Coyecque, E. Code administrative des Bibliothèques d'Etudes. Vol. 1, Introduction. Paris: 1929. |

NOTES

| | |
|---|---|
| 113 | Berwick-Sayers, W.C. The Paris Pilgrimage. *Library Association Record*, vol. 1, 1923, p. 167. |
| 114 | Coyecque, E. Les bibliothèques municipales de Paris... op.cit., p. 17. |
| 115 | Ibid., pp. 10-11. |
| 116 | Ibid., p. 13. |
| 117 | Piquard, Maurice. Journée du 20 novembre 1956. (In Association des Bibliothécaires Français: 1906-1956: Manifestations du cinquantenaire 20 et 21 novembre 1956. Paris: Association des Bibliothécaires Français, 1957, p. 3) |
| 118 | Vidier, A. Annuaire des Bibliothèques et Archives. Paris: 1927. pp xxi-xxiv. |
| 119 | Morel, E. La Librairie Publique, op.cit., pp. 304-305. |
| 120 | Morel, E. L'enseignement post-scolaire ... op.cit., p. 3. |
| 121 | Morel, op.cit., p. 304. |
| 122 | Ibid., pp. 23-25. |
| 123 | Morel, E. L'enseignement post scolaire ... op.cit., p. 1. |
| 124 | Munford, op.cit., p. 23. |
| 125 | Morel, E. La Librairie Publique, op.cit., pp. 304-305. |
| 126 | Morel, E. L'enseignement post-scolaire ... op.cit., p. 3. |
| 127 | Ibid. |
| 128 | Morel, E. Municipal libraries for France, op.cit., p. 109. |
| 129 | Ibid., pp. 110-111. |
| 130 | Ibid., p. 111. |
| 131 | Certificats issued on 16th December, 1913 by the Library Assistants' Association for E. Morel's election of Honorary Fellow of the Library Assistants' Association, signed by W.C. Berwick-Sayers. See Appendix B. |
| 132 | Berwick-Sayers, W.C. The Paris Pilgrimage: *Library Association Record*, vol. 1, 1923, p. 99. |
| 133 | Ibid., pp. 103-104. |
| 134 | Ibid. |
| 135 | Lemaitre, Renée. Des livres pour tous. *Association des Diplomée de l'Ecole des Bibliothécaires, Documentalistes, Bulletin d'Information*, no. 8, 1975, p. 13. |
| 136 | Ibid. |
| 137 | Esquer, Gabriel. Les bibliothèques publiques en Algérie. *Bulletin de l'Association des Bibliothécaires Français*, 1ère année, mars 1912, pp. 1-32. |
| 138 | Ibid., pp. 15-32. |
| 139 | C.S. Les Bibliothèques publiques en Algérie. *Bulletin de l'Association des Bibliothécaires Français*, 1ére année, mars 1912, p. 73. |
| 140 | Ibid., pp. 73-74. |
| 141 | Dainotti, op.cit., p. 486. |
| 142 | Morel, E. La Librairie Publique, op.cit., pp. 314-316. |

| | |
|---|---|
| 143 | Morel, E. La Librairie Publique en Angleterre et aux Etats Unis, op.cit., pp. 218-219. |
| ** | These were organized by Morel at the Ecole de Hautes Etudes, 1910-1915. |
| 144 | Michel, Henri. Les Bibliothèques municipales (In Association des Bibliothécaires Français. Bibliothèques... op.cit., p. 158.) |
| 145 | Ibid., p. 159. |
| 146 | Morel, E. Ligue pour la creation de librairies publiques. (In Morel, E. La Librairie Publique, op.cit., pp. 314-316.) |
| 147 | Morel, E. Bibliothèques, 2 vols. Paris: Mercure de France. Vol. 1, 390p; & vol. 2, 475p. |
| 148 | Morel, E. La Librairie Publique, op.cit., pp. 103-112. |
| 149 | Morel, E. Ibid., pp. 103-111. Bibliothèques, op.cit., vol. 1, pp. 97-110, pp. 200-204. |
| 150 | Morel, E. Bibliothèques, op.cit., vol. 1, p. 222; vol 2, pp. 325-329. |
| 151 | Ibid., vol. 1, p. 222. |
| 152 | Ibid., p. 57. |
| 153 | Ibid. |
| 154 | Ibid., vol. 1, p. 56. |
| 155 | Ibid., vol. 1, pp. 230-313; p. 342. |
| 156 | Ibid., vol. 1, pp. 209-229; pp. 194-199; pp. 346-347; vol. 2, p. 349; p. 49. |
| 157 | Grolier, G. op.cit., p. 146. |
| 158 | Morel. Bibliothèques, vol. 2, pp. 173-198. |
| 159 | Ibid., p. 198. |
| 160 | Morel, E. La Librairie Publique, op.cit., pp. 2-3. |
| 161 | Ibid., p. 3. |
| 162 | Morel, E. Catalogue de la Bibliothèque de Levallois-Perret, 1925, op.cit., p. 11. |
| *** | At a general meeting of the French Library Association held on 14th April 1912, he operated a "*bibliophote*" which showed Morel's colleagues what benefits libraries could reap by using this piece of equipment which could enlarge things on a screen with the use of projectors. (Assemblée Générale de 1912 tenue le 14 avril, 1912. *Bulletin de l'Association des Bibliothécaires Français*, vol. 6, 1912, p. 34). |
| 163 | Coyecque, E. Un grand bibliothécaire français... op.cit., pp. 141-142. |
| **** | *La Revue du Livre* was a monthly review which promoted librarianship, bibliography and the knowledge of books published under the editorship of a reputed librarian, G. de Grolier. |
| 164 | Morel, E. Les machines au secours de la Bibliographie. *Revue du Livre*, no. 1, 15 novembre 1933, pp. 14-19. |
| 165 | Ibid., p. 16. |

NOTES

166  Ibid.

## Chapter VII: Morel and Legal Deposit

1   GUILLAUNE BUDE: *Encyclopedia Britannica*. Chicago: William Benton, 1964. Vol. 4, p. 362A.
2   DUPUY, Suzanne. L'activité bibliographique et document à la Bibliothèque Nationale. Revue des Bibliothèques, tome 42, 1932, p. 8.
3   FRANCE. In, PAFFORD, J.H.P. Library Cooperation in Europe, London: The Library Association, 1935, p. 297.
4   GAUTIER, Jean. Nos bibliothèques publiques – leur situation légale. 2nd rev.ed. Paris: Librairie Chevalier et Rivière, 1903, p. 119.
5   Ibid., p. 120.
6   GAUTIER, Jean. Op.cit., p.6. The footnote no. 2, p. 6 shows the inferiority of the Bibliothèque Nationale's acquisition funds compared with those of Berlin, London and Washington.
7   LEMAITRE, Henri. Histoire du Dépôt Légal. Lère partie (France) Paris: A. Picard & file, 1910.
8   VIDIER, A. Publications nouvelles concernant les Bibliothèques Françaises. Rapports présentés aux Assemblées Générales des 23 avril 1911 et 14 avril 1912. In, *Bulletin de l'Associaton des Bibliothécaires Français*, vol. 8, 1912, p. 78.
*   The reviewer even advised the reader to compare Lemaitre's work with that of Charles Mortet who published an extract from the journal *Bibliographie Moderne* as a pamphlet entitled: *Les Origines du depot legal. Observations sur les ordonnances du 28 décembre, 1537 et du 17 mars 1538* (Besancon: 1911. 7p. Extrait du *Bibliographie Moderne*)
9   LEMAITRE, Henri. Op.cit., p. LIV.
10  LEMAITRE, Henri. Copyright Office de Washington. *Revue des Bibliothèques*, no. 1-3 1912. pp 1-19.
11  C.S. Chronique. Le fonctionnement du Copyright Office à Washington. In, *Bulletin de l'Association des Bibliothécaires Français*, 6e année, vol. 6, 1912, pp. 72-73.
12  MOREL, E. Le livre français et la production mondials. *Mercure de France*, vol. 95, 1912, p. 772.
13  MOREL, E. Dépôt Légal In *Les Bibliothèques*, vol. 2, pp. 160-172.
14  MOREL, E. op.cit., p. 162.
15  Ibid.
16  Ibid.
17  Ibid., p. 163.
18  Ibid., p. 184.

| | |
|---|---|
| 19 | Ibid., p. 187. |
| 20 | Ibid., p. 170. |
| 21 | Ibid., p. 171. |
| 22 | Ibid., p. 172. |
| 23 | MOREL, E. Les Bibliothèques. Vol. 2. Chapter 9, p. 311-312. |
| 24 | Ibid., p. 312. |
| 25 | Ibid., p. 326. |
| 26 | Ibid., p. 327. |
| 27 | Ibid., p. 319. |
| 28 | La Situation des Bibliothèques d'après, le Rapport de M. Steeg, In, *Bulletin de l'Association des Bibliothécaires Français*. Lère année, no. 6, novembre-décembre. 1907, p. 136. |
| 29 | Assemblée Générale du 3 avril 1910. In, *Bulletin de l'Association des Bibliothécaires Français*, vol. 4, 1910. p. 29. |
| 30 | VITRAC, Maurice. Le Dépôt Légal, *Bulletin de l'Association des Bibliothécaires Français*, vol.4, 1910. p. 58. |
| 31 | Ibid. |
| 32 | Ibid., p. 61. |
| 33 | Ibid., pp. 61-62. |
| 34 | Ibid., p. 62. |
| 35 | Chronique. In, *Bulletin de l'Association des Bibliothécaires Français*, 6e année, vol. 6, 1912, p. 72. |
| 36 | French Librarians' Association – Library Course: *The Library Journal*, December 1912, p. 684. |
| 37 | MOREL, E. Le Livre français et la production Mondiale: Essai de statistique des imprimés, *Mercure de France*, vol.95, 1912, p. 760. |
| 38 | MOREL, E. Le Production de l'imprimerie française, en 1909, *Mercure de France*, vol. 84, 1910, p. 466. |
| 39 | Ibid. |
| 40 | Ibid. |
| 41 | DEHERAIN, H. Chronique. *Bulletin de l'Association des Bibliothécaires Français*, janvier-février, 7e année, no. 1. |
| ** | RUBEN DE COUDERC published a series of articles on *Du Dépôt Légal des imprimés, estampes, et autres productions* in *Bulletin de l'Art Ancien et Moderne* nos janvier 18 and 25, février 1,8 and 15, 1913. |
| 42 | VIDIER, A. Publications nouvelles concernant les Bibliothèques Françaises en 1912. Rapport présenté à l'Assemblée Générale du mars 1913. *Bulletin de l'Association des Bibliothécaires Français*. 7e année, no. 1, 1913, pp. 46-47. |
| 43 | MORTET, Ch. Allocution. *Assemblée Générale de l'Association des Bibliothécaires Français de 1914*. *Bulletin de l'Association des Bibliothécaires Français*, no.2, mars-avril 1914, p. 35. |

NOTES

| | |
|---|---|
| 44 | *Journal Officiel* quoted in Le Parlement et les Bibliothèques: II: Sur La Bibliothèque Nationale et le dépôt legal, In *Bulletin de l'Association des Bibliothécaires Français,* no. 3, mai-juin, 1914, p. 64. |
| 45 | Ibid., pp. 64-65. |
| 46 | Ibid., pp. 64-67. |
| 47 | MORTET, Charles. Un nouveau pas vers la réforme du Dépôt Légal. *Bulletin de l'Association des Bibliothécaires Français,* jan-avril, 1918, pp. 5-13. |
| 48 | Bibliothèque Nationale Suisse de Berne. Chronique. *Bulletin de l'Association des Bibliothécaires Français.* Jan-avril, 1918, pp. 29-31. |
| 49 | MORTET, Charles, op.cit., pp. 5-13. |
| 50 | Ibid. |
| 51 | MOREL, E. Projet de loi sur le dépôt legal. *Bulletin de l'Association des Bibliothécaires Français,* 12 année, vol. 12, jan-avril, 1918, pp. 14-22. |
| 52 | Séances du Comité. *In, Bulletin de l'Association des Bibliothécaires Français,* jan.-avril, no. 1-2, 1918, p. 25. |
| 53 | Assemblée Générale de 1918, In, *Bulletin de l'Association des Bibliothécaires Français,* mai-aout, 1918, pp. 33-41. |
| 54 | Ibid., p. 66. |
| 55 | La Reception de l'Association des Bibliothécaires Français par l'American Library Association. *Bulletin de l'Association des Bibliothécaires Français,* no. 5-6, septembre-décembre, 1918, p. 69. |
| 56 | MOREL, E. Allocution de M. Eugène Morel, president. *Bulletin de l'Association des Bibliothécaires Français.* Janvier-février, 1919, p. 13. |
| 57 | MOREL, E. Le Dépôt Légal ou le droit d'imprimer pour soi tout seul. *Mercure de France,* vol. 155, 15 avril, 1922, p. 414. |
| 58 | Ibid., pp. 417-418. |
| 59 | Ibid., p. 415. |
| 60 | Ibid. |
| 61 | Ibid., p. 421. |
| 62 | GIRARD, Georges. Eugène Morel: Notes bio-bibliographiques: *Bulletin de la Maison du Livre Français,* 5e anné 3, no. 64, ler avril, 1924, p. 886. |
| *** | The documents on the *Loi Destrée 1921* can be found in the following booklet: COYECQUE, Ernest. *L'Oeuvre internationale d'organisation des Bibliothèques Publiques.* (Paris: Imp. de P. Dupont, 1922.) In it can be found copies of the following: (a) Reports of the Commission set up by the decree of August 30, 1920; (b) Report of M.J. Destrée, April 5, 1921; (c) Report of M. Heymann to the *Chambre* on June 21 and that of M. Derbaix to the *Senat,* August 23, 1921; (d) The law of October 7, 1921 (called La Loi Destrée) and the decrees relating to the setting up of the *Conseil Supérior* and the application of the law, all of these in October, 1921. |

Jules Destrée was a Belgian politician and writer born in Marcinelle in 1863. He was an active member of the group called Jeune Belgique; founder with Vandervelde of the *Cercle des Etudiants Progressistes;* became Member of Parliament in 1894; worked towards the organization of the popular libraries. At the *Societé des Nations,* he formed part of the *Commission de Coopération Intellectuelle.* He founded at Marcinelle a popular university where his wife taught with him. Author of many books on politics and literature. (LAROUSSE du XXe siècle. Tome II Paris: Librairie Larousse, 1929, p. 814.)

63. Ibid.
64. Congrès International des Bibliothécaires et des Bibliophiles. p. 20.
65. Ibid., p. 29.
66. Ibid.
67. LECLERC, Max. La Réforme du Dépôt Légal. *Bulletin de la Maison du Livre Français,* p. 887. (probably 1924.)
68. Ibid., p. 888.
69. Ibid., pp. 887-890.
70. GROLIER, E. de & GROLIER, G. de. L'Oeuvre d' Eugène Morel. *Revue du Livre,* 2e année, no. 6. avril, 1934, p. 146.
71. MOREL, E. Les machines au secours de la Bibliographie. *Revue du Livre Français,* 1933, no. 1, p. 17.
72. Ibid., pp. 17-1.
73. LAROUSSE du XXe siècle, vol. 12, Paris: Librairie Larousse, 1929. p. 780.
74. VILLENEUVE-TRANS, R. F. Comte de. Le role social des Bibliothèques. *Mercure de France,* vol. 252, mai 15, 1934. p. 87.
75. Ibid.
76. MOREL's letter dated September 7, 1926, Paris, to Miss Bogle.
77. MOREL, E. Le Domaine Public Payant. *Mercure de France,* 38e année, tome 197, no. 699, 1er auto 1937, p. 518.
78. Ibid., p. 519.
79. Ibid.
80. Ibid., p. 516.
81. Ibid., p. 517.
82. Ibid., p. 536.
83. MOREL, E. Note sur l'etablisssement d'une statistique de la production intellectuelle. In, Prime Congresso mondiale delle Bibliotheche e di Bibliografia. Rome-Venesia, 15-30 guigno, 1929. A vii, Atti pubblicata a cura del Minstro della Educasione Nazionale. Vol. 5. Memorie e Communicazione IV Roma La Libraria della Stats, 1929, p. 301.

# NOTES

84  Congrès International des Bibliothécaires et des Amis du Livre tenu a Prague du 28 juin au 3 juillet 1926. Procès verbaux et mémoires publiée par le Comité Executif du Congrès. Tome II. Communications et mémoires, rédigé par Bohuslaw Koutnik. Prague: Imprimerie d'Etat, 1928. p. 395.

85  COYECQUE, E. Un grand bibliothécaire français: Eugène Morel 1869-1934. *Revue du Livre,* 2e année no. 6, avril, 1934. pp. 140-143.

86  GROLIER, G. de and GROLIER, E. de. L'oeuvre... op.cit., pp. 144-146.

87  RICCI, Seymour de. Le Problème des Bibliothèques Françaises: Petit manuel pratique de bibliothécomie. Paris: L. Giraud-Badin, 1935, 89p.

88  RICCI, Seymour de. Eugène Morel: notice nécrologique. *Beaux Arts,* 30 mars, 1934.

89  SECHE, Alphonse. Dans la mélée litteraire. Paris: Nalfère, 1935. pp. 77-78.

# Bibliography

ASSOCIATION DES BIBLIOTHECAIRES FRANCAIS 1906-1956; Manifestations du cinquantenaire (20 et 21 novembre 1956): compte rendu, texts des communications suivi de l'annuaire des members de l'Association. Paris: 1957. 136p.

ASSOCIATION DES BIBLIOTHECAIRES FRANCAIS: Bibliothèques, livres et librairies. Paris: Marcel Rivière, 1912. 274p.

BAUDRILLART, H. Du role des bibliothèques et de l'extension qu'elles pourraient prendre. Paris: A. Picard, 1890. 27p.

BAUDRILLART, H. Les bibliothèques et les cours populaires. Paris: Hachette, 1867. 52p.

BENEDETTI, J. Le Quartier du Marais: III le Maris au XIXe siècle. Paris: Imp. Municipale, 1960. pp. 17-21.

BENGE, R.C. Public libraries in Paris. *Library Association Record,* March 1950, pp. 85-87.

BERENGER, Henri. L'éducation du people en France et en Angleterre, *Revue de Paris,* 15 septembre 1897, pp. 266-298.

BERWICK SAYERS, W.C. The Easter visit to Paris. *Library Association Record* (new series), vol. 1, 1923, pp. 33-34.

BERWICK SAYERS, W.C. The Paris Pilgrimage: part I. The Easter excursion. *Library Association Record,* vol. 1, 1923, pp. 98-104.

BERWICK SAYERS, W.C. The Paris Pilgrimage: part III: The Public libraries in the devastated areas. *Library Association Record,* vol. 1, 1923, pp. 165-171.

BLOCH, Camille. Les bibliothèques populaires en Angleterre. *Revue Bleue,* 4e série, tome II, no. 8, 25 fev. 1899, pp. 244-249.

BOGLE, Sarah C.N. Library development in France, *Library Occurent* (Indiana Public Library Commission), vol. 7, 1924, pp. 13-15.

BORDEN, Arnold K. The sociological beginnings of the library movement. *The Library Quarterly,* vol. I, no. 3, July, 1931, pp. 278-282.

BOUVY, Michel. Hassenforder (Jean). Dévelopment compare des bilbiothèques publiques en France, en Grande Bretagne et aux Etats Unis dans le seconde moitié du XIX siècle, 1850-1914. Paris: Cercle de la Librairie, 1967. (A review): (In *Bulletin de Documentation Bibliographique,* 14e année nos. 9-10, septembre-octobre, 1969, no. 2180, pp. 766-770)

BOWERMAN, George F. Municpal popular libraries of Paris. *Public Libraries,* vol. 12, 1907, pp. 395-96.

BRISCOE, J. Potter. Libraries and reading circles. *Library Association Record,* vol. 5, no. 5, 15 May 1903, pp. 219-224.

BUDGET des bibliothèquess populaires à Paris et à l'étranger. *Bulletin des Bibliothèques et des Archives,* 1884, pp. 113-114.

*BULLETIN de la Société Franklin: Journal des bibliothèques populaires*, no. 144, ler Juillet 1878.

*BULLETIN de l'Association des Bibliothécaires Français,* lère année no. 1-8, janvier-décembre 1907.

*BULLETIN de l'Association des Bibliothécaires Français,*vol. 4, no. 1-6, janvier-décembre 1907.

*BULLETIN de l'Association des Bibliothécaires Français,* vol. 5, no. 1-3, janvier-décembre 1911.

*BULLETIN de l'Association des Bibliothécaires Français,* 6 année, vol. 6, no. 1-6, janvier-décembre 1912.

*BULLETIN de l'Association des Bibliothécaires Français,* 7e année, vol. 7, no. 1-6, janvier-décembre 1913.

*BULLETIN de l'Association des Bibliothécaires Français,* vol. 8, no. 1-6, janvier-décembre 1914.

*BULLETIN de l'Association des Bibliothécaires Français,* vol. 9, 1915, pp. 5-48.

*BULLETIN de l'Association des Bibliothécaires Français,* vol. 9, 1915, pp. 56-101.

*BULLETIN de l'Association des Bibliothécaires Français,* vol. 12, no. 1-6, janvier-décembre 1918.

CAILLET, Maurice. L'inspection générale des bibliothèques. *Bulletin des Bibliothèques de France,* 15e année, no. 12, décembre 1970, pp. 597-608.

CAIN, Jules. Les bibliothèques. (In Encyclopédie Française. Paris: Librairie Larousse, 1939, vol. 18, 18, 46-4.)

CARON, C. Les bibliothèques populaires en Angleterre. *Revue Pédagogique,* vol. 47, 1905, pp. 457-463.

CARSON, Jessie. Report of the sub-committee on children's work. *Bulletin of the American Library Association,* vol. 16, 1922, pp. 200-204.

CARTER, J. F. Our libraries delight the children of France. *Public Libraries,* vol. 26, 1921, pp. 252-255.

CHAMPENOIS, Michele. Le Marais, au-dela du décor. *Le Monde,* 3 novembre 1973, p. 13.

CHAPOT, V. Organisation des Bibliothèques. *Revue de Synthèse Historique,* vol. 19, no.2, octobre 1909, pp. 129-149.

CHAPOT, V. Organisation des Bibliothèques. *Revue de Synthèse Historique,* vol. 20, no.58, 1910, pp. 1-7.

CHATELAIN, Emile. Bibliographie: (Review of Morel's) *Bibliothèques...deux mondes,* 2 vol. *Revue des Bibliothèques,* vol. 19, 1909. pp. 188-194.

CHEVALLEY, M.A. L'éducation populaire des adultes en Angleterre. Paris: Hachette, 1896.

CHILDREN'S LIBRARIES IN FRANCE. *Library Journal*, October 1920. pp. 831-2.

CHRONIQUE: bibliothèques. *Bulletin des Bibliothèques et des Archives*, 1884, pp. 113-117.

CLARKE, Archibald, (translator). The Municipal Libraries of Paris. *The Library*. Vol. 4, 1892, pp. 243 251.

CLARKE, J.A. French libraries in transition, 1789-95. *Library Quarterly*, vol. 37, no. 4, 1967, pp. 366-372.

CLAVIE, Marcel. Bibliothèques. *Mercure de France*, no. 498, 16 mars 1919, pp. 332-336.

CLAVIE, Marcel. La reorganization de la lecture publique en France. Paris: La Pensée Française, 1924. 94p.

CLAVIE, Marcel. La vie nouvelle des bibliothèques municipales de la ville de Paris. Paris: Alcan, 1916. 38p.

COEYTAUX, V. Le centenaire es bibliothèques parisiennes. *Bulletin des Bibliothèques de France*. IIe.année, no. 2, février 1966, pp. 64-70.

COMMISSION Supérieure des Bibliothèques. *Bulletin de l'Association des Bibliothécaires Français*, vol. 6, no. 6, novembre-décembre 1912, pp. 114-119.

CONGRESS International des Bibliothécaires, Paris, 1900. Congrès International des Bibliothécaires, tenu à Paris du 20 au 23 aout, 1900. Procès-verbaux et mémoires, publiés par Henry Martin, Paris: H. Welter, 1901. 267p.

CORDEY, Jean. La Bibliothèque Nationale et son adaption aux necessities actuelles. (In Congrès International des Bibliothécaires et des amis du livre tenue à Prague du 28 juin au 3 juillet 1926. Procès-verbaux et mémoires publiés par le Comité Executif du Congrès. Tome 2.

Communications et mémoires redigé par Bohustaf Koutnik. Prague: Imprimerie d'Etat, 1928. pp. 112-117.)

COYECQUE, Ernest. Association des bibliothécaires français: code administrative des bibliothèques d'étude. Paris: E. Dros, 1929.

COYECQUE, Ernest. Les bibliothèques municipales de Paris. *Revue des Bibliothèques,* 1928,pp. 19-30.

COYECQUE, Ernest. Les bibliothèques municipales de Paris. Aujourd'hui. Demain. Paris: Imprimerie du Palais, 1915. 30p.

COYECQUE, Ernest. L'oeuvre française d'une bibliothécaire Americaine: Miss Jessie Carson. *Revue des Bibliothèques,* vol. 34, 1924, pp. 257-270.

COYECQUE, Ernest. Préface (In Gruny, Marguérite. Beaux Livres: Belles histories. Paris: Bourrelier, (1937). pp. VII-IX.)

COYECQUE, Ernest. Un grand bibliothécaire français: Eugène Morel. 1869-1934. *Revue du Livre,* 2e année, no. 6, avril 1934. pp. 140-143.

CUTTER, Charles A. The Franklin Society of Paris. *Library Journal.* Vol. 1, 1976, pp. 3-5.

CUTTER, Charles A. Library association in France and America. *American Library Journal,* vol. 1, 1876, pp. 389-391.

DAINOTTI, Virginia Carini. *La biblioteca publia in Italia tra cronaca e atoria.* Vol. 2, Firense: Leo S. Olschki, Editore,k 1969. p. 486.

DANA, John Cotton. Some French libraries. *Public Libraries,* vol. 13, 1906, pp. 19-21.

DANA, John Cotton. Some French libraries. *Public Libraries,*1908,pp. 344-347.

DEFOUX, Leon. A propos du"Journal des Goncourt." *Mercure de France,* Tome 117, no. 438, 16 septembre 1916, pp. 289-297.

DELISLE, Leopold. Souvenirs de jeunesse (translated) *The Library* (new series). Vol. 9, 1908, pp. 201 211, 245-256.

DETROIT CONFERENCE. *Bulletin of the American Library Association*, vol. 16, 1922, pp. 194-195, 200 204.

DEWEY, Melvil. Library conditions in America. *Public Libraries*, vol. 9, no.8, 1904, pp. 363-365.

DEWEY, Melvil. The profession. *Library Journal*, vol. 1, 1876, pp. 5-6.

DITZION, Sidney. The anglo-american library scene. A contribution to the social history of the library movement. *Library Quarterly*, vol. 16, no. 4, October 1948, pp. 281-301.

DOCUMENTATION FRANCAISE. La Lecture publique en France. Paris: 1948. 20p. (*Notes Documentation et Etudes*, no. 918)

DUPUY, Suzanne. L'activeté bibliographique et documentaire à la Bibliothèque Nationale. *Revue des Bibliothèques*, Tome 42, 1932, pp. 5-20.

THE EASTER EXCURSION. *Library Assistant*, vol. XVI, no. 296, May 1923. pp. 264-266.

EDWARDS, Edward. Public libraries in Paris and London. *British Quarterly Review*, August 1847, pp. 72-114.

ESQUER, Gabriel. Les bibliothèques publiques en Algérie. *Annales Universitaires de l'Algérie*, lére année, mars 1912, pp. 1-32.

FAIRCHILD, Salone Cutler. What American libraries are doing for children and young people. *Library Association Record*, no. 11, 15 November 1903, pp. 541-551.

FAMIN, M.M. Bibliothèques enfantines aux Etats Unis. *Revue du Livre*, le année, no. 2, décembre 1933, pp. 43-46.

FARE, Henry. Rapport présenté...populations libres. See ROBERT Charles.

FERGUSON, John. Libraries in France. London: Clive Bingley, 1971. 120p.

FRENCH public libraries. *Library World,* vol. 13, 1911, pp. 275-6; 306-308.

GAUSSEN, Frédéric. Des bibliothèques sans lexteurs. *Le Monde,* 29 juillet, 30 juillet etler aout 1967.

GAUTIER, Jean. Nos bibliothèques publiques: leur situation légale. 2nd rev.ed. Paris: Librairie Chevalier & Rivière, 1903. 181p.

GIRARD, Georges. Notes bio-bibliograhpiques: Eugène Morel, *Bulletin de la Maison du Livre Française,* 5e année, no. 64, ler avril 1924. pp. 883-886.

GIRARD-MANGIN. Les Bibliothèques municipales devant l'opinion. *Bulletin de l'Association des Bibliothécaires Français,* no. 1-2, janvier-avril, 1912, pp. 17-18.

GLENN, F. M. Technical training in librarianship in England and abroad, *Library Association Record,* vol.12, 1910, pp. 120-121; 124-125.

GROLIER, R. & GROLIER, G. de. Les bibliographies nationals françaises. *Revue du Livre,* no. 1, novembre 1933, pp. 7-13.

GROLIER, G. & GROLIER, E. de L'oeuvre d'Eugène Morel. *Revue du Livre,* 2e année, no. 6, avril 1934, pp. 144-146.

GRUNY, Marguérite. Beaux Libres: belles hisoires. Paris: Bourrelier, (1-37). Introduction pp. xi-xiii.

GRUNY, Marguérite. Eugène Morel et les bibliothèques pour enfants, *Bulletin d'Analyses de Livres Pour Enfants,* no. 16, septembre-octobre, 1969, pp. 21-24.

GRUNY, Marguérite. "L'Heure Joyeuse." *Les Enfants et les Livres,* numéro special de l'Education Nationale, novembre 1952, pp. 20-21.

GRUNY, Marguérite, Melle. *Renseignements fournis par Melle Marguérite Gruny, niece of Eugène Morel and librarian of l'Heure Joyeuse:* author's correspondence with Miss M. Gruny.

GRUNY, Marguérite. Un pionnier des bibliothèques: Ernest Coyecque (1864-1954.) *Bulletin d'Informatoins de l'Association des Bibliothécaires Français,* no. 13, mars 1954, pp.1 1-12.

HASSENFORDER, Jean. Bibliothèques et développement Culturel. *La Table Ronde,* mai 1963, pp. 87-92.

HASSENFORDER, Jean. Comparative studies and the development of public libraries. *Unesco Bulletin for Libraries,* vol. 22, no. 2, January-February, 1968, pp. 13-18.

HASSENFORDER, Jean. Développement compare des bibliothèques publiques en France, en Grande Bretagne et aux Etats Unis dans la seconde moitié du XIXe siècle, Paris: Cercle de la Librairie, 1967. 210p.

HASSENFORDER, Jean. Histoire d'une tentative pour la promotion des bibliothèques populaires: La Société Franklin. *Education et Bibliothèques,* no. 8, mars 1983, pp. 21-36.

HASSENFORDER, Jean. Reflexions sur l'eévolution compare des bibliothèques en France et en Grande Bretagne Durant la seconde moitié du XIXe siècle. *Bulletin de l'Union Française des Organismes de Documentation,* no. 4, juillet-aout 1958, pp. 10-22.

HASSENFORDER, Jean. Un pionnier des bibliothèques publiques. *Lectures et Bibliothèques,* no. 12, -décembre, 1969, pp. 5-13.

HEINTZE, Ingeborg. French public libraries through Swedish eyes (translated by Michael Dewe.) *Library World,* vol. 64, no. 841, April 1968, pp. 246-250.

HENRIOT, Gabriel. La formation professionnelle des bibliothécaires. (In Primo Congresso Mondiale della Bibliotheche e di Bibliografia. Roma-Venezia, 15-30 Guigno, 1929, vol. 15: Memorie e Communicazioni. Roma: La Libreria della Stato, 1929, pp. 91-99.)

HENRIOT, Gabriel. France (In BOSTWICK, Arthur E. Pupular libraries of the world. Chicago: American Library Association, 1933, pp. 100-109.)

HENRIOT, Gabriel. L'Association des bibliothécaires français: un bilan de vingt années (1906-2926), *Revue des Bibliothèques,* vol. 34, no. 9, 1926, pp. 97-110.

HENRIOT, Gabriel. Note on French libraries. *Bulletin of American Library Association,* vol. 20, 1926. pp. 201-202.

HERBAY, J. Les bibliothèques municipales. *La Vie Française,* no. 1380, 18 novembre 1971.

HOBSON, A. Great Libraries. London: Weidenfeld & Nicholson, 1970. pp. 14-15.

HOT SPRINGS CONFERENCE. *Bulletin of American Library Association,* vol. 17, 1926, pp. 168-170.

HUCHET, Claire. La Bibliothèque enfantine:"L'heure Joyeuse", 3 Rue Boutebrie, Paris (Ve arrondissement). *Revue des Bibliothèques,* vol. 34, no. 121, 1927, pp. 270-276.

J.H.P. Libraries in France. *Public Libraries,* 1904, pp. 403-404.

KEOGH, Andrew. English and American Libraries – a comparison! *Public Libraries,* vol. 6, no. 7, July 1901, pp. 388-395.

LAHY, J.H. Public library situation in France. *Public Libraries,* 1919, pp. 203-204.

LANGLOIS, Ch. V. Les bibliothèques des écoles publiques. *Revue Politique et Littéraaire.* (Revue Bleue) no. 5, 3 aout 1907, pp.1 129-132.

LANGLOIS, Ch. V. Programmed u bulletin. *Bulletin des bibliothèques populaires,* janvier-février, 1906, pp. 154-157.

LANGLOIS, Ch. V. Projet sur le personnel des bibliothécaires. *Bibliothèques de l'Ecole des Chartes,* 1906, pp. 154-157.

LANGLOIS, Ch. V. Projet sur le personnel des bibliothécaires. *Bibliothèques de l'Ecole des Chartes*, novembre-décembre 1905, pp. 750-758.

LAUDE, Jules. Les bibliothèques publiques: leur importance et leur role. Chermont-Ferrand: G. Mont Louis, 1902, 25p. (Extrait de *La Revue d'Auvergne*. Septembre-décembre 1901.)

LAUDE, J. Quelques mots sur les bibliothèques françaises à propos de la proposition de loi portent reorganization générale des archives en France. *La Bibliographie Moderne*, mai-aout 1904, pp. 157-176.

LEAVITT, Maria V. Some French libraries as seen by a goodwill delegate. *Library Journal*, vol. 48, 1923, pp. 865-866.

LECLERC, Max. La réforme du dépôt légal. *Les Nouvelles Littéraires*, 3e année, no. 72, samedi ler mars 1924, p. 4.

LETOS, E.G. M. Leopold Delisle et la Bibliothèque Nationale. *Revue des Bibliothèques*, vol. 34, no. 12, 1924, pp. 116-121; 142-151.

LEFEBRE, Ernest. Jules Radu, Fondateur des"bibliothèques communales" precurseur de Jean Macé. *Bulletin de la Société d'Etudes Historiques, Géographiques et Scientifiques de la Region Parisienne*. 33e année, nos. 102-103m habvuer-juin 1959, pp. 19-37.

LEMAITRE, Henri. Histoire du dépôt legal. Lère partie (France). Paris: A. Picard & Fils, 1910, 128p. (Publication de la Société Française de Bibliographie.)

LEMAITRE, Henri. La Bibliothèque enfantine de la Rue Boutebrie: L'Heure Joyeuse. *Revue des Bibliothèques*, vol. 32, 1925, pp. 29-54.

LEMAITRE, Henri. Richesses des bibliothèques municipales de France. *Zentralblatt fur bibliothekswesen*, vol. 50, janvier-février 1933, pp. 94-106.

LEMAITRE, Reneé. Des livres pour tous. *Association des Diplomés de l'Ecole de Bibliothécaires Documentalistes. Bulletin d'Information*, no. 8, septembre 1975, pp. 11-15.

LIBRARY ASSISTANTS' ASSOCIATION. Certificate of Honorary Fellowship granted to Eugène Morel. 22nd May, 1912.

LIBRARY ASSISTANTS' ASSOCIATION. Minute Book 1910-1914. Seventeenth Session, 22nd May 1912, p. 148. (Meeting at which Morel gained his fellowship.)

LOUANDRE, Charles. La Bibliothèque royale et les bibliothèques publiques. *Revue des Deux Mondes,* 15 mars 1946, pp. 1045-1067.

MACFARLANE, J. Confiscated libraries of the French Revolution, *The Library,* vol. 8, 1896, pp. 102 104.

MACFARLANE, John. The National Libraries of Great Britain and France and their Catalogues. *The Library* (1st series) vol. 40, 1898, pp. 37-41.

MARCHEVILLE, R. de. Notes sur l'état de la lecture populaire en France et sur la situation des bibliothèques en 1866 d'après les rapports des préfets et des inspecteurs d'académie. *Bulletin de la Société Franklin,* no. 50, 15 juin 1872, pp. 180-189 & no. 152, 15 juillet 1872, pp. 214-224.

MASSON, A. and SALVAN, P. Les bibliothèques. Paris: P.U.F., 1961. 128p. (Que sais-je? No. 944)

MAURY, Lucien. L'avènement du livre. *Revue Politique et Litteraire* (Revue Bleue), 1910, pp. 247-251.

MAZEROLLE, F. Le Congrès international des bibliothécaires et des bibliophiles. 8p. (Extrait de *L'Illustration* des 7 et 14 avril 1923) Paris: L'Illustration, 1923.

MICHEL, Henri. Les Bibliothèques municpales (In Association des Bibliothécaires Français. *Bibliothèques, livres et librairies.* Paris: Rivière, 1912, pp. 137-173.)

MICHON, L.M. Les bibliothèques française. (1932-33). (In IFLA Publications vol. 5. Actes du Comité International des Bibliothèques. 6e session, Chicago, 14 octobre; Avignon, 13-14 novembre 1933; La Haye; M. Nijhoff, 1934, pp. 178-181.)

THE MONTH at Headquarters. *Bulletin of the American Library Association*, vol. 10, 1916, pp. 67-69.

MOORE, Annie Carroll. Children's libraries in France. *Library Journal*, 1920, pp. 831-832.

MOREL, Eugène-Alphonse né à Paris le 21 juin 1869. Licencié en droit. (salary record card)

MOREL, Eugène. Allocution de M. Eugène Morel, President. *Bulletin de l'Association des Bibliothécaires Français,* janvier-février 1919, pp. 9-13.

MOREL, Eugène. *Bibliothèques: essai sur le développement des bibliothèques publiques et de la librairie dans les deux mondes.* 2 vols. Paris: Mercure de France, 1908. 390p. + 475p.

MOREL, Eugène. Cadre et index de classement decimal réduit à 3 chiffres. Paris: Ecole de Bibliothécaires. 1925. xxxp.

MOREL, Eugène. Catalogue de la Bibliothèque de Levallois-Perret. 1925. paris: L'Emancipatrice (Imprimerie Cooperative), 1925.

MOREL, Eugène. Certificate of appointment as *sous-bibliothécaire de 4e classe*. Direction de la Bibliothèque Nationale. 1st March 1900.

MOREL, Eugène. Conservation et utilization de la presse qoutidienne. *Revue du livre,* no. 5 mars 1934, pp. 119-125.

MOREL, Eugène. Curriculum vitae partiel non date établi probablement en 1926, relative aux activités d'E. Morel touchant les bibliothèques.

MOREL, Eugène. Dame Baleine. *Vers et Prose*, vol. 11, 1907, pp. 112-118.

MOREL, Eugène. Jules Verne. *La Nouvelle Revue*, vol. 33, 1905, pp. 439-449.

MOREL, Eugène. *La Librairie Publique,* Paris: A. Colin, 1910. 322p.

MOREL, Eugène. La"Librairie Publique" en Angleterre et aux Etats Unis. (In Association des Bibliothécaires Français. *Bibliothèques, Livres et Librairies*. Paris: Marcel Rivière, 1912. pp. 197-220.)

MOREL, Eugène. La loi sur le dépôt légal (19 mai 1925). Paris: Librairie Ancienne Honoré Champion, 1925, pp. 5-33.

MOREL, Eugène. La production de la librairie française et le dépôt légal en 1908. *Mercure de France,* vol. 78, 1909, pp. 181-184.

MOREL, Eugène. La production de l'imprimerie française en 1909. *Mercure de France,* vol. 84, 1910, pp. 466-482.

MOREL, Eugène. La production et les huits heures. Paris: Confédération Générale du Travail, 1928, pp. VII-XIV.

MOREL, Eugène. Le dépôt légal: etude et projet de loi. Paris: Editions Bossard, 1917, pp. 5-46.

MOREL, Eugène. Le dépôt légal ou le droit d'imprimer pour sci tout seul. *Mercure de France,* vol. 155, 15 avril 1922, pp. 411-421.

MOREL, Eugène. Le Domaine Public Payant. *Mercure de France, 38e année,* tome 197, no. 699, ler aout 1927,pp. 513-537.

MOREL, Eugène. Le livre françaiset la production mondiale: essai de statistique des imprimés. *Mercure de France,* vol. 95, 1912, pp. 760-774.

MOREL, Eugène. L'enseignement post-scolaire: la Bibliothèque Moderne. Paris: Durand, 1927. 14p.

MOREL, Eugène. Le Théâtre ou l'instinct d'être autre. *Revue d'Art Dramatique et Musical,* 20 juin 1906, pp. 413-448.

MOREL, Eugène. Letter dated 24 March 1882 to his brother Frédéric.

MOREL, Eugène. Letter dated 21 January 1884 to his brother Frédéric.

MOREL, Eugène. Letter dated (?) July 1884 to his brother Frédéric.

MOREL, Eugène. Mounet-Sully. Mercure de France, vol. 114, 1916, pp. 630-648.

MOREL, Eugène. Municipal libraries for France. *Library World*, vol. 14, 1911, pp. 109-111. (The following article by M. Morel the author of *Bibliothèques: essai sur le développement des bibliothèques publiques et de la librairie dans les deux mondes*. Appeared in *Le Matin* and is here translated as an interesting view of library activity in England, America and the Continent.)

MOREL, Eugène. Notes sur l'établissement d'une statistique de la production intellectuelle. (In Primo Congresso mondialedella Bibliotheche e di Bibliografia. Roma-Venezia, 15-30 Guigno, 1929, pp. 301-304.)

MOREL, Eugène & LORDE, André de. Terre d'épouvante. Paris: L'illustration, 1907, 18p.

MORTET, Charles. Les Bibliothèques publiques en France. (In Congrès International... (continues in CORDEY, Jean, op.cit)pp. 392-411)

MORTET, Charles. Projet d'association entre les bibliothécaires français. *Revue des Bibliothèques*, avril 1891, pp. 23-26.

MORTET, Charles. The public libraries of France; national, communal and university. *Library Association Record*, September 1925, pp. 147-159.

MUHLENFELD, O. The library schools of the continent. *Library Assistants*, vol. 10, 1913, pp. 154-160.

MUNFORD, W.A. Penny Rate: aspects of British Public Library History, vol. 52, no. 9. September 1950, pp. 311-321.

NAUDE, Gabriel. Advis pour dresser une bibliothèque. Leipzig: VEV Edition, 1963, 148p. Reprint of the 1st edition of 1627.

NEVEUX, Pol. Origines de nos bibliothèques provincials. *Revue des Bibliothèques*, Tome 42, 1932, pp. 140-221.

OGER, H. Plans for libraries in France. *Library Journal,* vol. 40, 1915, pp. 414-5.

OURSEL, C. A propos de la reorganization des bibliothèques et des archives, *Le Bibliographe Moderne,* septembre-octobre 1905, pp. 363-372.

OURSEL, C. Le statut des bibliothèques municipales classes. *Revue des Bibliothèques,* vol. 36, no. 12, 1929, pp. 163-171.

OVERMAN, Ruth Anne. Childrens librarians section. *Bulletin of American Library Association,* vol. 20, 1926, pp. 500-501.

PAFFORD, J.H.P. Library cooperation in Europe: France. London: The Library Association, 1935, pp. 297-307.

PAPERS & PROCEEDINGS. Fiftieth anniversary conference, 1926. Philadelphia Atlantic City, October 4-9. (American Library Association) General Sessions – Proceedings. Vol. 20, 1926. pp. 117-182; 196-200; p. 500.

PELLISSON, Maurice. Les bibliothèques populaires à l'etranger et en France. Paris: Imprimerie Nationale, 1906. 220p.

PELLISSON, M. Les bibliothèques intercommunales circulantes. Paris: Imp. Nationale, 1915. 37p. (Publications du Musée Pédagogique. Nouvelle Série XXI.)

PETIT, Edouard. Rapport sur l'éducation populaire en 1901-1902 adréssé à M. Chaumie, Ministre de l'Instruction Publique. Paris: Imp. Nationale, 1902. 69p. (Ministère de l'Instruction Publique et des Beaux Arts.)

PICHOIS, Claude. Pur une sociologie des faits littéraires: les cabinets de lecture à Paris Durant la première moitié du XIXe siècle. *Annales, Economies, Société, Civilisations,* septembre 1959, pp. 521-534.

PIPER, Cecil. Training for librarians in France. *Library World,* vol. 12, 1910, pp. 421-422.

POLNAY, Peter de. Aspects of Paris. London: W.H. Allen, 1968, 240p.

PROPOSED Associatoin of French Librarians. *Library Journal,* vol. 31, April 1906, pp. 173-174.

PUBLIC library movement in France. *Public Libraries,* vol. 21, 1915, pp. 311-312.

PUBLIC libraries for France. A commission and its task: the need for a Carnegie. *The Observer,* Sunday, 12 January 1930, p. 11.

PUBLIC libraries in Paris. *Library Journal,* vol. 17, May 1892, pp. 169-170.

RAMSDEN, M. History of the Association of Assistant Librarians: 1895-1945. London: AAL, 1973. pp. 77-78.

RAUX, Henri F. Un initiater de la lelcture publique en France: Eugène Morel (1869-1934) (In Festshrift Eugen Strollreither. Erlangen: Universititatsbibliothek, 1950, pp. 197-202.)

RICCI, Seymour de. Eugène Morel: notice nécrologique. *Beaux Arts,* 30 mars 1934.

RICCI, Seymour de. Ee problème des bibliothèques françaises: petit manuel pratique de bibliothéconomie. Paris: L. Giraud-Badin, 1933. 93p.

RICHOU, Gabriel. Traité de l'administration des bibliothèques publiques, historique, organization, legislation. Paris: Paul Dupon, 1885. 421p.

ROBERT, Charles. La lecture populaire et les bibliothèques en 1861, *Bulletin de la Société Franklin,* no. 35, ler avril 1892, pp. 100-110.

ROBERT, Charles and FARE, Henry. Rapport présenté au Conseil d'Administration de la Société Franklin par...à l'appui d'un projet de loi relatif à la foundation et au fonctionnement des bibliothèques populaires libres. *Bulletin de la Société Franklin,* no. 144, ler juillet 1978, pp. 115-208.

ROSS, J. Technical training in librarianship in England and abroad. *Library Association Record*, vol. 12, 1910. pp. 113-114.

RUDORFF, Raymond."Belle Epoque": Paris in the Nineties. London: Hamish Hamilton, 1972. 365p.

SALVAN, P. Les Bibliothèques. See MASSON, A. and Salvan, P.

SECHE, Alphonse. Dans la melée littéraire. Paris: Malfère, 1935. pp. 77-78.

SIMON, Jules. L'instruction et les bibliothèques populaires. *Revue des Deux Mondes*, 15 septembre 1863, pp. 349-375.

SMITH, George. Gabriel Naudé: a librarian of the seventeenth century. *Library Association Record*, vol. 1, July 1899, pp. 423-431.

STATISTIQUES des bibliothèques populaires. *Bulletin Administratif du Ministère de l'Instruction Publique*, no. 1549, 13 décembre 1902. pp. 1103-1105.

SUSTAC, Charles. Situation des bibliothèques de province. Conclusions d'un questionnaire. *Bulletin de l'Association des Bibliothécaires Français*, 1ère année, no. 1, 1907, pp. 1-14.

THOMAS, Ernest C. The popular libraries of Paris. *Library Chronicle*, vol. 1, 1884, pp. 12-15.

THOMAS, Marcel. Les bibliothèques de France. *Tendances*, no. 24, aout 1963, pp. 1-31.

TURNBULL, T.E. The libraries of France. *Library World*, vol. 12, 1909, pp. 125-127.

TYLER, Moses C. The historic evolution of the free public library in America and its true function in the community. *The Library Journal*, vol. 9, no. 3, march 1884, pp. 40-47.

VILLENUEVE-TRANS, R.F. Comte de. Le role social des bibliothèques. *Mercure de France*, vol. 252, mai 15 1934, pp. 86-96.

WYER, J.P. Library reform in France, *Library Journal*, vol. 31, May 1906, pp. 215-217.

# Index

Academic Libraries
   *See* Libraries, academic
*Académie de Paris*, 11
American Book Committee of the Art
   War Relief Association, 98
American Committee for Devastated
   France, 98, 74, 76, 79, 81-82,
   94, 123
American Committee on Children's
   Libraries, 94
American Libraries (France)
   Aisne, 80
   Paris, 79, 80
   Rue de l'Elysee, 81
American Library Association, 71, 74,
   76, 78, 80, 81, 82, 116, 124,
   179
*American Library Association Bulletin*, 78
American Library of Soissons, 77
Anderson, Edwin, 78
Anglo-Saxon public libraries, 56, 59,
   102, 104, 105, 107, 110, 111,
   112, 116, 121, 135-136
*Annales Universitaires de l'Algérie*, 138
Antoine, André, 26
Archivist-paleographers, 34, 52, 60, 63,
   119, 148
*Ardoisières de l'Anjou*, 3
Association des Bibliothécaires Français, 13,
   59, 60, 64, 65, 67, 71, 72, 76,
   83, 86, 101, 116, 120, 149
*Association des Gens de Lettres*, 163
*Association Polytechnique*, 49
*Attaché payé à la journée*, 13
*Auskunftasbureau*, 143
Balzac, Honoré de
   *Honorina*, 1
Barrau'Dihigo, L, 60
Baudry, Miss, 77
Bertaut, Jules, 127
Berwick-Sayers, W.C., 93, 98, 129,
   130, 137
*Bibliographie la France*, 152, 167, 188

*Bibliophote*, 75, 145
*Bibliothèque d'Art et d'Industrie
   Forney*, 46, 81
*Bibliothèque de l'American Library
   Association*, 179
*Bibliothèque de l'Arsenal*, 19
*Bibliothèque Historique de la Ville de Paris*, 1
*Bibliothèque Nationale*, 10-12, 14-19, 21-
   25, 28-32, 34, 40, 71-74, 86,
   87, 101, 111, 123-124, 139,
   142-143, 145, 147-151, 153,
   156-160, 163, 165-168, 188-
   192
*Bibliothèque Royale* (Later *Bibliothèque
   Nationale*), 37, 147
*Bibliothèque Sainte Geneviève*, 19, 63, 93,
   120, 161
*Bibliothèques Classées*, 33, 52
*Bibliothèque, Livres et Librairies* (1912), 68,
   71, 81, 104
*Bibliothèques non-classées*, 33
*Bibliothèques populaires Municipales*, 51
*Bibliothèques Publiques de
   Paris*, (Arsenal, Nazarine, Sainte
   Geneviève), 169
Bloch, Camille, 68
Bluysen, Paul, 160-161
Bogle, Sarah C.N., 74-75, 76, 80, 94,
   189
Book Committee of the American War
   Relief Association, 93
Book Committee on Children's
   Libraries of New York, 94
Bourrelier, Michel, 68
Bouvy, Michel, 36, 109, 113
British Library Association,
   *See* Library Association (England)
British Mechanic's Institute, 47, 49, 116
British Museum, 23, 28, 29, 142-143
British Penny Rate, 135
Brock, Thomas, 9
Brown, J.D.
   *Guide to Librarianship*, 57

Buchon, J.A., 47
Buckerhalle, 105
Bude, Guillaume, 147
*Bulletin d'Analyses de Livres Pour Enfants*, 87
*Bulletin de Documentation Bilbiographique*, 109
*Bulletin de la Maison du Livre Français*, 31, 181, 183
*Bulletin de l'Association des Bibliothécaires Français*, 32, 60, 64, 65, 116, 138, 148, 153
*Bulletin des Bibliothèques de France*, 36, 96
*Bulletin d'Information de l'Association des Bibliothécaires Français*, 122
*Bulletin of the American Library Association*, See *American Library Association Bulletin*
*Bureau des Bibliothèques*, 122
Caillet, Maurice, 87
Cain, Jules, 98
*Caisse des Bibliothèques Publiques*, 154
Capen, S.T., 78
Capet, M. 71
Carnot, Hippolyte, 49
Carnot, Lazare, 49, 85
Carson, Jessie, 75, 76-77, 79, 80, 81, 93, 126
*Catalogue de la Bibliothèque de Levallois-Perret*,
    (1913), 117
    (1925), 118
*Catalogue des Imprimés* (1896), 18, 28, 29
*Cercle de la librairie*, 72, 167, 184
*Cercle des Editeurs de Musique*, 184
Chapot, Victor, 93, 120
    *L'Organization des Bibliothéques*, 120, 122
Champenois, Julien, J., 78
Chatelain, Emile, 112, 122
Chevalley, M.A., 40, 41, 59
    *Education Populaire des Adultes en Angleterre* (1896), 41
Chevrillon, André, 126
Children's Libraries,
    Committee for Children's Libraries of New York, 128
    England, 88
    Morel & Children's Libraries, 85-100
    Paris: First Children's Library, 94
    Story Hours, 99
    United States, 88, 93
Coeytaux, Violette, 96
*Comité Consultatif du Dépôt Légal*, 189
*Comité de la Bibliothèque Moderne*, 86, 126
*Comité des Régions Dévastées*, 82
*Comité du Salut Public*, 85
*Comité d'Instruction Pour La Formation de Bibliothécaires*, 81
*Commission de L'Enseignement*, 183
*Commission Supérieure des Bibliothécaires*, 182
*Confédération des Travailleurs Intellectuels*, 184
*Conférence de l'Institut de Documentation* (1933), 188
*Conferences sur les Bibliothèques Modernes*, 65
*Congrès de Bibliothécaires et de Bibliophiles*, (1923), 129, 182
*Congrès des Bibliothèques* (1910), 89
*Congrès du Livre*
    (1917), 86, 163, 180, 184
    (1921) 86, 179
*Congrès International de la Lecture Publique* (1931), 60
*Congrès International des Bibliothécaires*, 149
*Congrès International des Imprimeurs de France*, 149
*Congrès International des Bibliothécaires et des Amis du Livre* (1926), 191
*Convention Nationale*, 43
*Congrès de l'Art Théâtrale* (1900), 33
*Congrès des Bibliothèque* (1900), 38
Copyright, 148, 149, 151
Copyright Office (Library of Congress), 150, 151, 189
Cordey, Jean, 191
Coutts, Henry T., 74
Couvreur, André, 156
Coville, M., 185
Coyecque, Ernest, 60, 70, 75, 76, 80, 82, 83, 86, 87, 94, 101, 103, 104, 118, 122, 125-126, 129-130, 131, 192
Croiset, M., 66

# INDEX

Croydon Public Libraries, 98
Dainotti, Virginia Carini
    *La Bibliotheca Publica in Italia tra cronoca e storia*, 139
Daudet, Alphonse, 1
Davis, Mary, 76
Decourcelle, Pierre, 184
Decrees concerning Libraries,
    (1789, November 2) National Assembly, 43
    (1838, February 12) *L'Ordonnance Royale*, 48
    (1862, June 1) 53, 85
    (1870, J. Ferry Decree) 51
    (1881, July 29) 148, 155
    (1885, June 17) 12-14
    (1888, January 23) 15
Delessert, François Marie, 49
Delisle, Leopold, 15, 25, 29, 30, 38, 64
    *Instructions pour la redaction d'un nventaire des incunables conserves dans les bibliothèques publiques de France*, (1886), 16
    *Instrucitons élémentaires et techniques pour la mise et le mantien de ordre des livres d'une bibliothèque* (1890), 16
Denniker, J., 60, 67
Descaves, Lucien, 7
Destrée, Jules
    *Loi Destrée de 1921*, 181, 190
Dewey Decimal Classificaiton, 117, 145
Dewey, Melvil, 64, 113
Dieudonné, 64
*Directeur du Secrétariat et de la Comptabilité, Ministry of Public Instruction*, 33
*Direction de l'Enseignement Primaire*, 85
*Direction des Beaux Arts*, 158
*Direction des Bibliothèques Municipales et des Bibliothèques Administratives de Paris et de la Seine*, 70
Documentation centers, 144
Dourver, Odette, 82
Duggan, Stephen, 78
Duproix, Lydia, 77-78, 79
Duruy, Victor, 50
*Ecole de la Bibliothèque Moderne*, 71
*Ecole de l'Elysée*, 83-84
*Ecole des Bibliothécaires de Paris*, 83-84, 98

*Ecole des Chartes*, 17, 19, 20, 31, 52, 63, 64, 71, 161
*Ecole des Hautes Etudes Sociales*, 19, 27, 57, 59, 65, 67, 71, 72, 87, 97, 101, 102, 104, 117, 139, 156
*Ecole International des Bibliothécaires*, 71
*Ecole National Supérieure des Mines*, 3
*Ecole Polytechnique*, 3
Education Act (1870), England, 52
Education, Library See Library Education
Edwards, Edward, 12, 34, 37, 40, 45, 113, 116, 119, 132
*Emigrés*, 33, 63
Esquer, Gabriel
    *Les Bibliothèques Publiques en Algérie*, 138, 139
Ewart Law, 52, 132, 138
*Exposition Technique de Bibliothèques*, 182
Falloux Act (Public Education Act, 1850), 50
Falloux, Frederic Alfred de, 50
Faye, M., 14
Febvre, Lucien
    *Combats pour l'histoire* (1965), 114
Fénéon, Felix, 28
Ferry, Jules, 51, 85
Féssart Library, 126-128
Festival International du Livre, (1975), 138
Film Silf, 145
Finn, Mary, 78
Firmin-Ros, M., 76, 94
Fonds d'Etat, 24
Fonds de ville, 24
Forney, Samuel, 46, 59
Fournière, M., 66
Free public libraries, 35, 36, 38, 40, 41, 44, 55, 88, 101, 102, 104, 105, 106, 107, 121-123, 129, 132, 134, 135, 138, 140
French National Library
    See *Bibliothèque Nationale*
French Revolution, 34, 43, 47, 52
Gaussen, Frederic, 58, 86 ? (I didn't find a reference for the index in diss. 187)
Gautier, Jean, 64, 67, 71

*Nos Bibliothèques Publiques* (1903), 147-148
Glenn, F.M., 19
Concourt, Academie de, 21
*Grand Livre des Bibliothèques Publiques en France*(1838), 47
Grandes Ecoles de Paris, 15
Gréard, Octave, 11
Greens, Marion, 93
Grenier Goncourt, 10
Griffiths, J.L., 94, 98
Grolier, G. & E. de, 70, 187, 188, 192
Grunebaum-Ballin, M., 185
Gruny, Marguerite, 20, 77, 82, 83, 87, 97, 98, 99, 101, 122
Gaell, Paul, 94
Guizot, François, 44-45, 47
Halle aux Draps, 49
Hannique, Léon, 6
Hassenforder, Jean,
    *Developpement compare des bibliothèques en France, en Grande Bretagne et aux Etats Unis dans la seconde moitié du xixe siècle: 1850-1914*, 36, 37, 38, 39, 61, 108, 113, 115
    *Education et Bibliothèques* (1963), 38, 57, 58
Heintze, Ingeborg, 86
Henriot, Gabriel, 75, 81, 82
Henriot, H., 59
Herrick, Myron, 126
Hitchler, Theresa, 76
Hollebecque, Professor, 96
    *Education thru books according to American methods in Public Libraries* (1919), 72, 154
*Hotel des Sociétés Savantes*, 72, 154
Hotel Lamoignon of Le Marais, 1
Huchet, Claire, 85, 98-99
Humblot, A.F., 68
Information bureaux, 144, 145
*Institut Interantional de Bibliographie*, 72, 73
*Institut Bibliographique*, 152-153
*Institut Pédagogique National*, 58
Johnstone, W. Dawson, 75
Jules Ferry Decree (1870), 51
Julliard, M., 126

*Jury International de l'Exposition Universelle*, (1878), 53
Keogh, Andrew, 40
Lacoste, Miss, 77
La Fontaine, 67
La Librairie Claire, 127
La Maison du Livre, 127, 182
Langlois, C.V., 17, 18, 21, 53, 59, 85
La Place Voltaire Library, 104
*La Revue des Bibliothèques*, 112
*La Revue Politique et Littéraire*, 112
*La Revue Scientifique*, 111
*L'Argus Soissonnais*, 124, 125-126
Laude, Jean
*Les Bibliothèques Publiques*, 114
League For the Creation of Public Libraries
    See Ligue pour la Création des Librairies Publiques
Learned Libraries, 43
Leavitt, Maria V., 74
Leclerc, Max, 183, 185, 187
Lecture Publique, 101, 102, 103, 107, 118
Ledos, Gabriel, E., 29
Legal deposit, 145, 147-155, 156, 161, 162, 163-187
Lemaitre, Henry, 59, 68, 99
*Histoire du Dépôt Légal* (1910), 148-149
Lemaitre, Jules, 71, 94-95, 150
Lemaitre, René
    *Des Livres Pour Tous* (article - 1975), 138
*Le Marais*, 1
*Le Matin*, 64, 102
*Le Monde*, 58, 86, 113
Leschalle, 105, 135
*Le Temps*, 17, 21, 41, 59
Levallois-Perret Library, 70, 117, 118, 192
Leygues, Georges, 32
L'Heure Joyeuse, 85, 92-96, 98-99, 128
Libraries, academic, 143
Libraries, Government, 48
Libraries, municipal, 34, 36-37, 39-41, 43, 45-46, 47, 48, 53-55, 57-58, 60-61, 63, 77, 104, 109-

# INDEX

110, 111, 113, 116, 119, 122, 129, 131, 135
Libraries, parish, 34, 50
Libraries, popular, 34, 35, 38-40, 41, 49, 51, 53-55, 57, 60, 90, 103, 108, 116-117, 119, 122, 128, 135, 139
Libraries, private, 51
Libraries, public, 43-45, 46, 50, 57-58, 61-62, 114
Libraries, school, 34, 39, 41, 50, 53-54, 85-86, 90, 93
Libraries, special, 142-143
Libraries, town, 43, 51
Library Assistant, 65, 73
Library Assistants' Association, (England), 74-137
Library Association (England), 28, 29, 73, 116, 130, 137-138
Library Association, French
 *See Association des Bibliothécaires Français*
Library Charter, 52
Library Commission (France)
 (1838) 48
 (1839) 52
 (1879) 52
Library Decrees
 *See* Decrees concerning Libraries
Library Education, 19, 20, 24, 74
 Morel & Library Education, 63-70
 Courses (1910), 65
 Courses (1911), 67, 68-70
 Courses (1911-1912), 71
 Summer Training School, Paris, 74
 Scholarships, 76
*Library Journal*, 72, 116
*Library occurent*, 74, 75, 76, 94
Library of Congress, 143, 149-150, 165
Library Pioneers, 43, 61, 102, 113, 114-115
Library Surveys
 *See* Surveys, Library
*Library World*, 64, 66, 102, 135
*Ligue de l'Enseignement*, 46, 50, 143
*Ligue Pour La Création de Librairies Publiques*, 141-142

*L'Oeuvre*, 77
London,
 Public library situation (1895), 23
 In 1895, 21-22
Lorde, André de, 27
Macé, Jean, 50, 54
Macfarlane, John, 28
*Manuel Général de l'Enseignement Primaire*, 41, 59
Marais, Paul, 178
Marais Quartier, 1
Marcel, H.,
 *La Bibliothèque Nationale* (1907), 14
Marcel, Pierre, 66
Marcel, Roland, 189
Martin, Henry, 67
Marty, Henriot, 86
Massé, M., 143
Masson, A.
 *Les Bibliothèques*, 29
Maury, Michel, 112, 121
May, Dick, 66
Mechanization in libraries, 144-145
Mellottee, Paul, 68
*Mercure de France*, 33-34, 41, 150, 157, 180
Meudon, Library, 117
Mezières, M., 148
Michel, Henri, 60, 110, 140
Minister of Education, 51
Minister of the Interior, 166, 169, 183, 186
Minister of Public Instruction, 13, 44, 45, 47, 49, 52-53, 160-161, 166, 169, 183
Moore, Annie Carroll, 78-79
Morel, Charles Adolphe, Father, 1, 2, 3, 4
Morel, Eugène
 birth, 3
 childhood, 4-5
 death, 70, 102, 192
 employment not in a library
  attorney at law, 8, 10
  Lawyer (1889), 8
  journalist *See* Morel - journalism/articles
 Library education, 19-20

Military service (1890-1891), 8-9
Student - lycée & university, 4-7
Morel, Eugène
　Articles
　　Le Domaine Public Payant, 189-191
　　La Livre Français et la Production Mondiale, 150, 157
　　La Production de l'Imprimerie Française, 157
　　Production et Le Dépôt Légal, 157
　　Le Dépôt Légal, etude et projet de loi, 161-179, 187
　　Le Dépôt Légal ou le droit d'imprimer pour soi tout seul, 180
　　Projet de loi sur le Dépôt Légal, 187
　　On the aid machines can bring to bibliography, 70
　　Municipal libraries for France, 102, 135
　　L'Enseignement post scolaire: La Bibliothèque Moderne, 124, 128, 135
　　Books on librarianship, 22-23
　　La Librairie Publique, 22-23, 35, 38, 88, 96, 106-109, 110-111, 120-121, 123, 130
　　Bibliothèques (2 vol.) 83, 102, 106-109, 111-112, 117, 120, 122, 130, 142-143, 152, 157
Morel, Eugène
　Employment - *Bibliothèque Nationale*
　　Attaché (1892), 10
　　1892-1900, 11-42
　　Stagiaire, 12
　　sous bibliothécaire - 4e classe (1900), 25, 32
　　sous bibliothécaire -3e classe (1911), 64
　　sous bibliothécaire - 2e classe (1911), 64
　　sous bibliothécaire - 1e classe, 64
Morel, Eugène
　Journalism
　　La Revue Blanche, 11-12
　　La Revue du Livre, 70
　　La Revue Moderne, 6-7
　　Mercure de France, 11
Morel, Eugène
　Lectures on librarianship
　　La Bibliothèque Royale de Berlin, 71-72
　　La Libraire Publique en Angleterre et aux Etats Unis, 55, 57, 68, 81, 104, 140
　　The French Books in France: Statistics, 72, 156
Morel, Eugène
　Library activities
　　Morel & Library education, 63-84
　　Morel & children's libraries, 85-100
　　Morel & advocacy of public libraries, 101-217
　　Morel & legal deposit, 147-193
　　Chairman, French Library Association, 86, 101
　　Vice-chairman, Comité de la Bibliothèque Moderne, 86
Morel, Eugène
　Literary activities - Publications
　　Artificielle, 20, 27
　　Dans la nuit, 27
　　Ignornace Acquise, 6
　　La Femme Adultère, 27
　　La Prisonnière, 32
　　La Rouille du sabre, 193
　　Les Boers, 31
　　Les Morfondus, 193
　　Loreau est acquitté, 28
　　Petits Français, 9, 87
　　Projet de Théâtre Populaires, 33
　　Terre Promise, 30
Morel's niece
　See Gruny, Marguerite
Morel, Eugène
　Social activities
　　Salon Goncourt, 10
　　Société des Gens de Lettres, Vice-chairman, 86
Morel, Frédéric, brother, 2, 8-9, 21
Morel, Jean François, grandfather, 2
Morel, Louisa, Morel's mother

INDEX

*See* Salanson, Louisa
Morgan, Anne, 78
Mortet, Charles, 52, 60, 154, 158, 161-162, 169
*Un nouveau pas vers la reforme du dépôt légal,* (article -1918) 161
Mounet-Sully, 26-27
Muhlenfeld, O., 65, 73
Muhlfeld, Lucien, 12
Napoleon III, 49-50
National bibliography, 145
National Library (France)
   *See* Bibliothèque Nationale
Naudé, Gabriel
   *Advis pour dresser une bibliothèque*, 44
Neveu, Pol, 60, 176
Newcomb, Virginia, 78
*Nouvelle Ecole des Bibliothécaires*, 83
*Nouvelle Revue*, 41
O´Connor, Alice K., 76, 79, 93
*Office National des Universités Françaises*, 77-78, 80
Ogle, J.J.,
   *The Free Public Library*, 23
Oldy, William,
   *The British Librarian*, 12
*Ordonnance de Montpellier* (1537), 29, 147, 149
Otlet, Paul, 67, 73
Pafford, J.H.P., 147
Paris,
   in 18th century, 1
   in 1869, 1
Paris, Library System, 51, 55, 104, 116, 118, 191-192
Parsons, Mary, 76, 81
*Pavillon de Maison*, 138
Pellison, Maurice, 16, 37, 44-45, 46, 51, 56, 60, 86, 113, 140
Pench, Louis, 126
Perdonnet, M., 49
Perreyve, L´Ábbé, 41, 115
Philanthropy,
   Bonnemain, 46
   Coignet, Léon, 46
   Edelstand du Méril, 46
   Forney, Samuel, 46
   Foussier, 46

Groud, M., 46
Mocomble, 46
Parent de Rozan, 46
Tridon, Gustave (Mrs=), 46
Philippon de la Madeleine, Louis, 44-45
   *Vues pratiques sur l'éducation du tant des villes que des campagnes*, 45
Picot, 149
   *Le Dépôt Légal: Comptes rendus de l'Académie des sciences morales et politique* (1883), 148
Piolet, Le Père, 41, 115
Piper, A.C., 18-19
Plaisant, Marcel, 185
Plummer, Mary Wright, 89
Popular Libraries,
   *See* Libraries, Popular
Primary Education,
   Decree, (1880-1881), 85
Private libraries
   *See* Libraries, Private
Public Libraries Act, England (1919), 57-58, 131-133, 135
Quiri, Miss, 77
Ramsden, Michael,
   History of the Association of Assistant Librarians (1895-1945), 73
Raux, Henri F., 84, 102, 111, 113
Ravaisson, J.G.F., 47
Redenbacher, Fritz, 84
*Régie du Dépôt Légal*, 183, 189
Reims,
   In 1829, 2
Renan, Ernest, 50
*Réunion des Bibliothèques de Paris*, 189
*Revue Blanche*, 30
*Revue Bleue*, 85
*Revue d'Art Dramatique*, 33, 192
*Revue des Bibliothèques*, 80, 83, 94, 99, 149, 166
*Revue de Synthèse Historique*, 93
*Revue du Livre*, 70 87, 145, 187, 192
*Revue Moderne*, 33
*Revue Politique et Littéraire*, 121
Ricci, Seymour de,
   *Problème des bibliothèques françaises: petit manuel de bibliothéconomie* (1933), 192

Rivière, Marcel, 68, 104
Rolland, Romain, 18, 27, 66
Rosny, Seraphin Justin, 7
Rouanet, Gustave, 159-161
Ruben de Couderc, 158
Rudorff, Raymond
    *Belle Epoque*, 8, 30
Rue Féssart Library, 70, 76-77, 96
Rue Sorbier Library, 96
Sainte Beuve, Charles Augustin, 50
Sainte Geneviève Library
    See *Bibliothèque Sainte Geneviève*
Salanson, Alphonse, Morel's uncle, 3, 5
Salanson, Louise, Morel's mother, 3
Salon Goncourt, 10, 11, 34
Salvan, P.,
    *Les Bibliothèques*, 29
Salvandy, Narcisse Achille de, 44, 47, 48
Sauvage, E., 67
Scholarly libraries, 103, 108, 119
School libraries
    See Libraries, School
School of librarianship, 65, 70, 73, 75, 76, 78, 81-84, 97-98
*Section des Bibliothèques Modernes*, 20, 27, 66, 156
Select Committee on Public Libraries, Great Britain (1849), 45
Self-instruction, 118, 120, 132
Simon, Jules, 51
*Société des Amis de la Bibliothèque Nationale et des Grandes Bibliothèques de France*, 157, 182
*Société des Bibliothèques Communales*, 49
*Société des Bibliothèques Populaires du Haut Rhin*, 54
*Société des Gens de Lettres*, 171, 179, 184, 191
    Morel: Vice President, 86, 94
*Société des Libraires et Editeurs de la Suisse Romande*, 161
*Société des Omnibus de Londres*, 3
*Société d'Histoire Moderne*, 149
*Société du Mercure de France*, 31
*Société Française de Bibliographie*, 148-149
*Société Franklin*, 38, 39, 46, 53-54, 58
*Société Pour L'Instruction Elémentaire*, 85
*Sociétés d'Amis des Bibliothèques*, 140

*Soirées de Medan*, 6
Soissons, 79, 124-125, 127, 128
Solberg, Thorvald, 150
Sorbonne, 129
    Faculté de Lettres, 19
    Library, 112
*Sou des Bibliothèques*, 46
*Stagiaire commissioné*, 13, 25
Steeg, M., 153
Stevenson, Burton E., 179
Summer Training School, 74, 76
Surveys, Library
    Enquête (1873), 51
Sustrac, Charles, 60, 67
Svilikossitch, Michel, 67
Swiss National Library, 161
*Syndicat de la Propriété Intellectuelle*, 179-180, 185
*Syndicat des Editeurs*, 179, 184
*Syndicat pour la Protection de La Propriété Littéraire*, 185
Technical Exhibition, 138
Theodore-Vibert, P., 68
Thoroval, J.,
    *Grande Etapes de la Civilisation Française*, 25
Thorigny, Rue, 2, 3
Tolstoi, Leo, 193
Tourneaux, Maurice, 68
Tradieu, André, 126
Tyler, Alice S., 78
Varthon, Louis, 129
Veber, M., 159-161
Verne, Jules, 8, 9, 10
Vidier, A., 60, 67, 71, 72, 131, 148, 157, 176
Vidier, Etienne,
    *L'Eglise et les oeuvres socials en 1900*, 115
Villemain, François, 44
Vitrac, Maurice, 68, 154, 156
Volksbibliotheken, 35
Vuibert, 180
Washington Library
    See Library of Congress
Williams, Mabel, 76
Zola, Emile,
    *Soirée de Médan*, 6

www.ingramcontent.com/pod-product-compliance
Lightning Source LLC
Chambersburg PA
CBHW071406300426
44114CB00016B/2206